CONTEMPORARY PROTESTANT THOUGHT

 CONTEMPORARY THEOLOGY SERIES

GENERAL EDITORS:

J. FRANK DEVINE, S.J.
RICHARD W. ROUSSEAU, S.J.

CONTEMPORARY PROTESTANT THOUGHT is one of the volumes in the Ecclesial Theology section of this Series.

Contemporary
Protestant Thought

C . J . CURTIS

PASTOR, IMMANUEL LUTHERAN CHURCH

ASSOCIATE PROFESSOR, DE PAUL UNIVERSITY

THE BRUCE PUBLISHING COMPANY / NEW YORK

Library of Congress Catalog Card Number: 72-87991
Copyright © 1970 The Bruce Publishing Company
Made in the United States of America

Editors' Introduction

This series begins with the presupposition that theology is necessary. It is necessary if Christian intelligence is to search for meaning in its dialogue with God, man, and the world. Since Christian intelligence is not the exclusive possession of the theological specialist or the cleric, the search must be carried on in all those areas of life, secular as well as religious, including the college situation, where meaning is to be found.

This search is a peaceful one, for in some mysterious way it has already achieved its goal: the vision of faith and the fullness of love. Still it remains a relentless and universal search. Its inner certainty must radiate out not only to the edges of the mind but also into the farthest recesses of the world. We could call it "lay" theology, but this word seems too pale a description for such an exciting enterprise of the Christian life.

In view of this, the editors of this series are convinced that new questions had to be asked, new structures created, and new books written. These books would be neither catechetical nor apologetic. They would be purely and simply theological. The primary audience would be believers, but all thinking men would find them useful. In scope they would be broad enough to ensure perspective. They would be scholarly enough to be intellectually relevant. They would avoid pedantry. In short, they would try to present a rich and deep understanding of Christian revelation in such a way that today's college students would be able to respond with a Christian faith and life that are both culturally mature and scientifically precise. Finally, the authors of these books would be, for the most part, teachers in colleges and universities where much of the contemporary theological dialogue is now going on.

The series falls into four parts: biblical, historical, ecclesial, and ethical. The divisions were not predetermined by the editors. They follow the shape of the most vigorous theological work now being done.

The books in the biblical section are intended to go beyond the traditional treatment of Bible history and the now familiar perspectives of salvation history. They concentrate on various books of the Bible. Their method has been especially designed for college work. Tentatively it might be called "exegetical theology." Every verse is not considered after the fashion of a commentary, nor are narratives developed as a biography, nor is there any attempt to create large theological syntheses. Rather the individual books are studied in chronological sequence; key passages are treated in detail and the rest are summarized. At the same time some attention is paid to the growing theological synthesis.

Since scholastic theology is already represented by individual works and sets of textbooks, the books in our historical section study dogmatic questions from a developmental point of view. In this way the editors hope to make the college students more aware of the great wealth of theological thinking that recent historico-theological studies have uncovered. This method, which is more inductive than deductive, should happily coincide with the thought processes of the college student. The three basic poles for synthesis are: God, Christ, and Man. In each area the historical development will be studied and a significant number of basic source texts presented. The problems raised in these studies will range all the way from Augustinian pessimism to Teilhardian optimism.

The textbooks for the third part of the series will deal with issues of great contemporary importance. They will examine questions discussed by the Second Vatican Council. As the name implies, ecclesial theology must first concern itself with the Church, what the Church knows herself to be, as expressed in the insights of the new *Constitution on the Church* and with the more significant of the Church's allied concerns: other world religions, American Protestantism, its history, its motivating forces and spirit, and finally the new sacramental theology so enriched by the many magnificent liturgical advances. All of this growth has brought a wider and deeper appreciation of the nature of the Roman Catholic Church and her relationship, rooted in understanding and love, with the whole world.

The fourth and final section of the series is devoted explicitly to Christian moral response. The editors subscribe to the position that the proper place for the Catholic college or university to examine ethical questions is in a revelational rather than in a purely philosophical context. In addition to the "virtue" divisions of the *Summa* or the classic moral theology text, designed primarily for confessors, there is a need and a place for a "Christian ethics" that reflects the new insights which both biblical and dogmatic theology can provide. These books will strive to be openly Christian in spirit, eclectic in approach, up to date in scholarship, and will address themselves to those ethical problems which are most real to the modern American mind.

Finally, the editors would like to express their thanks to all those whose interest, advice, and cooperation have made this series possible. They are especially grateful to Dr. William May who initiated the project and sustained it through the inevitable disappointments and complications, and to W. Robert Abbott, for his invaluable editorial assistance. To the individual authors who so graciously added to their heavy burden of academic responsibility by undertaking these books, we can only express the hope that their share in the shaping and influencing of the American Catholic community of today and of tomorrow will be far more meaningful to them than any meager thanks of ours.

The Editors,
REV. J. FRANK DEVINE, S.J., Boston College
REV. RICHARD W. ROUSSEAU, S.J., Fairfield University

ACKNOWLEDGMENTS

The editor and publishers of *Contemporary Protestant Thought* are grateful to the following for permission to reprint copyrighted materials:

George Allen & Unwin, Ltd., London, for excerpts from Martin Buber's *The Knowledge of Man;*

Association Press, New York, for excerpts from William Hamilton's *The New Essence of Christianity;*

Geoffrey Bles, Ltd., London, for excerpts from Nicholas Berdyaev's *The Beginning and the End, Truth and Revelation, Spirit and Reality, The Meaning of History;*

The Bobbs-Merrill Company, Inc., Indianapolis, Ind., for excerpts from *Radical Theology and The Death of God*, copyright © 1966, by Thomas J. J. Altizer and William Hamilton, reprinted by permission of the publishers, The Bobbs-Merrill Company, Inc.;

T. & T. Clark, Edinburgh, for excerpts from Karl Barth's *Church Dogmatics;*

Wm. Collins Sons & Co., Ltd., London, for excerpts from Thomas J. J. Altizer's *The Gospel of Christian Atheism* and from Dietrich Bonhoeffer's *Act and Being;*

Commonweal, New York, for excerpts from *Commonweal* editorial "Dr. King's Legacy," *Commonweal* (April 19, 1968);

European Literary Bureau, Surrey, for excerpts from Nicholas Berdyaev's *The Divine and the Human;*

EVZ Verlag, Zurich, for excerpts from Karl Barth's *Die Kirchliche Dogmatik* and *Die Theologie und die Kirche;*

Fortress Press, Philadelphia, for excerpts from John D. Godsey's *Preface to Bonhoeffer;*

Harper & Row, Publishers, New York, for excerpts from Nicholas Berdyaev's *The Destiny of Man;* from pp. 157–184 in *No Rusty Swords* by Dietrich Bonhoeffer, translated by John Bowden, copyright, 1947 by Christian Kaiser Verlag. Copyright © 1965 in the English translation by William Collins Sons & Co. Ltd., London, and Harper & Row, Publishers, Incorporated, New York. Reprinted by permission of Harper & Row, Publishers; from Dietrich Bonhoeffer's *Act and Being, Christ the Center* translated by John Bowden, *The Communion of Saints,* and *Life Together* translated by J. W. Doberstein; from Rudolf Bultmann's article "The Case of Demythologizing" in *Kerygma and Myth,* Volume II, edited by H. W. Bortsch and translated by R. H. Fuller; from Martin Buber's *The Legend of the Baal-Shem,* translated by M. Friedman; from Martin Luther King, Jr.'s *Why We Can't Wait* and *Strength to Love;* from Schubert M. Ogden's *Christ Without Myth* and *The Reality of God;* from Alfred North Whitehead's *Process and Reality;*

Harvard University Press, Cambridge, for excerpts from a speech by Alfred North Whitehead recorded in the *Symposium in Honor of the Seventieth Birthday of Alfred North Whitehead;*

The Harvill Press, Ltd., London, for excerpts from Hans Urs von Balthasar's *Martin Buber and Christianity;*

John Knox Press, Richmond, Virginia, for excerpts from Karl Barth's *Anselm: Fides Quaerens Intellectum,* translated by Ian W. Robertson;

Johnson Publishing Co., Inc., Chicago, for excerpts from *What Manner of Man: A Biography of Martin Luther King, Jr. 1929–1968* by Lerone Bennett, Jr., Copyright Johnson Publishing Co., 1963, 1968;

Lutterworth Press, London, for excerpts from John B. Cobb's *A Christian Natural Theology;* and from Emil Brunner's *The Divine Imperative;*

The Macmillan Company, New York, for excerpts reprinted with permission of The Macmillan Company from *Martin Buber and Christianity* by Hans Urs von Balthasar, translated by Alexander Dru, copyright © Hans Urs von Balthasar, 1958, copyright © in the English translation by Harvill Press, 1961, first published in The United States of America by The Macmillan Company; for excerpts reprinted with permission of The Macmillan Company from *Creation and Fall* by Dietrich Bonhoeffer, © by SCM Press, Ltd., 1959; for excerpts reprinted with permission of The Macmillan Company from *The Cost of Discipleship* by Dietrich Bonhoeffer, © by SCM Press, Ltd., 1959; for excerpts reprinted with permission of The Macmillan Company from *Ethics* by Dietrich Bonhoeffer, © Chr. Verlag 1949, © SCM Press 1955, published in the U.S. by The Macmillan Company; for excerpts reprinted with permission of The Macmillan Company from *Letters and Papers From Prison* by Dietrich Bonhoeffer, © by The Macmillan Company 1953, © by SCM Press, Ltd. 1967; for excerpts reprinted with permission of The Macmillan Company from *The Secular Meaning of the Gospel* by Paul M. Van Buren, © by Paul Van Buren 1963; for excerpts reprinted with permission of The Macmillan Company from *The Secular City* by Harvey Cox, © by Harvey Cox 1965; for excerpts reprinted with permission of The Macmillan Company from *The Aims of Education* by Alfred North Whitehead, Copyright by The Macmillan Company renewed 1957 by Evelyn Whitehead;

New American Library, Inc., New York, for excerpts from Louis Fischer's *Gandhi;*

James Nisbet and Company Limited, Hertfordshire, for excerpts from H. R. Mackintosh's *Types of Modern Theology;*

Oxford University Press, London, for excerpts from Nathan Söderblom's *The Nature of Revelation,* translated by F. C. Pamp;

Philosophical Library, New York, for excerpts from Martin Buber's *Hasidism* and from Alfred North Whitehead's *Science and Philosophy;*

Fleming H. Revell Company, Old Tappan, N.J., for excerpts from Nathan Söderblom's *Christian Fellowship;*

Author's Introduction

My purpose in writing this book is to provide students of theology and the general reader, particularly students in Catholic colleges and universities and Catholic readers, with an ecumenically ordered introduction to the thought of the most significant representatives of Protestant theology in the twentieth century. Although my major focus is on the development of Protestant theology, I have included chapters devoted to an investigation of a Roman Catholic thinker (Teilhard de Chardin), a Jewish philosopher-theologian (Martin Buber), and a great Russian Orthodox spokesman (Nicolas Berdyaev). I have included a discussion of these men inasmuch as their influence has been pronounced on Protestant thought. Teilhard has greatly influenced the rise of "process theology," Buber has contributed both to the personalist and existentialist strains within Protestant theology, and Berdyaev has contributed to the historical, existential approach.

The material of this book grew out of lectures and courses which I gave at Chicago's DePaul University, one of the ten largest Catholic Universities in the world. I was the first Lutheran and Protestant to teach in the previously all-Catholic theological faculty of the University. This provided me with an ideal setting for ecumenical dialogue and creative interchange with both faculty and students. It has greatly enhanced my ecumenical vision and immeasurably enriched my understanding of the complexity and surprising parallelism of contemporary Roman Catholic, Eastern Orthodox, Jewish, and Protestant thought.

My method has been to let the primary sources speak as much as possible in order to permit adequate understanding of the great multiplicity of concerns which animate contemporary religious thought. It has not been my intention to assume a partisan view on the subject of twentieth-century religious reflection, although undoubtedly my evangelical-catholic predilections and my preferences for ecumenism and process thought were bound to show through. My concern has been to present as broad and as intensive a picture of the modern religious scene as possible. It is my hope that these pages will contribute to the construction of the ecumenical theology of the great church of the future and inspire the present generation to rise to the magnificent vision of the universal church in the high priestly prayer of our Lord: "that they may all be one."

C. J. CURTIS

CONTENTS

CHAPTER I

ECUMENICAL THEOLOGY: SÖDERBLOM

Pope John XXIII will go down in history as the most significant pope of our century. He ushered in the ecumenical reformation of the Roman Catholic Church. If we look in Protestantism for his equal, we immediately come upon the name of Nathan Söderblom, Archbishop of Uppsala, Sweden, from 1914 to 1931. He was one of the founding fathers and pioneers of the ecumenical movement which began in Protestantism, Anglicanism, and Eastern Orthodoxy during the early part of the twentieth century. The date to remember here is the year 1910, when the International Missionary Council, which met in Edinburgh, Scotland, initiated the first ecumenical overtures. But it was not until Archbishop Söderblom convened the Stockholm Conference on Life and Work in 1925 that the ecumenical movement really got off the ground.

Nathan Söderblom was born in 1866, the son of a Lutheran pastor. He studied theology at the University of Uppsala and was ordained to the priesthood in 1893. He served as chaplain of the Uppsala Mental Hospital, and after that as chaplain to the Swedish legation in Paris, France. In Paris he studied in the field of the history of religions at the famed Sorbonne University, where he received his doctorate—the only Swede ever to be awarded the highest academic honor by the Protestant theological faculty of the Sorbonne. After teaching theology at the universities of Uppsala, Sweden, and Leipzig, Germany, Söderblom was consecrated as Archbishop of Uppsala, the most prestigious ecclesiastical post in Lutheranism. Together with the archdiocese of Canterbury, England, the archdiocese of Uppsala, Sweden, was, and still is, the great ecclesiastical center of world-Protestantism, a position highlighted in 1968 when the Fourth Assembly of the World Council of Churches was held in Uppsala.

Archbishop Söderblom at once began to transform the role of the archdiocese of Uppsala into that of a powerhouse of world-ecumenism. His parish was the world, his vision a united Christendom, his goal social justice and lasting peace for all men and nations. The terror of World War I filled the first four years after Söderblom became archbishop. Although safe in neutral Sweden, he suffered greatly from the fact that the youth of Europe and America were being sacrificed on the altar of hatred erected by the so-called Christian nations of the West. Under his leadership the social concerns of the ecumenical Life and Work movement received a tremendous impetus. Although interested in the ecumenical Faith and Order movement, which had grown out of the Edinburgh Conference of 1910 and was led by Bishop Charles Brent of the Protestant Episcopal Church in the U.S.A., Söderblom was primarily concerned with the social and moral issues of the Life and Work movement. He felt that what the modern world needs most is Christian love and concern, not the endless quarrels over theological and doctrinal differences. His vision of a Christendom united in love and service of suffering and confused mankind triumphed at the Stockholm conference of 1925, when Anglican, Protestant, and Orthodox ecclesiastical leaders met in one of the most impressive ecumenical gatherings of the twentieth century.

Despite his arduous tasks as archbishop, Söderblom found time to continue to write in the fields of theology, church history, and the history of religions. His prominent role in the spiritual and intellectual life of Sweden and of the world was given recognition by his election to the Swedish Academy of Sciences in 1921, and by the invitation to give the famous Gifford lectures on natural theology at Edinburgh in 1931. A brief illness led to his death on July 12, 1931, a few weeks after these lectures. On his deathbed he spoke of the great work which had occupied him during the last years and which was to be his scholarly testament. Its title was to be *The Living God.* "I know that God lives," he said in the hour of his death, "I can prove it by means of the history of religions."

There are five major areas of theological interest in the life and thought of Archbishop Söderblom. They are: (1) ecumenism, (2) the reality of revelation, (3) the social gospel, (4) the life and thought of Luther, and (5) the history of religions. In each one of these areas he made a monumental contribution to contemporary theology. The influence of his over 700 published writings is increasing rather than decreasing as the years go by and the ecumenical movement continues to transform the denominations of the world.

Archbishop Söderblom became famous for the phrase, "Doctrine divides —service unites." This ecumenical motto summarized his conviction that a united Christian response to the needs and problems of the world is the only feasible way to achieve the unity of Christendom. In his book entitled *Christian Fellowship,* first published in 1923, he expressed his view that while theological discussions are vitally necessary for the promotion of Christian unity, the debate over theological differences will never bring the churches closer together. Warming up ancient theological quarrels and their fruitless issue can only divide Christians who find themselves on different denominational lines. The subsequent development of the ecumenical movement leading up to the World Council of Churches shows that every significant step forward was taken in practical cooperation and united service, not by settling any of the major denominational differences in theology.

Martin Luther spoke of the visible church, which is a mixture of believers and hypocrites, and the invisible church, which is the true church. Today we would make the same distinction in terms of the sociological and the theological aspects of the church. Theologically speaking, there is only one church: the one, holy, catholic, and apostolic church. Archbishop Söderblom conceived of it as "a spiritual fellowship," that is, "a temple not built by human hands, but erected by God Himself on the foundation of the Apostles and Prophets, whose corner-stone is the Lord Jesus Himself (Eph 2:20–22)."[1] And if you ask out of what material this temple of God is erected, Söderblom answers: "All sincere souls in all Christian congregations are living stones in the Lord's house. Praying and loving hearts— those who have fallen asleep as well as those yet living—form that house of God which is the true Church."[2]

Archbishop Söderblom held that the spiritual fellowship of the true church exists already today, and that there was no need and no human possibility to create the one true church. From the theological point of view, he said, "no organization can be equivalent to the true Church of

[1] Nathan Söderblom, *Christian Fellowship* (New York: Fleming H. Revell Co., 1923), p. 11.
[2] *Ibid.*

Christ. Only faith, which sees the invisible with the unclouded eye of truth, is aware that it belongs to the one flock which Christ has redeemed and which one day shall be assembled from all peoples and nations."[3]

Thus the unity of the one true church in one sense already exists and in another sense is an eschatological reality which will be actualized fully only at the end of time. The end of time in Söderblom's thought signified the goal toward which the entire vast process of the universe is moving. This goal was the final fulfillment of the historical process.

Perhaps you wonder why we need the ecumenical movement for Christian unity if the one true church already exists or if only God can bring forth its unity at the end of time. At this point we must move over to the sociological aspect of the church. This aspect includes the divisions of the churches and denominations of the world. These are divisions of doctrine, of social class, of race, and of nationality. Archbishop Söderblom considered disunion among Christians to be "really a crime and sin,"[4] and union "a sacred, inescapable duty."[5] Those who asked him why he thought so, he referred to the high-priestly prayer of our Lord in the seventeenth chapter of St. John's Gospel. Here visible, sociological unity among Christians is demanded in order that

> the world may believe that God did send Christ. . . . By our divisions we Christians are a hindrance to our Saviour in His work of salvation. We prevent men from believing in Him. Christian unity is imperatively needed that the world may see and acknowledge the Lord. Our divisions crucify Him anew. They expose Him to derision and contempt. Our divisions are not merely a drawback: they are a crime. Unity is not only a beautiful idea. It is Christ's plain command and our unconditional duty. When you once perceive this, your conscience can never more be reconciled to division. The lack of unity will burn you like fire. The desire for unity is not a fashion, a phenomenon of the time, nor a pious wish whereby men seek to conceal from themselves and others the hard reality, the cleft which history and the world crisis of our time have driven between men. No, unity is a sacred obligation. The way to it is long and steep and stony. It leads through many hardships, great and small. Each one of these by itself seems impossible to overcome. But faith overcomes all hindrances if only we are genuinely penitent.[6]

These powerful and passionate words announced the arrival of the ecumenical dawn. Archbishop Söderblom, however, was aware not only of the absence of unity in the empirical church, but also of the profound elements of unity that already exist and which Roman Catholics, Protest-

[3] *Ibid.*, p. 12.
[4] *Ibid.*, p. 17.
[5] B. N. Karlström, *Kristna Samförståndssträvanden* (Stockholm, 1947), p. 6.
[6] Söderblom, *op. cit.*, pp. 17–18.

ants, and Orthodox are beginning to discover as they draw closer together in the wake of the ecumenical transformation of the churches in our time. On the theological level there has been, thanks largely to men like Archbishop Söderblom, a rediscovery of the essential catholicity of all denominations—not just the Roman Catholic. Söderblom, a Lutheran archbishop, thought of himself as an evangelical catholic. He used the word in the sense of "universal." He conceived of the church as a thoroughly historical process, which evolves in three main sections—the Orthodox Catholic, the Roman Catholic, and the Evangelic Catholic. Just as in the evolution of each human being in the course of the history of a lifetime there are at first important stages which lie dormant until the body is ready and the mind has matured sufficiently, so also in the historical evolution of the church there are stages and phases which emerge as God's plan for the church gradually unfolds in the process of history. Not that the evolution of the church is or was completed when Protestantism emerged on the scene. No, the ecumenical reformation of the churches is also to be considered a new and significant phase in the historical evolution of the church.

Söderblom saw it as the sacred obligation of each modern Christian to witness to the ecumenical and universal unity of the church in its three historical branches. He called for an end to the shortsighted denominational perspectives which see only the differences. Denominational divisiveness and short-sightedness fail to see that even in the midst of the Babel of denominations—there are about 200 of them in our country—the unity of Christians is not without witness. He observed that this unity "is seen, first and foremost, in its forgetfulness of self, in its patience and self-sacrifice. Furthermore, our Christian unity is visible in our common recognition of the same Holy Scriptures, in faith and in prayer—above all, in the Lord's Prayer and in the Holy Sacraments."[7]

Archbishop Söderblom gave a great deal of thought to the question as to how this visible unity of Christendom is to be realized in contemporary history. In his day there was a twofold ecumenical thrust. On the one hand, there was the so-called "Faith and Order" movement, headed by the Protestant Episcopal Bishop Charles Brent. This branch of the ecumenical movement tried to achieve visible unity by settling the theological and doctrinal differences which separate the churches. On the other hand, there was the ecumenical "Life and Work" movement of practical Christianity, led by Archbishop Söderblom. Its aim was to find Christian unity by uniting all Christians, regardless of creed, color, or nationality, in a common effort to meet the world's need in economics, social justice, civil

7Ibid., p. 12.

rights, international law and peace, individual and social ethics, etc. In a sense, the Life and Work movement was the action-oriented "social gospel" in ecumenical dress.

Söderblom was an ecumenical genius who saw the need for both of these approaches without relativizing and paralyzing his zeal for practical Christianity and the social gospel as the way to achieve immediate, small victories on the way to a visibly united church embracing all Christians everywhere. Christians today are summoned by Christ by two calls.

> The one runs: "Let us sit at the Master's feet like Mary, listen to Him, quietly pray and talk together about what unites us and what divides us. Thus we shall come to an agreement at the end." But union around the Saviour cannot wait until such agreement has been reached. The Lord has another distinct call: "Rise, and follow me." This call goes now to every one of us, to every Christian communion. Let us rise and follow Him in His footsteps. The world is craving for love and justice. . . . We are asked to come out. Let us rise and follow Him—healing, helping, learning, teaching. In following Him and forgetting ourselves, onward bound, we shall come nearer to our Master, and thus inevitably to each other, and become one.[8]

The second call of our Lord is embodied in Söderblom's "method of love"[9] which he espoused as the most effective way to reach Christian unity in our generation. He termed it "the path of Christian co-operation."[10] This path is marked by the recognition that "love needs wisdom. Effort needs clear insight and direction. Otherwise much noble endeavour, much precious sacrifice is wasted."[11]

The goal of Archbishop Söderblom's "method of love" is "spiritual unity" based on the realization that "neither big forms nor big words can repair the injuries of our epoch. Only a true Christian spirit and a truly Christian life can do this."[12] Hence the primary objective of Söderblomian ecumenical theology is to promote unity of Christian action while permitting diversity of doctrinal positions and dogmatic formulations. This distinguishes his approach from what he termed "the method of faith"[13] on the one hand, and "the method of absorption"[14] on the other.

The method of faith insists that for complete Christian unity we must "become of one mind, not only in love, but also in the doctrinal expressions for the revealed truth, and to sit all together at our Saviour's feet, listening

[8] *Ibid.*, pp. 18–19.
[9] *Ibid.*, pp. 155–180.
[10] *Ibid.*, p. 155.
[11] *Ibid.*, pp. 176–177.
[12] *Ibid.*, p. 171.
[13] *Ibid.*, pp. 122 ff.
[14] *Ibid.*, pp. 121 f.

to His voice with burning hearts."[15] Söderblom's objection to this method was that the sacred obligations of the love-commandment cannot be set aside until doctrinal agreements are reached. Furthermore, the method of faith tended to concentrate on old, divisive dogmas, whereas Archbishop Söderblom recognized the urgent need for "a new creed" which would replace the obsolete and irrelevant elements of the old traditional creeds while preserving their true spirit and essence. Irrelevance and obsolescence stem largely from the failure of Christians to obey the love-commandment and to actualize the universal brotherhood of all men regardless of race, color, religion, and nationality.

"The simplest thing is the most difficult," Söderblom said.

Brotherhood of men, how evident! The great commandment of love even of enemies, of Samaritans, of those belonging to another nation, or to a despised race, how beautiful! But if we look around, it seems doubtful whether such a doctrine has really been issued and recognized in our civilization. Ought not brotherhood of men to be preached and brought about by the Church? Nationalistic prejudices are to be combated as earnestly as any other heresy. Does not the extension of lawful order to international relations and the organization of a supernational commonwealth concern the Church? Is it not implied in the very principles of Christianity? The Christian ideal of peace against war must belong to the elementary teaching in Church and school as well as other essential parts of our faith.[16]

The method of absorption seeks to create Christian unity by absorbing all denominations into one great institution or organization. Archbishop Söderblom, aware of the demonic possibilities of such a vast centralization of power, rejected the view according to which "the unity of the Church can only be accomplished by all the other communions' abolishing their holy doctrines and ceremonies in order to join the only saving sect."[17] The bitter tone of his discussion of the method of absorption indicates his unyielding opposition to it. And yet this method is enjoying a certain popularity among Protestants who have been eager to merge denominations. Since the Second Vatican Council and Pope John XXIII, the Roman Catholic Church has given up the hope of absorbing all other denominations into itself. But the Protestant merger movement has taken over the idea underlying the method of absorption, modified it to fit the Protestant situation, and is seeking to apply it with great eagerness and remarkable success.

The mergers within Lutheranism in the U.S.A., for instance, give instructive examples of the Protestant version of the method of absorption. The

15 *Ibid.*, pp. 123 f.
16 *Ibid.*, pp. 177–178.
17 *Ibid.*, p. 121.

same is true of the merger of Congregationalists and the Evangelical and Reformed Church into the new United Church of Christ. And negotiations are under way to create a 25-million-member super-church through a six-way merger involving Episcopalians, Methodists, and Disciples. The very way in which Archbishop Söderblom and the Church of England established intercommunion in 1922, based on the recognition that the apostolic succession had been preserved in both the Church of England and the Lutheran Church of Sweden, showed that he was not a champion of mergers. To him "organization is not the important thing." He warned that "if too much importance is attached to organization, we run the risk of being enticed into the prison of statutory religion, abandoned long ago by Jesus, Paul, Luther, and others, but still attractive."[18]

Against the dangerous ideal of organizational and institutional unity Archbishop Söderblom set his vision of "spiritual unity."[19] Although himself an archbishop and prince of the church, he was the ardent champion of the federative approach to Christian unity based on spiritual unity. "The Spirit communicated to men through the Word of God is more important than organization,"[20] he insisted. "The Word of God means more than organization—the Word that was made flesh."[21] He denied that either Jesus or Luther had any interest in founding a new religion or a new church.

In the case of Jesus and the twelve disciples, Söderblom observed that Jesus did not found a religion or a church organization. Neither did any or all of the twelve disciples. If we want to speak of a founder of the Christian religion we must speak of a man who probably never saw the Lord Jesus during his earthly ministry and who was not one of the twelve chosen disciples. That man was the apostle Paul. "But," Söderblom reminds us, "even with regard to his importance to the world, we must bear in mind that this was fundamentally due to his personal and spiritual influence, and only in the second, or perhaps only in the tenth place, to the organization he introduced or improved in the communities."[22]

In the case of Luther, of whom Söderblom says that he "has had a deeper influence on the West than any man after Jesus,"[23] we note that he was primarily a prophet calling for reform in the name of the Word of God. Luther was not a religious organizer, and the need to organize his followers arose only because his plea for reform was rejected by the

18 *Ibid.*, p. 157.
19 *Ibid.*, pp. 159 ff., 171 ff.
20 *Ibid.*, p. 159.
21 *Ibid.*, p. 158.
22 *Ibid.*
23 *Ibid.*

Roman Catholic Church of his day. Certainly the worldly Renaissance popes and cardinals and archbishops had little appreciation for Luther's Evangelic Reformation. Archbishop Söderblom points out that

it is true that Luther has left evidence of ingenuity also as an organizer—a fact which has, especially lately, been emphasized; for instance, his ideas on the duties of a bishop, as expounded and put into practice by him, deserve attention wherever in Evangelic Christendom this office exists or is about to be founded, whether, like Luther, we call it by the name of visitor, or prefer other names, such as president, superintendent, or whatever other temporal titles we may be able to invent, or whether we venture to use the Biblical and old-established word bishop. But, on the whole, Luther had no inclination to organize a new religious community. His calling was purely spiritual. Peace within, perfect peace, was the object of his work. With outward establishments and institutions his work had little to do.[24]

There were those in Söderblom's day, and they are still with us, who say that the most important requisite for Christian unity is the historical episcopate. All Christians must submit to those bishops who stand in the apostolic succession. Anglicans, Roman Catholics, Eastern Orthodox, and numerous Protestants say and have said this. Archbishop Söderblom, who himself stood in the apostolic succession of the historic episcopate, rejected this notion as a manifestation of the method of absorption and therefore contrary to the spiritual unity he envisioned. He raised the question whether in Methodism, for instance, the decisive difference is between episcopal and non-episcopal Methodists, or whether a fundamental change took place when the Lutheran superintendents of Estonia, Latvia, and Saxony were consecrated as bishops by Archbishop Söderblom and other episcopal dignitaries.

"Does it mean so much if one uses a Latin or a Greek word," he asked. "Does it mean so much if one uses the Biblical term *episkopos* (bishop) or some other one?" Söderblom did not think so. He believed that the decisive line of division ran between those who considered a certain external order, in this case the historic episcopal office, necessary for the existence of the true church and Christian unity, and those who did not. "The former," he stressed,

favour statutory religion, the latter have an Evangelic view. The former group has its strong and consistent prototype in Rome, which identifies the Roman Catholic Church with its hierarchy and sacrament with God's kingdom on earth, and which must therefore consistently demand that every true Christian shall abandon his own spiritual home and range himself beneath the dominion of the Pope and his bishops. But there is something of the same spirit wherever episcopacy or the unbroken succession of bishops through the ages is made an essential condition for the unity of the Church.[25]

Important for Söderblom's understanding of ecumenism in an evangelic as well as a catholic spirit are two basic emphases. The first is on the core of the Christian religion, which is God, and God alone. No organization, no institution, no form of church government can be called essential to the welfare of the church. The one and only thing that is essential to the church is the Word of God which became a human being in Jesus Christ our Lord. Therefore, "a difference must be made between what is precious to us but unessential and what is essential, in other words, between that which belongs to God's other good gifts and the one thing needful."[26]

The second Söderblomian emphasis in his ecumenical theology is on freedom. His basic principle was: "unity in essentials, freedom and diversity in all else." The Christian unity Archbishop Söberblom sought did not mean uniformity. To him the deepest division ran across denominational lines between those who believed in a certain type of church organization as the requisite of Christian unity, and those who did not. He firmly upheld his conviction that "the unity of the Church can be brought about without her organization's being everywhere the same. One can find advantages and disadvantages in every form of Church organization. None is ideal. God has led us in different paths. Each has special experiences to preserve and make use of. Unity ought not to be uniformity. It would then be poorer."[27] And, he would add, such unity would not be in the spirit of evangelic catholicity, because evangelic means freedom, the kind of freedom St. Paul spoke of when he said that "where the Spirit of the Lord is, there is liberty" (2 Cor 3:17).

Following the French Protestant theologian, Auguste Sabatier, under whom Söderblom studied at the Sorbonne in Paris, the archbishop made a distinction between "statutory religion and spiritual religion."[28] Sabatier had made a similar distinction between "the religions of authority and the Religion of the Spirit." Deeper than the divisions caused by creeds, doctrines, and differing forms of worship and church administration is the division that separates the adherents of a religion of law and organization from the protagonists of a religion of freedom, spirit, and gospel. The former demand unity based on authority and uniformity. The latter seek unity in freedom and diversity. "It is to be noted in this connection," Archbishop Söderblom points out,

---

[25] *Ibid.*, pp. 134–135.
[26] *Ibid.*, p. 135.
[27] *Ibid.*, p. 136.
[28] *Ibid.*, p. 137.

that a Scottish Presbyterian insists on the unbroken connection between his elders and the Apostles by means of the laying on of hands just as strongly as an Anglican or Roman Christian insists on the apostolic succession of the bishops. Nevertheless they can respect the freedom of the Gospel and say, "Our form of communion is tested and found good, but it is not necessary for the true congregation of Christ, not necessary for the unity of the Church." They are then on the same side of the frontiers as we are.[29]

The concept of revelation is of decisive significance for any theological system. It answers the question, "On what basis do you make your affirmations about God, the Incarnation, the Last Judgment, etc.?" Söderblom's answer was: "I know that there is a living God, because I can see and demonstrate the continuous process of his self-revelation in nature, in history, and in the inner, personal life of man."

One of the clearest evidences of God's universal revelation was for Söderblom the emergence of genius. From the dawn of history to the present day there have arisen in virtually every part of the world men and women with extraordinary powers of creativity and leadership. Through them something really new emerged in history. Their tremendous natural endowments bear witness to God's continued creation. No matter whether the material with which genius works is stone, tone, color, words, armies, states, or the hearts of men, "something new emerges, something original, not found before."[30] Söderblom was fully aware that

it is not always easy to determine wherein the new thing consists. But the fact that it is new distinguishes the work of genius from that of the merely talented. We can see this distinction more clearly if we but note the fact that the work of talent, be it ever so remarkable, but still merely talent, consists in a skillful reproduction according to rules and patterns. The work of genius, however, gives rise to new rules, which analysis afterwards discovers. *Creation* comes first, in revelation, in beauty of character, in social structure, in the work of art. Exactly as in nature, [so in] the world of God's material creation; first flowers, then botany. Genius emerges as an essential element in the continuing creation of the Almighty. Genius is often also conscious of participation in a miracle.[31]

Söderblom spoke of St. Paul and Martin Luther as examples of men of religious genius, and of George Washington and Abraham Lincoln as men of political genius. Men of genius open up a new vision and hope before the eyes of their fellowmen, and the power of the new thing that emerged with them takes generations until it has spent its force.

---

[29] *Ibid.*, p. 136.
[30] Nathan Söderblom, *The Nature of Revelation*, trans. F. C. Pamp (New York: Oxford University Press, 1933), p. 151.
[31] *Ibid.*

Söderblom spoke of an

organic connection between the continuing creation of God and the work of men of genius. *Men of genius are the appointed interpreters of God's creation.* Existence is difficult to interpret and easily appears meaningless, bitterly meaningless. Through their powers of penetration, through their personalities and their creations, men of genius aid us to see or to surmise a meaning in life. This they do, not merely as thinkers. No, not primarily as thinkers, but as doers, as heroes, martyrs, prophets, saints, as artists, inventors, composers, poets. Their unique endowment reveals thus a mysterious connection with creation itself.[32]

Revelation, according to Archbishop Söderblom, did not stop with the biblical accounts of natural miracles. Revelation is a continued and continuous process which extends as far as creation. Men of genius interpret creation as at bottom a divine miracle, a revelation of the Creator, God, who at no time and in no place has left himself without a witness. Both creation and revelation are co-extensive processes.

Typically Söderblomian is the emphasis on revelation as an act rather than primarily as a thought. Men of genius, says Söderblom, are instruments of the revelation of God not primarily through their thoughts, but rather through their deeds. Revelation is a matter of action, and only later does reflection begin to analyze what has been revealed.

Söderblom transferred this concept of revelation as act to his ecumenical program. He insisted that practical Christian cooperation across denominational lines must precede doctrinal agreement. First comes the flower, then botany. A program of united Christian action on an interdenominational, worldwide scale was all the more necessary for two reasons. First, the world's need for love, justice, and peace is so great that only the united action of all the Christians in the world can hope to make a real contribution to the future of the world. Second, to begin with attempts to harmonize conflicting Christian doctrines is to do things backwards and to condemn the ecumenical reformation of our time to futility. First, ecumenical action must renew our hearts and minds and give us a new vision of the unity of the churches of Jesus Christ. Then we can sit down and think about the miracle of ecumenical transformation and spiritual renewal that has taken place. First the ancient walls of fear and prejudice must crumble and fall. Then we will be ready to embrace each other across denominational lines and fashion together a new ecumenical creed that will be catholic in substance, evangelical in outlook, and relevant to the needs and hopes of modern men in the space age.

The matter of a new, ecumenical creed which is to replace all those

[32] *Ibid.*, p. 152.

creedal affirmations which have traditionally divided Christians and set brother against brother brings us to the third focus of Söderblom's life and thought which we have called "the social gospel" for lack of a better word. The concern for social justice and international peace and goodwill characterized the archbishop's entire life and work. In 1930 he was awarded the Nobel Peace Prize for it. In 1925 he channelled the pioneering energies of the ecumenical movement into constructive channels of Christian "Life and Work." The world needs compassionate and relevant action, not another creed or doctrine for men to argue about—this was one of Archbishop Söderblom's most cherished convictions.

It would be erroneous to assume that he undervalued the significance of doctrinal agreement. Ecumenical unity must be unity in loving deed and in the truth of faith and revelation. But he never tired of saying that first comes God's overpowering revelation, then come our poor and inadequate human attempts to capture the meaning for all time and eternity. Söderblom saw the ecumenical movement as a contemporary instance of God's continued revelation. To try to squeeze this movement into the shape of doctrines which grew out of ancient and long forgotten controversies would be tantamount to pouring new wine into old wineskins. The result can only be that the new wine will burst the old skins, if it is really new wine.

"What we need is a new confession of faith," Söderblom said. "I do not mean any alteration in the old creeds of the Church, but a clear expression of the teaching of Christ and our Christian duty with regard to the brotherhood of nations, to the fundamental moral laws for the shaping of society, and to the activity of Christian love and charity."[33] During his lifetime Söderblom was an ardent supporter of the League of Nations which was later superseded by the United Nations. He saw in the creation of one world government in freedom and justice an essentially Christian ideal and calling. Beside giving energetic support to the League, the archbishop tried to bring about reconciliation between nations through the influence of Christian churches and personalities. During World War I he tried to arrange a summit conference of ecclesiastical leaders to demonstrate that the faith and love of Christianity transcends hatred and chauvinism. He failed in this noble undertaking: neither the bishops of England and France, nor those of Germany and Austria could see beyond their own national interest. Only bishops from the neutral nations supported Söderblom's call for a united Christian witness before a world torn by hatred, war, poverty, and bloodshed.

Generally speaking, the "social gospel" can be defined as the sincere

[33] Söderblom, *Christian Fellowship* (New York: Fleming H. Revell Co., 1923), p. 179.

attempt of socially conscious Christians to make Christian faith and love dynamically relevant in contemporary life. The social gospel seeks to apply the teachings of our Lord to the needs of men in the modern world. Söderblom noted that in contemporary society

> there is a division that is more momentous even than the mutual opposition of nations. It runs through every nation and country and threatens our whole civilization. It is due to the economic and social situation. In the Gospel our Saviour says much about Mammon. Ought not the Christian Church as such to have a clear and powerful programme in connection with the reconstruction of society?[34]

The archbishop was aware of the fine statements on social issues which individual denominations had proposed. He knew that Pope Leo XIII (1878–1903) had issued a famous encyclical in 1891, *Rerum novarum*, which awoke wide Roman Catholic concern with the issues of social justice. He was aware of the fine work of the Lutheran "inner mission" on behalf of the neglected and unfortunate members of our modern industrial society. But he knew that unless these fine beginnings of a social gospel could be united in ecumenical cooperation, they would be inadequate expressions of what Söderblom called "Christianity's new confession of faith in a supernational brotherhood and Christian principles for social and economic life."[35]

God's revelation in our time moves like a titanic process. Individual acts of rescue are no longer adequate. God discloses himself and his plan for mankind in great movements. Therefore the church must learn from this changed situation, abandon the older individualism of its approach to social problems and issues, and begin to organize and to move in a united, concentrated, interdenominational, worldwide effort. To implement this kind of international Christian cooperation on moral and social issues was one of the primary objectives of the Ecumenical Life and Work Conference at Stockholm in 1925.

Nowhere is the need for all-embracing, interdenominational action more evident than in the question of international peace. Söderblom stressed that "a united Christendom would be the mightiest champion of peace on earth."[36] The message of peace and justice must become an integral part of the contemporary message of the churches to the world. Lack of unity in this matter can only mean the paralysis of the churches' witness for peace and the Prince of Peace. It gives the world an excuse to follow the path of war unto its very end—the self-immolation of the human race. The

---

[34] *Ibid.*, p. 178.
[35] *Ibid.*, pp. 179–180.
[36] Nathan Söderblom. *The Church and Peace* (Oxford: Clarendon Press, 1929), p. 58.

church, if it is to be a faithful witness and interpreter of God's revelation to the modern world, must be united in word and deed, with Christians across denominational lines working together hand in hand for social justice, civil rights, and international peace and goodwill.

Archbishop Söderblom's emphasis on ecumenism and on what unites Christians of various denominations rather than what divides them may give the impression that he did not care much about the specifically Lutheran tradition out of which he came. But nothing could be farther from the truth. Söderblom's vision of ecumenicity was that of unity within diversity. He did not see any conflict between cherishing his Lutheran heritage, on the one hand, and total commitment to the modern ecumenical reformation on the other. As a contemporary of Sigmund Freud and Carl Jung, Söderblom was very keenly interested in the historical and psychological sources of Luther's thought. He wrote a substantial scholarly volume on Luther's humor and melancholy. Luther's melancholy or terrors of conscience (*terrores conscientiae*) were for Söderblom not a psychological aberration, but the authentic sign of "personal mysticism."

The revelation of God, according to Söderblom, can be received directly through mystical religious experience. This view aroused much controversy among those Lutherans and Protestants who limit the revelation of God exclusively to the Word of God as recorded in Holy Scripture. Söderblom saw the revelation of God also outside of the Bible. He held that Luther stood in continuity with the evangelical or personal mysticism of the Middle Ages, such as was practiced by John Tauler and the Brethren of the Common Life. After Luther, men such as Blaise Pascal, John Bunyan, and Søren Kierkegaard continued this strand of personal mysticism.

One of Söderblom's great contributions to the discussion of the concept of revelation in the twentieth century was the recovery of the way of mysticism as a way of divine revelation. He made this possible by distinguishing carefully between personality mysticism, as we find it in St. Augustine, Luther, Pascal, and Kierkegaard, and infinity mysticism as represented by Dionysius the Areopagite, St. Bernard of Clairvaux, Meister Eckhart, St. Theresa, and Wordsworth. The contrast between the mysticism of infinity and the mysticism of personality Söderblom described as follows:

The identifying marks of the mysticism of infinity are "pleasant delights, tranquillity, devotion, piety" (*blanda, tranquilla, devota et religiosa*). St. Francis heard the angel drawing the bow across the strings of the celestial violin. The infinite sweetness and beauty of the tone was such, that one more stroke would have brought him death in complete blessedness. The mysticism of infinity in its pure form, seeks its way out to the point of union with the divine by leaving, by degrees, the creaturely, divesting itself of all qualities, pushing slowly out beyond the sole distinction of existence and non-existence, being and non-being. Beyond the last cliffs of conscious life lies the goal, wrapped in mist. It is without space and form, without name and outline that can be remembered. The moments spent in genuine ecstasy cannot even be described, for consciousness is extinguished. They are surrounded by an inexpressible sanctity and given an ethereal fragrance. During the time that Porphyry abode with his admired master, Plotinus four times experienced union with that divine life which is in all that exists. The purest element of ecstasy consists in a liberty, won step by step, until the outermost limits of life are reached.

How different is the world of personal mysticism! Jeremiah, St. Paul, St. Augustine, Luther, Pascal, Kierkegaard, cry out: "Lord, spare me! Depart from me! My guilt!" (*O, culpa mea!*) The miserable human creature quakes and shivers, bleeds and moans. In the mysticism of infinity we see an outstretched hand, a longing, dreaming gaze. In the mysticism of personality we see a man, who shrinks back in dread and dares not even lift up his eyes. In the former there is an ascension, in the latter a struggle in the darkness of death. Under the mighty grasp of God the recipient of God's grace shudders. He cannot escape and he would not escape. He kisses and blesses the hand of God, for it lifts him up into another world, into the blessed kingdom of life and so holds him secure, so safe, that he can defy sin and death and the Devil. In the former we have liberty in the dim spaces of infinity; in the latter, liberty in the mighty hand of God. In the former a struggle toward the One, the great and unutterable One: in the latter, a meeting in quiet places perhaps, but also in the desert, in work, with an attacking, living, active Will; with an overflowing, empowering fulness of a personal life of holiness and love, in comparison with which all else that is called life is but a disappointment, an illusion. In the one, the great stillness, the distant, unfathomable depths of Divinity; in the other, a living God, unutterably active, who crushes us, but also saves us.[37]

The concept of personal mysticism was of basic importance both for the typically Söderblomian understanding of Luther and for his conception of the living God. While infinite mysticism has won for itself a certain place in Christianity, the pulse of authentically Christian religious experience is personal mysticism. Personal mysticism is Christ's way to God and with God. By placing Luther in the context of medieval Roman Catholic mysticism of the evangelical type, Söderblom stressed the catholicity of Luther. Luther was for Söderblom the evangelical catholic *par excellence*. He stood in essential and historical continuity with what was most authentically catholic and evangelical in the medieval Roman Church.

Prior to Söderblom the tendency among Protestants had been to view Luther in isolation. After the days of the apostles, and especially the

[37] Söderblom, *The Nature of Revelation*, pp. 94–96.

Apostle Paul, Christianity had degenerated until Luther suddenly appeared and restored the pure gospel to the church. Against this unhistorical and unfair view of a great leap from St. Paul to Luther, Söderblom set his face. He demonstrated by means of his scholarly Luther studies that Luther was as much a son of the Catholic Church of the Middle Ages as he was a disciple of St. Paul and the pure gospel. The effect of this discovery was to throw a totally new light on the relationship of Luther to the Roman Catholic Church. Once the Söderblomian emphasis on Luther as a loyal son of evangelical catholicity in the Roman Church had won widespread acceptance, the way was made smoother for a new, ecumenical assessment of Luther. Where formerly Roman Catholic accounts of Luther were highly polemical—and the same was true of Protestant accounts—there now appeared interpretations of Luther's life and thought which attempted to be historically sound and even sympathetic.[38] This change in attitude toward Luther is increasingly gaining ground in Roman Catholicism as well as in Protestantism. It has helped to smooth the way for better ecumenical understanding and cooperation.

Typical of Söderblom's reinterpretation of Luther is his work on *Martin Luther's Small Catechism*. The archbishop there emphasizes the ecumenical or catholic spirit of this popular presentation of the Christian faith. He notes that there is not a single polemical reference in the *Small Catechism*—an amazing witness to the catholicity of the Reformer's faith. Every denomination in Christendom could accept and teach the *Small Catechism,* for it represents what Christians across denominational divisions have always believed and taught. For Söderblom the *Small Catechism* was the literary classic of evangelical catholicity: simple in form, practical in language, evangelical in outlook, catholic in substance.

We now come to the last of the five great themes of the life and thought of Archbishop Söderblom: the history of religions. This field was Söderblom's great love, and already quite early, while he was still a student at the University of Sorbonne in Paris, he established an international reputation as an historian of religions. His area of specialization was the ancient Persian religion of Zoroastrianism, which today has followers among the Parsees of Bombay, India. The prevalent view among Christians in Söderblom's day was that Christianity was the one and only true religion, and all the other religions of the world were devilish error which led pagans straight into the jaws of hell. To convert the heathen to the

[38] Examples of the former polemical attitude are the comprehensive works of the Roman Catholic Luther scholars Heinrich S. Denifle and Hartmann Grisar. Examples of an ecumenical appraisal of Luther are the works of Joseph Lortz and Adolf Herte who, in the 1940's, turned their backs on the tradition of polemical Roman Catholic study of Luther by their fair and objective and sympathetic attitude toward the Reformer.

blessings of Christian religion and culture had been the great aim of Roman Catholic, Orthodox, and Protestant missions during the nineteenth century.

Against this judgmental attitude toward non-Christian religions Söderblom set his great discovery that the living God reveals himself in every religion. No religion is simply the product of man's cultural activity and literary imagination. In the case of Zorastrianism, he demonstrated a relatively close affinity between the prophetic message of Zarathustra and that of the Hebrew prophets, and gave forceful expression to his conviction that both Zarathustra and the prophets of Israel are instances of the special revelation of God. In other words, the special revelation of God is not confined to the Bible and the Tradition of the Church.

Of course, there were important differences between Zarathustra and the Hebrew prophets. The Persian prophet had no successor; therefore, Söderblom contends, his special insight into the revelation of the living God did not develop as in Israel and consequently was eventually lost and modified almost beyond recognition. On the positive side, Söderblom stresses especially one among the differences between the prophet Zarathustra of Persia and the biblical prophets of Israel, one in which Zarathustra had an advantage over the prophets of the Old Testament. Moses and the earlier prophets know nothing of God's power beyond the grave. Their gaze loses itself in the gloom of Sheol until, by a process unique in the history of religion, the craving for righteousness and trust in God by their own irresistible necessity burst upon the gates of Sheol, above all in Psalm 73, without their being guided by conceptions of heaven and hell. From the outset Zarathustra is aware of paradise as well as a place of punishment after death. He makes an unconscious contradiction of the Psalmist's words: " 'In Sheol who shall give thee thanks?' Beyond the gates of death is exactly the place where the 'House of Song' is situated."[39]

There has been speculation that the Hebrew prophets took over the idea of heaven and hell and life after death from Zoroastrianism in Persia. Söderblom showed in his scholarly analysis of Hebrew and Persian documents that the Persian and Hebrew conceptions of life after death were arrived at independently, first in Persia, then in Israel. His works on *The Fravashis,* or guardian angels, and *The Future Life according to Mazdaism* were especially influential in supporting his thesis about the independent development of Persian and Hebrew prophetic religion.

The same emphasis on the manifold character of God's revelation can also be found in Söderblom's view of, and faith in "a general revelation of God. No religion is a product of culture," he said, "all religion depends on a revelation."[40] At all times, and in all places, wherever there has been

[39] Nathan Söderblom, *The Living God* (Boston: Beacon, 1962), p. 203.
[40] Söderblom, *The Nature of Revelation,* p. 8.

religion, there has been the presence and revelation of the living God. In every generation, from time immemorial,

> even pagans have known that "we are also his offspring." And "he has not let himself be without witness." We ought to read Origen's interpretation of such texts. It is high time in this age of world missions and world communications and the final flow of world history in one deep stream, that the Church acquaint itself with the thought of the general revelation of God.[41]

Belief in general revelation means that God's revelation is not confined to the Holy Scriptures and the sacred tradition of the church universal or catholic. If God is the living God, Söderblom argued, then "it is absurd to look upon God's Revelation as finished with Christ or the Bible."[42] God continues to reveal himself to this day. However, his revelation is in conformity with the cultural conditions of the times. "Every higher religion," Söderblom observes, "demands as a necessary condition a certain measure of culture. This includes the religion of prophecy. No phenomenon in the history of religions, no revelation has sprung forth as a *Deus ex machina* without given cultural conditions."[43] To the Chinese, God reveals himself in terms of Chinese culture, and to the Americans in the forms of Western culture.

Did Söderblom hold that all religions are essentially on the same level and of equal worth? Here the answer must be both "yes" and "no." "Yes," insofar as all religion is dependent on a revelation of the living God. Buddhism, Islam, Judaism, Christianity—all are the result of God's revelatory activity in nature, in history, and in the human soul. "No," insofar as biblical revelation is unique—and this uniqueness of Christianity Söderblom believed could be demonstrated by an objective study of the history of religions. "The history related in the Bible," he contended, "is God's Revelation in a fuller, richer, weightier sense than any other history. The uniqueness of God's Revelation in the history recorded in the Bible seems impossible and unlikely to reasoning *a priori;* but still it is a fact, which comparative religion will make more and more evident."[44]

Söderblom judged the uniqueness of Christianity to consist in the fact that in the Christian religion the revealed way of salvation is not a law which must be kept, nor a noble truth which must be believed, nor an eightfold path which must be followed, but a historical human figure, the man Jesus Christ. Nature, but more especially history, national and personal history, is the place where God reveals himself and his will for mankind. The highest, richest, and central manifestation of the living God

---

[41] *Ibid.,* pp. 10–11.
[42] Söderblom, *The Living God,* p. 351.
[43] Söderblom, *The Nature of Revelation,* p. 11.
[44] Söderblom, *The Living God,* pp. 350–351.

must therefore be in the form of a man. The history of the world's religions is the history of God's universal revelation, "inside which we can discern the special revelation,"[45] the special revelation of God through the prophets of Israel, through Christ, through the apostles and the church. Both general and special revelation are processes which, as the history of religions shows, have continued at all times and in all places to this day, and will continue in the future of the human race.

[45] *Ibid.,* p. 351.

Chapter II

Ecumenical Theology: Bonhoeffer

Dietrich Bonhoeffer is one of the most interesting modern theologians. As a prophetic voice of the twentieth-century church he thought ahead of his time and sought to prepare the church for the ecumenical future in the space age.

Bonhoeffer was born on February 4, 1906, in Breslau, Germany, the son of a well-known physician, psychiatrist, and neurologist. He and his twin sister were the sixth and seventh of eight children.

When Dietrich Bonhoeffer was six years old, his family moved to Berlin, in 1912, where his father became professor of psychiatry at the University of Berlin. In Berlin the Bonhoeffers lived next door to the family of the famed theologian and church historian Adolf von Harnack. Young Dietrich enjoyed sports, played the piano very well, and was a good student with an amazing capacity for work and astounding powers of concentration. Already at an early age he demonstrated the ability of uniting love and joy of living with a strong sense of ethical responsibility.

Having decided at a relatively early age to devote himself to the study of theology, Bonhoeffer, at age seventeen, enrolled in the theological field at the University of Tübingen. During the two semesters at Tübingen he was influenced by the biblical theology of Adolf Schlatter.

German universities generally have two semesters: a winter semester which runs from October to March, and a summer semester which lasts from April through July. Bonhoeffer, after completing the summer semester at Tübingen University, travelled for several months through Rome and North Africa. He was deeply impressed by the glory of the Roman liturgy. The Lutheran liturgy of his church in Berlin seemed poor by comparison. The young student of theology also felt the powerful appeal of the monastic life; and later in his life, when he was head of the evangelical brotherhood seminary at Finkenwalde in Pomerania, he tried to translate some of the good points of monastic life into a Protestant framework.

In 1925, at the age of nineteen years, Bonhoeffer decided that it was time for some really serious theological study. He went to the University of Berlin, then a center of liberal theological scholarship, and studied under the Lutheran theologians Reinhold Seeberg and Karl Holl. The great light of the theological faculty was Adolf von Harnack, but with characteristic independence Bonhoeffer did not follow the Ritschlian liberalism of Harnack. He espoused rather the dialectical theology of Karl Barth, whom he had never heard, but about whose theology he had read a good deal.

When Bonhoeffer was twenty-one years of age he submitted his thesis to the theological faculty of the University of Berlin. Entitled *Sanctorum Communio,* or *The Communion of Saints,* it presented an examination of the structure of the church from a Barthian point of view. Taking issue with Ernst Troeltsch's distinction between church and sect, Bonhoeffer argued that the church can be understood neither sociologically nor out of the experience of fellowship among its members, but only as a divine act. The church is the body of Christ, a collective person, realized in Christ and actualized by the Holy Spirit.

The following year the twenty-two-year-old Bonhoeffer went to Spain to become assistant pastor to the German-speaking congregation in Barcelona. He tried his hand at bullfighting, and collected samples of children's games which reflected the old struggle between Moslems and Christians in Spain. At the same time he was engaged in pastoral work and theological studies, preparing his thesis for the press. Bonhoeffer's amazing capacity for work is demonstrated by the fact that in addition he worked on his inaugural dissertation (*Habilitationsschrift*), entitled *Act and Being,* which was to admit him to the position of lecturer in theology at the University of Berlin.

In 1930, at age twenty-four Bonhoeffer actually became a lecturer in systematic theology. But before starting his courses, he was given a leave of absence to accept a Sloan Fellowship to study theology at Union Theological Seminary in New York City for one year. Union was, and still is, the leading Protestant theological school in the United States. Bonhoeffer helped to introduce and interpret Barthian dialectical theology in this center of American theological life, which was then experiencing a severe crisis of its liberal outlook.

One might expect that Bonhoeffer spent most of his time in the theological library of Union Seminary. But that was not so: Bonhoeffer was supremely interested in life in North America. The situation of the Negroes in Harlem fascinated him. He spent the Christmas holidays in Cuba. After the term at Union had ended, he, together with a German student of theology and a French pastor, drove in an old Oldsmobile across the United States from New York to Mexico.

The reaction of Bonhoeffer to the life and thought of the American Protestant church was largely critical. He was disturbed by the lack of theological rigor and the lax attitude toward the question of the truth value of the affirmations of Christian faith. The vitality of church life in the U.S.A., the active and relevant social concern of the churches, the concrete fellowship, and the democratic spirit of U.S. Protestantism impressed Bonhoeffer very much. In many ways American Protestant church life was much closer than the German to the ideal of the church which Bonhoeffer had outlined in his two works, *The Communion of Saints* and *Act and Being*. But Bonhoeffer was critical of U.S. Protestantism as a "Protestantism without Reformation," i.e., without concern for pure doctrine and right confession.

In the autumn of 1931, the twenty-five-year-old Bonhoeffer began lecturing on twentieth-century theology at the University of Berlin. At the same time he served as campus pastor at the Berlin Institute of Technology. In addition to this he took on the job of teaching a confirmation class of some fifty boys in the poverty-stricken district of Wedding. This confirmation class had been so unruly that Bonhoeffer's predecessor had given up. Bonhoeffer, however, made his confirmation instruction a genuine success. He moved into the slums of the Wedding district, visited every family of his fifty confirmands, and made friends with the boys by inviting them to his apartment, playing games with them, serving refreshments, and talking about the Bible and Luther's *Cathechism*.

The following year Bonhoeffer lectured on the first three chapters of the Bible, Gen 1–3. These lectures were later published under the title of *Creation and Fall*.

In 1933, when Bonhoeffer was twenty-seven years old, Hitler came to power. Bonhoeffer's opposition to the Nazi regime, which he voiced through radio and press, led to his increasing isolation at the University of Berlin. His lectures of that year were published from the notes of his students under the title, *Christ the Center*. It was the absolute centrality of Christ in the life and thought of Bonhoeffer which made him adamantly opposed to Hitler, in whom he saw the manifestation of the Antichrist.

In addition to his opposition to the Hitler regime, there were a number of other factors which jarred Bonhoeffer loose from his academic post as lecturer in theology. One of these was his association with the theology of Karl Barth, which made him suspect at Berlin and prevented him from finding theologically congenial colleagues. Another factor which made Bonhoeffer increasingly uncomfortable at Berlin was a personal theological crisis, which initiated a movement away from dogmatic theology and toward simple, biblical exegesis. The fruit of this movement was his famous book, *The Cost of Discipleship*.

The convergence of these factors caused Bonhoeffer to take a leave of absence, in October of 1933, in order to become pastor of two German-speaking congregations in London. This ministry to the congregations of Sydenham and St. Paul's made it possible for Bonhoeffer to make a complete break with the Nazi Christians who were increasingly dominating the German Evangelical, or Protestant, Church. Especially detestable to Bonhoeffer was the so-called "Aryan Paragraph," which prevented anyone of Jewish descent, or married to a Jew, from being a pastor in the Protestant church of Germany. In England, Bonhoeffer was able to get away from all of the Nazi abominations. But he kept in close touch with the so-called Confessing Church, which, unlike the so-called "German Christians," opposed Hitler and National Socialism in the name of the Lordship of Christ. Bonhoeffer became the leading ecumenist of the Confessing Church and developed many contacts in Great Britain which he later was to use for his political activities aimed at the assassination of Hitler and the overthrow of the Nazi dictatorship.

After about one and one-half years in England, the call came to the twenty-nine-year-old Bonhoeffer to take over the leadership of a seminary of the anti-Nazi Confessing Church. The call came at a time when he was planning to go to India to study Gandhi's nonviolent method. India or Finkenwalde in Hitler's Germany—Bonhoeffer wrestled with himself which way to go; but finally his love for the brethren won out, and he went back to Germany.

During the years as head of the seminary of the Confessing Church at Finkenwalde near Stettin in Pomerania, Bonhoeffer wrote *The Cost of Discipleship*. When this book was first published in 1937, its author became famous at once in all of Germany. Two years later Bonhoeffer, then thirty-three years old, published the most monastic of all his writings, *Life Together*. This work outlines the principles of communal life as it was lived at the Finkenwalde seminary of the Confessing Church.

The clouds of the approaching war were gathering in 1939, and American friends of Bonhoeffer, who knew that he would refuse to bear arms if drafted in the event of war, wanted to get the immensely able and gifted theologian out of Germany before World War II would break out. They succeeded in getting an invitation for Bonhoeffer to preach and lecture at Union Theological Seminary in New York City for the next two to three years. Bonhoeffer accepted and went to New York in order to keep open the ecumenical contacts between the U.S. and the Confessing Church of Germany.

But when it became inescapably clear that war would break out soon between Germany and Britain and France, he decided to return to Germany, for the brethren there needed him in their fellowship of suffering. He knew already, then, that the war meant either the total defeat of Germany or the end of Western Christian civilization. Bonhoeffer was thus put into the strange position of feeling compelled to pray for the defeat of Germany, and he was willing to suffer through this defeat. Only in this way did he believe that he would have the right to participate in the reconstruction of Germany along democratic and Christian lines.

Once back in Germany, Bonhoeffer again assumed the leadership of the Finkenwalde seminary of the Confessing Church. Less than a year later, in March of 1940, the seminary was disbanded by order of the Gestapo. Bonhoeffer, then thirty-four years of age, was forbidden to speak, lecture, or publish anywhere in Germany. Since 1938 he had already been prohibited from residing in Berlin.

This was a decisive point in Bonhoeffer's life. He still could escape into religious piety, withdraw from the wicked world, and cultivate his own holiness in the seclusion of a religious life. But he decided to become an active participant in the political underground resistance movement and to devote himself full-time to working for the anti-Nazi Confessing Church in Germany. In the service of the ecclesiastical and political movement of resistance he went to Geneva, Switzerland. There he met with Visser 't Hooft, who later was to become the first General Secretary of the World Council of Churches. Together the two religious leaders drew up a statement[1] pleading for peace terms other than total surrender in order to strengthen the activities of the resistance in Germany. This joint statement was sent to English friends in the hope that it would influence Allied military and political decisions.

---

[1] Dietrich Bonhoeffer, "The Church and the New Order in Europe," *Gesammelte Schriften* (Munich: Chr. Kaiser Verlag, 1958), I, pp. 362–371.

The following year Bonhoeffer flew to Sweden in behalf of the resistance. He was equipped with courier identification papers through the office of Admiral Canaris, head of the German counter intelligence, and a leading figure in the resistance movement. In Sweden Bonhoeffer met his old ecumenical friend, Bishop Bell of Chichester, in a secret meeting at Sigtuna near Stockholm. He revealed to him the plans of the resistance to overthrow Hitler, and asked him to obtain assurances from the British government that the Allies would give Germany a chance to negotiate an honorable peace if the *coup d'état* was successful.

On April 5, 1943, Dietrich Bonhoeffer was arrested in Berlin at his parents' house. He was imprisoned at the Tegel military prison in Berlin. There friendly prison guards and medical orderlies provided him with contact with the outside world, which enabled him to keep in touch with friends as well as do a great deal of reading in the Bible, especially the Old Testament, in theology, nineteenth-century philosophy, science, literature, history, and music. Bonhoeffer also experimented with literary forms of expression, such as poetry, drama, and the novel. He wrote a good many of the fragments which later were published under the title of *Ethics*.

In 1944, following the unsuccessful attempt on the life of Hitler, Bonhoeffer was moved to the much stricter prison in the Prinz Albrechtstrasse in Berlin. Here he wrote down some of the radical theological ideas which have made him famous as a seer of the shape of the church in a religionless world. These radical ideas frightened and alarmed Bonhoeffer himself, but he had to write them down in order to clear the way for a positive, constructive statement which he never lived to make. But they have been picked up by the radical "God is dead" theologians and thus gained enormous publicity and given profound stimulation to present-day theological thought.

Shortly after his thirty-ninth birthday, in February of 1945, Bonhoeffer was taken to Buchenwald concentration camp, where he was herded together with a whole galaxy of stars: the Russian flyer Vassilli Kokorin, nephew of Molotov, who taught Bonhoeffer Russian; the English intelligence officer Payne Best and the squadron leader Hugh Falconer; and the German General von Rabenau, General von Falkenhausen, former Secretary of State Pünder, and Dr. Josef Müller.

Two months later, in April of 1945, just a few days before the American troops came, Bonhoeffer was transferred to Flossenbürg concentration camp in Bavaria. There he was executed by hanging on April 9, 1945, less than a month before the Nazi empire signed its declaration of total surrender.

It has been customary to distinguish three periods in the life and thought of Dietrich Bonhoeffer. Eberhard Bethge, a close personal friend of Bonhoeffer who has edited and reconstructed most of his extant writings, gives the following threefold division: during phase one, which covers the period from 1906 to 1931 (when Bonhoeffer began lecturing in theology at the University of Berlin), Dietrich Bonhoeffer "said to the theologians: Your theme is the church!" The second phase, which runs from 1932 to the outbreak of the Second World War in 1939, has Bonhoeffer saying to the church: "Your theme is the world!" The final phase covers the period from 1940 until Bonhoeffer's martyrdom in 1945. Here "Bonhoeffer said to the world: Your theme, foresakenness, is God's own theme."[2]

The same German scholar proposed another similar division of the theological legacy of Bonhoeffer. The first period, from 1906 to 1932, is characterized by "the quest for the concrete nature of the [Christian] message."[3] The two great works of this early period are *The Communion of Saints* and *Act and Being*. Having located the concrete focus of the Christian message in the church, the body of Christ on earth, he then proceeds to concentrate on "the narrow gate" of authentic Christian faith and life in the church. Typical of this second period, which runs from 1933 to 1939, are the books *The Cost of Discipleship* and *Life Together*. The final period, from 1940 to 1945, is characterized by Bonhoeffer's theological liberation for a religionless Christianity in a world come of age. In this period belong his *Ethics* and the *Letters and Papers from Prison*.

Bonhoeffer has made an equally amazing impact on American theology. American interpreters, like the Methodist theologian John D. Godsey, have also argued for a threefold division of Bonhoeffer's work. The first phase, from 1906 to 1931, is marked by the emphasis on "Jesus Christ as the revelational reality of the church." Here Bonhoeffer speaks and thinks in terms of the church as the collective person of Christ, which is actualized on earth by the Holy Spirit. Phase two, from 1932 to 1939, is characterized by the concern with "Jesus Christ as the Lord over the church." Everything that Bonhoeffer said and wrote during this period bears the stamp of his stress on the Lordship of Jesus and the obedience which is demanded of those worthy to be called Christians, that is, followers of Christ. Phase three, from 1940 to 1945, has as its typical theme a this-worldly (*diesseitig*) vision of "Jesus Christ as the Lord over the world."[4] The experiences of the resistance and years of imprisonment

---

[2] Quoted by John D. Godsey, *The Theology of Dietrich Bonhoeffer* (Philadelphia: Westminster Press, 1960), pp. 19, 80, 195.
[3] Eberhard Bethge, "The Challenge of Dietrich Bonhoeffer's Life and Theology," *The Chicago Theological Seminary Register*, LI, No. 2 (February, 1961), p. 4.
[4] Godsey, *op. cit.*, p. 266.

have brought Bonhoeffer to the point where he views religion as an attempt to escape from reality. The modern world does in fact solve all of its major problems without recourse to the hypothesis "God"; it is a religionless world, that is, a world were religion no longer constitutes the indispensable center of life and reference as in former ages.

There is much to commend this triadic arrangement of Bonhoeffer's life and thought. However, we propose here a fivefold division of his work: 1. Bonhoeffer, the student of theology; 2. Bonhoeffer, the theological professor; 3. Bonhoeffer, the ecumenist; 4. Bonhoeffer, the resistance agent; and 5. Bonhoeffer, the theological radical. The advantage of this fivefold division over the traditional threefold division is that it permits a clearer focussing of some of the most characteristic concerns of Bonhoeffer's life and work.

Bonhoeffer always sought to be concrete; he had a genius for translating thought into concrete action. In few if any modern theologians is there a more intimate connection between the events of his life and his theology. The risk of the concrete decision was his great, secret passion. Time and again he called his church, as well as the ecumenical community of faith, to the daring adventure of concrete commitment to a definite course of action. He dared to regard the assassination of Hitler as an inescapable demand made by Christ upon his life. In the same spirit he defended the concrete decisions and pronouncements of the Confessing Church in Germany—against the sage warnings of wise old armchair theologians.

Bonhoeffer, the student of theology. The urge toward the concrete is already prominent in the two theological works which stand out among the writings of Bonhoeffer the student of theology: *The Communion of Saints* and *Act and Being.*

The Communion of Saints was the dissertation which the twenty-one-year-old Bonhoeffer submitted to the theological faculty of the University of Berlin, and which he published three years later at his own expense. Subsequently, this thesis was to be acclaimed by leading theologians as one of the theological miracles of our century.

The main argument of *Sanctorum Communio* is that the church can be understood more fully with the aid of the insights of modern sociology and social philosophy. For Bonhoeffer the church is more than a religious fellowship; it is the concrete body of Christ, Christ existing as community, a collective person. The church has a social dimension as well as a theological one, and both of these must be seen together in order to get a complete picture of the unique structure of the church.

What makes a person a person? Fellowship (*Gemeinschaft*), says Bonhoeffer; the personal relationship between my "I" and the other person's "Thou." Both as a human being and as a moral being a person exists only in an I-Thou relationship. No human person can emerge and exist in total isolation from God and fellow man. For the Christian understanding of man a person is never alone, but always lives and grows in community, in fellowship with others.

Bonhoeffer argues that the Christian concept of personhood refers to man after the Fall. Before the Fall and original sin man lived in unbroken fellowship with God and without ethical responsibility. Since the Fall, however, man must make moral decisions about good and evil. He must also recognize the valid claim of his fellow man, because the human Thou is a mirror, a copy (*Abbild*) of God's Thou.

God, personhood, and fellowship are inseparable one from the other. God wills each person in his wholeness and uniqueness. But "the individual belongs essentially and absolutely with the other, according to the will of God, even though, or even because, each is completely separate from the other."[5]

The individual needs the other in order to become a person. This need is most truly fulfilled in love and recognition of the other. Rejection of the other is the denial of his personhood. The I-Thou relationship and the collective personal reality of community are for the human person not an optional extra, but a matter of life and death.

Having established that community is the essential basis of personal human life, Bonhoeffer then proceeds to argue that the church, which is the community and communion of saints, is concretely grounded in that which is most basic and true about human life as such. The church is not an association (*Gesellschaft*) or a religious society consisting of separate individuals with a common goal. Tönnies' sociological distinction between *Gesellschaft* (society or association) and *Gemeinschaft* (community or fellowship) is of basic significance for Bonhoeffer's understanding of the church. A society serves its individual members as an instrument designed to achieve a certain end. In the eyes of the law, for instance, the church is a corporation, i.e., a society. In reality, however, the church is not a society but a community: the communion of saints, which is the communion of love and truth. A community does not serve as a means to a higher end; its fellowship is an end in itself. The purpose of the church is to be the body of Christ and the community of the Holy Spirit. In other words, the purpose of the church is to be itself.

The reason for Bonhoeffer's insistence that the church is a community and not a society is that, from the theological point of view, "the community as a collective person can expect eternal life, but the society is

[5] Dietrich Bonhoeffer, *The Communion of Saints* (New York: Harper & Row, 1964), p. 37.

dissolved."[6] "The community as a collective person is from God and to God, and . . . must be thought of as based on the will of God."[7]

As a good Lutheran and Barthian Bonhoeffer stresses that "only faith can create true experience of the church."[8] And where must we go to believe and experience the new creation, the church, the collective person of the body of Christ? Bonhoeffer's answer points to the concrete realities of our everyday experience.

> It is precisely in the commonplace surroundings of every day that the church is believed and experienced; it is not in moments of spiritual exaltation, but in the monotony and severity of daily life, and in the regular worship of God that we come to understand the church's full significance. All else merely veils the true state of things.[9]

In *The Communion of Saints* Bonhoeffer had spoken of the church as "Christ existing as community," as a collective person. In his work, *Act and Being,* he sets out to explore the significance of the community of the church for the Christian way of knowing. Knowledge of the truth of the Christian faith comes by revelation, that is, it comes from "outside of" man and his possibilities and capacities for knowing himself and his world. Revelation is the work of God by his word. Just as the church is to be thought of as a collective person, so God reveals himself in the church as person. The community of the church is created by and in Christ. In this fellowship Christ reveals himself as the new humanity.

Bonhoeffer relates this understanding of revelation in the community of faith to two great philosophical traditions. One of these, which has Immanuel Kant as its foremost representative, holds that knowledge of reality comes to us in the context of action. Truth exists only in act. The other tradition stresses reality as being. Truth is, whether we know it or not. St. Thomas and the modern philosopher Martin Heidegger are treated as examples of this view of how we know reality.

Bonhoeffer criticizes the individualism[10] of both Kant's and Heidegger's solutions. He also objects to the autonomous and closed character of their understanding of man, which does not leave room for revelation. Bonhoeffer points out that revelation occurs in the community of the church. The knowledge of the truth is here a social event which takes place in the community of faith.

Bonhoeffer now proceeds to unite the views of truth as act and truth

[6] *Ibid.,* pp. 199–200.
[7] *Ibid.,* p. 200.
[8] *Ibid.,* p. 198.
[9] *Ibid.*
[10] Dietrich Bonhoeffer, *Act and Being,* trans. B. Noble (London: Collins, 1962), p. 122.

as being in one conception of the church. He declares that, on the one hand, "to 'become' a member of Christ's Church man must believe (it being understood that this is not a human possibility, since faith is given by God). It is only in such faith that man 'has' God. And according to the measure of his faith man has much, little or nothing of God."[11] Here the emphasis is on the act of belief: the reality of God's revelation in the church is accessible only through an act of faith. On the other hand, "faith has being in the church as its condition. Faith invariably discovers itself already in the Church. When it comes to know that it is in the Church, it was already there. To believe is as much as to say: to find God, his grace and the community of Christ already present."[12] This means that the community of faith is prior to the act of faith.

Faith and revelation are both an act and an existing reality. Revelation is independent of faith, but "only in faith does man know that the being of revelation, his own being in the Church of Christ, is independent of faith."[13] Faith here means both believing certain truths and being in the communion of the church.

The final part of *Act and Being* is devoted to Bonhoeffer's statement of the doctrine of man. What is man? Bonhoeffer denies that there is a general abstract answer to this question—an answer like, "Man is a rational animal," or "Man is a tool-making animal." Man exists concretely either "in Adam" or "in Christ." To be "in Adam" means to be in sin, both as an individual who commits sinful acts and as a member of sinful humanity. Adam is "I" and humanity.[14] Hence sin is both an individual act and a universal reality. To be "in Christ" means on the one hand repentance and death of the old man, the old Adam, and on the other hand it signifies a great future "of life and sanctity."[15]

From our analysis of *The Communion of Saints* and *Act and Being* we conclude that Bonhoeffer's early period of theological creativity focused on the question of the authentic nature of the church. At the center of the church stood for him the living Lord, Jesus Christ, who calls men to faith and obedience. This "inward look" directed to the church's world of faith was to change as Bonhoeffer's theological development matured and to be complemented by the "outward look" to the world. Thus the man who at one time risked his life and liberty to train ministers for the church, later risked and lost both liberty and life in the attempt to assassinate Hitler and thus to save the world.

---

11 *Ibid.*, p. 127.
12 *Ibid.*, pp. 127–128.
13 *Ibid.*, p. 128.
14 *Ibid.*, p. 162.
15 *Ibid.*, p. 180.

The two works, *The Communion of Saints* and *Acts and Being*, reveal to us the young Bonhoeffer as a committed, loyal, and thoughtful member of the church, open to all the scientific and philosophical challenges of the modern world. Bonhoeffer the student of theology emerges as one of the most promising new theologians of our century. The famous American theologian and ethicist, Reinhold Niebuhr, who was a young professor when Bonhoeffer came to Union Theological Seminary in New York City, in 1939, characterized him as a "brilliant and theologically sophisticated young man."[16]

Bonhoeffer, the theological professor. A promising career in the privileged circles of German academic life stood open before Bonhoeffer. The twenty-five-year-old theological professor began with zeal and vigor, but from the beginning he was distracted by the political unrest which accompanied the rise of Hitler in the German Weimar Republic. Bonhoeffer's lectures of 1932–1933 on *Creation and Fall,* and his 1933 lectures on the doctrine of Christ, *Christ the Center,* afford an excellent insight into his thought during the early 1930's.

In *Creation and Fall* Bonhoeffer deals with man and his relationship to God as this is pictured in the first three chapters of Genesis. Man stands in the middle between a beginning and an end of which he can know only by hearing the word of God. In fact, God is the beginning, for God created man and the world out of nothing. Apart from God, nothingness is the only thing man can see as he tries to penetrate to the beginning. Therefore, Bonhoeffer, says, we must come to Christ in order to know the beginning of the universe and our own beginning. God is at the beginning; he creates the universe in freedom out of nothing. To know the beginning is to know God, and we "must go to Christ to know God."[17]

Bonhoeffer stresses the freedom of God in his work of creation. God does not have to create, he does not act under compulsion or necessity, he acts in freedom. He creates man in his image, so that to be truly human means to be truly free. And what does it mean to be truly free? Bonhoeffer answers that "freedom is a relationship between two persons. Being free means 'being free for the other,' because the other has bound me to him. Only in relationship with the other am I free."[18]

Freedom in personal relationship is at the same time a limitation of man's existence. "The other person is the limit placed upon me by God. I love this limit and I shall not transgress it because of my love. This

[16] See Reinhold Niebuhr's characterization of Bonhoeffer in the *Union Seminary Quarterly Review,* I, No. 3 (March, 1946), p. 3.
[17] Dietrich Bonhoeffer, *Creation and Fall,* trans. John C. Fletcher (New York: Macmillan Co., 1965), p. 14.
[18] *Ibid.,* p. 37.

means nothing except that the two, who remain *two* as creatures of God, become *one* body, i.e. belong to one another in love."[19] The common bond between man and his fellow man is understood by the biblical writer in connection with human sexuality. "Very clearly," Bonhoeffer explains,

> sexuality is the expression of the two-sidedness of being both an individual and being one with the other person. Sexuality is nothing but the ultimate realization of our belonging to one another. Here sexuality has as yet no life of its own detached from this purpose. Here the community of man and woman is the community derived from God, the community of love glorifying and worshipping him as the Creator. It is therefore the Church in its original form. And because it is the Church it is a community eternally bound together.[20]

Into this harmonious paradise of God's original creative design evil enters in the form of what Bonhoeffer terms "the religious question."[21] Religion for him is man's rebellion against God, man's perverse attempt to seize and control God. Religion, for Bonhoeffer, is man's final and supreme effort to glorify himself and to become *sicut Deus,* like God.

The result is the Fall. Bonhoeffer stresses that

> the Fall of man in God's creation is both inconceivable and unalterably inexcusable, and therefore the word "disobedience" does not exhaust the facts of the case. It is revolt, it is the creature's departure from the attitude which is the only possible attitude for him, it is the creature's becoming Creator, it is the destruction of creatureliness.[22]

The Fall is man's self-destruction. "The destruction of creation by the creature"[23] is the primordial source of evil in the world.

The question may be asked, why God permitted evil in a world which he created good and over which he has complete control? How can evil exist if God is both absolutely good and almighty? Bonhoeffer replies that

> the question of why evil exists is not a theological question, for it assumes that it is possible to go behind the existence forced upon us as sinners. If we could answer it then *we* would not be sinners. We could make something else responsible. Therefore the "question of why" can always only be answered with the "that," which burdens man completely.[24]

Bonhoeffer's point here is to keep us from trying to absolve ourselves from our own responsibility and guilt by making God ultimately responsible for

19 *Ibid.,* p. 61.
20 *Ibid.,* p. 62.
21 *Ibid.,* p. 64.
22 *Ibid.,* p. 76.
23 *Ibid.*
24 *Ibid.*

sin and evil in the world. Moreover, the question why God permits evil to exist in the world of which he is both creator and preserver is misleading because "the theological question does not arise about the origin of evil but about the real overcoming of evil on the Cross; it asks for the forgiveness of guilt, for the reconciliation of the fallen world."[25]

Traditional Christian dogmatics saw the Fall of man as the consequence of, and punishment for, man's original sin. The essence of original sin was seen in sexuality. In his innocence before the Fall man was naked and not ashamed. With the Fall, original sin, and sexuality, nakedness became something shameful. Estranged from his true nature, man could no longer be naked without shame.

Bonhoeffer believes that the traditional Christian triad of the Fall, original sin, and sexuality is basically valid. The knowledge of good and evil of which the third chapter of Genesis speaks

> is originally not an abstract knowledge of ethical principles, but sexuality; i.e. a perversion of the relationship between persons. And since the essential nature of sexuality consists in destruction the dark secret of the originally sinful being of man is in fact preserved from generation to generation in continuing procreation. The objection, which refers to the natural character of sexuality, is not conscious of the highly ambivalent character of all so-called "natural" things in our world. The sanctification of sexuality is given in its restraint by shame, i.e. in its covering and in the vocation of the restrained community of marriage in the Church. The deepest reason for this is that man has lost his creatureliness. His creatureliness has been corrupted in his being like God. All the world of creation is now veiled: it is mute and unresponsive, opaque and mysterious.[26]

Man now lives in the fallen world under the curse of God. Man's world is

> the changed, the destroyed, world. At odds with God, with the other person and with nature, man cannot live, yet in this division of *tob* [good] and *ra* [evil], he cannot live *without God*, without the other person, or without nature. In truth he lives in the world of the curse, but just because it is *God's* curse that burdens it, this world is not totally forsaken by God; it is the world of the preservation of life, blessed in God's curse, pacified in enmity, pain and work.[27]

The story of creation has ended. In the fallen world God no longer creates; rather, he preserves. "The Creator is now the Preserver. The created world is now the fallen, preserved world."[28] Into this world enters the great human drama of the story of Cain. Bonhoeffer notes that

25 *Ibid.*
26 *Ibid.*, p. 85.
27 *Ibid.*
28 *Ibid.*, p. 88.

Cain is the first man to be born upon the cursed ground. The whole story of death begins with Cain. Adam, preserved on the way to death and consumed with thirst for life, begets Cain, the murderer. . . . Why does Cain murder? Out of hatred towards God. This hatred is great. Cain is great, he is greater than Adam, for his hatred is greater, and this means that his yearning for life is greater. The story of death stands under the mark of Cain.[29]

According to Bonhoeffer, the end of the story of death is Christ. "Christ on the Cross, the murdered Son of God, is the end of the story of Cain, and thus the actual end of the story."[30] "The tree of life, the Cross of Christ, the middle of the fallen and preserved world of God, for us that is the end of the story of paradise."[31]

Bonhoeffer developed the concept of Christ hinted at in his lectures on *Creation and Fall* further in his lectures on Christology, the doctrine of the person and work of Christ. He begins in typically Lutheran fashion with the Christ *pro me,* for me. "Christ is present in the church as a person"[32] who lives, loves, suffers, and triumphs for me. Bonhoeffer stresses that "Christ is Christ not as Christ in himself, but in his relation to me."[33]

The emphasis on *what* Christ has done for me rather than *how* he was able to do what he did Bonhoeffer shares with the Reformers Luther, Calvin, and Melanchthon. In traditional Christian thought about Christ's presence and work among us today, "The What of the real presence easily turns into a How, and orthodoxy is equated with a theoretical alchemy of the incarnation."[34] Bonhoeffer rejects the traditional concept of the incarnation as inadequate. The classic speculations about the two natures of Christ, the divine and the human, are misleading because they asked, "How is Christ present?" instead of, or to the exclusion of, "What is Christ doing for me?" Bonhoeffer emphasizes Christ as act, whereas traditional orthodoxy speculated about Christ's being.

He states that Christ is concretely and really present here and now, in space and time, in the written and preached word of God, in the holy sacraments, and in the church. Christ here suffers and is victorious for me as the pioneer of God's new creation. He stands in my place before God, receiving the blows of God's judgment in my place and transferring to me the grace of God.[35] It is evident that, for a fully evangelical statement of

29 *Ibid.,* p. 93.
30 *Ibid.*
31 *Ibid.,* p. 94.
32 Dietrich Bonhoeffer, *Christ the Center,* trans. J. Bowden (New York: Harper & Row, 1966), p. 43.
33 *Ibid.,* p. 47.
34 Jaroslav Pelikan, "Bonhoeffer's *Christologie* of 1933," *The Place of Bonhoeffer,* ed. Martin E. Marty (New York: Association Press, 1962), p. 149.
35 Bonhoeffer, *Christ the Center,* pp. 48–49.

the doctrine of the person and work of Christ, act and being must be seen together. Christ is what he does, and he does what he is. But Bonhoeffer believed that in his day there was more need for emphasizing the dynamic act of Christ than for speculating about the divine and the human dimensions of Christ's being.

Christ is present as the center of our existence. This is true even when Christ appears to be pushed to the far edge of our lives. Bonhoeffer explains that "Christ as the center of human existence means that he is man's judgment and his justification."[36]

Christ is also present as the center of history. Bonhoeffer declares that

Christ is present to us in a double form, as church and as state. But this is true only for us, who receive him as Word and sacrament and community, for us, who, after the cross, must see the state in the light of Christ. The state is the rule of God "with his left hand" (Luther, Weimar edition, 36, 385, 6-9; WA 52, 26, 20-26). As long as Christ was on earth he was the rule of God. When he was crucified, the rule broke into two, one by his right hand and one by the left hand of God. Now his rule can be known only as twofold, as church and as state. But the whole Christ is present to his church. And this church is the hidden centre of the state. The state need not know that the church is at its centre, but in fact it lives from this centre and cannot continue without it.[37]

Because Christ is the new creation, he is the mediator between God and nature. The place where this is most clearly seen is in the sacraments. "Enslaved nature does not utter the Word of creation directly to us. But the sacraments speak. In the sacrament, Christ is the mediator between nature and God, and stands for all creatures before God."[38]

Following a survey of the history of the development of the doctrine of the person and work of Christ, Bonhoeffer concludes his lectures on Christology with an interpretation of Christ as "the Humiliated One" and "the Risen One." Christ is *incognito,* unrecognized in the world. And yet he bears the stamp of the power and glory of the living God. "We have the Exalted One," Bonhoeffer observes, "only as the Crucified, the Sinless One only as the one laden with guilt, the Risen One only as the Humiliated One. Were this not so, the *pro nobis* would be done away with, there would be no faith."[39]

How do we know all this? Bonhoeffer answers:

We know all this only from our encounter with the Lowly One. The church goes on its own way of lowliness with this Lowly One. It cannot strive for a

[36] *Ibid.,* p. 63.
[37] *Ibid.,* p. 66.
[38] *Ibid.,* p. 67.
[39] *Ibid.,* p. 116.

visible confirmation of its way while it renounces itself at every step. But as the lowly church, it may not look at itself in vain conceit, as though its lowliness were visible proof that Christ was present there. Lowliness is no proof, at least not a proof that one can refer to. There is no law or principle here which the church has to follow; this is a fact, in short, God's way with the church. As Paul says of himself that he can be either exalted or lowly so long as it happens for the sake of Christ, so too the church can be exalted and lowly, so long as it follows Christ's way. This way is the enemy of the proud, whether they wrap themselves in purple robes or set the martyr's crown upon their heads. The church always looks only to the humiliated Christ, whether it be exalted or lowly.[40]

This is a typically evangelical interpretation of Christ and the church. It emphasizes the humiliation, lowliness, and suffering of Christ and of the church in the world. Later, in Bonhoeffer's prison letters, the theme of humiliation and suffering of God at the hands of a godless world recurs again. Only here it is developed in a more radical and revolutionary way as the clue to the religionless existence of the modern Christian in the secular world.

The lectures on Christology of 1933 ended Bonhoeffer's career as a teacher of theology at the University of Berlin. He continued his work as theological professor at the clandestine seminary of the Confessing Church at Finkenwalde. Two characteristic works of this second phase of Bonhoeffer the professor of theology are *The Cost of Discipleship* and *Life Together*.

In *The Cost of Discipleship*, which aroused immediate attention at its first publication in the late 1930's, Bonhoeffer deals with the reality of sin and grace in interpersonal relationships. "The book," said Bishop Bell of Chichester, a close English friend of Bonhoeffer, "will show men by what fire this young German churchman was possessed."[41] Grouping his thoughts around the Sermon on the Mount, Bonhoeffer proposes "to tell how Jesus calls us to be his disciples."[42]

The first thing we must realize, Bonhoeffer insists, is that "cheap grace is the deadly enemy of our Church. We are fighting today for costly grace."[43] And what is cheap grace?

Cheap grace means grace sold on the market like cheapjacks' wares. The sacraments, the forgiveness of sin, and the consolations of religion are thrown away at cut prices. Grace is represented as the church's inexhaustible treasury, from which she showers blessings with generous hands, without

[40] *Ibid.*, pp. 117–118.
[41] G. K. A. Bell, "Foreword," Dietrich Bonhoeffer, *The Cost of Discipleship*, trans. R. H. Fuller (New York: Macmillan, 1966), p. 8.
[42] *Ibid.*, p. 39.
[43] *Ibid.*, p. 45

asking questions or fixing limits. Grace without price; grace without cost!
The essence of grace, we suppose, is that the account has been paid in advance; and, because it has been paid, everything can be had for nothing.
Since the cost was infinite, the possibilities of using and spending it are
infinite. What would grace be if it were not cheap?[44]

Costly grace, in contrast to cheap grace, is the grace of true discipleship.
"When Christ calls a man he bids him come and die. . . . When we are
called to follow Christ, we are summoned to an exclusive attachment to his
person. The grace of his call bursts all the bonds of legalism. It is a
gracious call, a gracious commandment."[45]

But the call to discipleship leads us in the narrow path of costly grace.

The path of discipleship is narrow, and it is fatally easy to miss one's way and
stray from the path, even after years of discipleship. And it is hard to find.
On either side of the narrow path deep chasms yawn. To be called to a life
of extraordinary quality, to live up to it, and yet to be unconscious of it is
indeed a narrow way. To confess and testify to the truth as it is in Jesus,
and at the same time to love the enemies of that truth, his enemies and
ours, and to love them with the infinite love of Jesus Christ, is indeed a
narrow way. To believe the promise of Jesus that his followers shall possess
the earth, and at the same time to face our enemies unarmed and defence-
less, preferring to incur injustice rather than to do wrong themselves, is indeed a narrow way. To see the weakness and wrong in others, and at the
same time refrain from judging them; to deliver the gospel message without
casting pearls before swine, is indeed a narrow way. The way is unutterably
hard, and at every moment we are in danger of straying from it. If we regard this way as one we follow in obedience to an external command, if we
are afraid of ourselves all the time, it is indeed an impossible way. But if we
behold Jesus Christ going on before step by step, we shall not go astray.
But if we worry about the dangers that beset us, if we gaze at the road
instead of at him who goes before, we are already straying from the path.
For he is himself the way, the narrow way and the strait gate. He, and he
alone, is our journey's end. When we know that, we are able to proceed
along the narrow way through the strait gate of the cross, and on to eternal
life, and the very narrowness of the road will increase our certainty. The
way which the Son of God trod on earth, and the way which we too must
tread as citizens of two worlds on the razor edge between this world and the
kingdom of heaven, could hardly be a broad way. The narrow way is bound
to be right.[46]

Walking along the razor edge of costly grace we can survive as Christians only if our eyes are exclusively fixed on Christ the Master. Therefore,
Bonhoeffer declares, as authentic followers of Christ,

[44] *Ibid.,* p. 7.
[45] *Ibid.,* p. 63.
[46] *Ibid.,* pp. 211–212.

we pay no attention to our own lives or the new image which we bear, for then we should at once have forfeited it, since it is only to serve as a mirror for the image of Christ on whom our gaze is fixed. The disciple looks solely at his Master. But when a man follows Jesus Christ and bears the image of the incarnate, crucified and risen Lord, when he has become the image of God, we may at last say that he has been called to be the "imitator of God." The follower of Jesus is the imitator of God.[47]

No one can fail to be affected by the powerful and simple Christian piety which enlivens Bonhoeffer's reflections on "the cost of discipleship" and "costly grace." The theme of costly grace is explored in its communal context in Bonhoeffer's book *Life Together.* "Christian community," Bonhoeffer emphasizes there, "is like the Christian's sanctification. It is a gift of God which we cannot claim."[48] Christian fellowship is not an ideal, but a reality created by God in Christ. And

> because Christian community is founded solely on Jesus Christ, it is a spiritual and not a psychic reality. In this it differs absolutely from all other communities. The Scriptures call "pneumatic," "spiritual," that which is created only by the Holy Spirit, who puts Jesus Christ into our hearts as Lord and Saviour. The Scriptures term "psychic," "human" that which comes from the natural urges, powers, and capacities of the human spirit.[49]

The limitations of our merely human efforts are only too apparent in the church. For example, no amount of good will and persuasion on the part of church members can keep within the fellowship someone who is determined to break away from the community of faith, hope, and love.

> Our brother's ways are not in our hands; we cannot hold together what is breaking; we cannot keep life in what is determined to die. But God binds elements together in the breaking, creates community in the separation, grants grace through judgment. He has put His Word in our mouth. He wants it to be spoken through us. If we hinder His Word, the blood of the sinning brother will be upon us. If we carry out His Word, God will save our brother through us.[50]

This is the costly grace that works through human fellowship and yet is not subject to our control.

Bonhoeffer, the ecumenist. During his years as professor Bonhoeffer was actively engaged in the ecumenical movement. In September, 1931, at the age of twenty-five years, he was a delegate to the ecumenical conference of the World Alliance for Promoting International Friendship Through the

[47] *Ibid.,* p. 344.
[48] Dietrich Bonhoeffer, *Life Together,* trans. J. W. Doberstein (New York: Harper, 1954), p. 30.
[49] *Ibid.,* p. 31.
[50] *Ibid.,* p. 108.

Churches. (The World Alliance was one of the three great ecumenical streams which were united later in the World Council of Churches. The other two were the Life and Work movement, led by Archbishop Söderblom, and the Faith and Order movement led by Bishop Charles Brent and other Anglicans.) The World Alliance's International Youth Conference elected Bonhoeffer International Youth Secretary for Germany and Central Europe.

Soon he became known as one of the most respected German ecumenists, because of his personal friendliness, theological astuteness, and linguistic ability. In his report from the ecumenical conference which elected him youth secretary Bonhoeffer indicated his encouragement over the fact that in the face of the moral and spiritual collapse of Europe during the 1930's, the churches united in the ecumenical movement "have their feet firmly planted on the ground and issue the call to truthfulness, faithfulness, and the keeping of promises."[51] It was precisely this kind of relevant, practical Christian concern for the world and the individual as a human being which Archbishop Söderblom had so effectively promoted in the Life and Work movement.

Bonhoeffer's ecumenical contacts as International Youth Secretary broadened his horizons and deepened his theological sensitivities. At the Theological Conference for Ecumenical Youth Work at Berlin, in 1932, he raised two important points against the prevalent concern for the structure of the ecumenical church of the future. First, ecumenical Christian youth are concerned that the question of truth and error be kept in mind when evaluating the differing perspectives of the churches. The concept of heresy has lost all meaning for the ecumenical movement. Second, the theological differences between the Protestant churches participating in the ecumenical movement are much more serious than were the most divisive issues separating Protestants and Roman Catholics at the time of the Reformation. Bonhoeffer's point was that ecumenists should worry more about the truth and error of contemporary Christian teaching and less about how many divided churches can be the one holy catholic church on earth.[52]

In July, 1932, Bonhoeffer participated in the ecumenical Youth Conference at Cernohorske Kupele in Czechoslovakia. There he presented a paper which outlined the structure of his ecumenical theology. He begins with the observation that

> there is still no theology of the ecumenical movement. As often as the church of Christ has reached a new understanding of its nature it has produced a

[51] Dietrich Bonhoeffer, *Gesammelte Schriften* (Munich: Chr. Kaiser Verlag, 1958), I, p. 113.
[52] *Ibid.*, I, p. 126.

new theology, appropriate to this self-understanding. A change in the church's understanding of itself is proved genuine by the production of a theology. For theology is the church's self-understanding of its own nature on the basis of its understanding of the revelation of God in Christ, and this self-understanding of necessity always begins where there is a new trend in the church's understanding of itself. If the ecumenical movement stems from a new self-understanding of the church of Christ, it must and will produce a theology. If it does not succeed in this, that will be evidence that it is nothing but a new and up-to-date improvement in church organisation. No one requires a theology of such an organisation, but simply definite action in a concrete task.[53]

Ecumenical theology, according to Bonhoeffer, must, first, begin with a new understanding of the nature and mission of the church. "The church as the one community of the Lord Jesus Christ, who is Lord of the world, has the commission to say his Word to the whole world. The territory of the one church of Christ is the whole world. Each individual church has geographical limits drawn to its own preaching, but the *one* church has no limits."[54] In other words, the church is ecumenical, that is, its claim embraces the *oikoumene,* the entire inhabited earth.

Second, on this foundation ecumenical thought must now raise the question of authority.

With whose authority does the church speak when it declares this claim of Christ to the whole world? With the authority in which alone the church can speak, with the authority of the Christ living and present in it. The church is the presence of Christ on earth, the church is the present Christ. For this reason alone its word has authority. The word of the church is the word of the present Christ, it is gospel and commandment. It would be the retrogression of the church to the synagogue if its proclamation were commandment alone, and it would be the lapse of the church into libertinism should it want to deny the commandment of God for the sake of the Gospel.[55]

Third, ecumenical theology must tell us how the gospel and commandment of God are concrete and real in our lives today. The demand that ecumenism be concrete and practical is typical of Bonhoeffer's entire theology. He makes two suggestions in this context. First, he notes,

someone can only speak to me with authority if a word from the deepest knowledge of my humanity encounters me here and now in all my reality. Any other word is impotent. The word of the church to the world must

---

[53] Dietrich Bonhoeffer, *No Rusty Swords,* trans. E. H. Robertson and J. Bowden (New York: Harper & Row, 1965), pp. 157–158.
[54] *Ibid.,* p. 161.
[55] *Ibid.*

therefore encounter the world in all its present reality from the deepest knowledge of the world, if it is to be authoritative. The church must be able to say the Word of God, the word of authority, here and now, in the most concrete way possible, from knowledge of the situation. The church may not therefore preach timeless principles however true, but only commandments which are true today.[56]

In other words, "what the sacrament is for the preaching of the Gospel, the knowledge of form reality is for the preaching of the sacrament. *Reality is the sacrament of command.*"[57] Second, *"the Gospel becomes concrete in the hearers, the commandment becomes concrete in those who preach it."*[58] This means that

if the church really has a commandment of God, it must proclaim it in the most definite form possible, from the fullest knowledge of the matter, and it must utter a summons to obedience. A commandment must be definite, otherwise it is not a commandment. God's commandment now requires something quite definite from us. And the church should proclaim this to the community.[59]

Fourth, the theology of ecumenism must not confuse the realization of certain concrete commandments, for instance international peace, with the partial realization of the kingdom of God on earth. Bonhoeffer charged that this confusion was especially prevalent among U.S. and British ecumenists. To them he said:

International peace is not a reality of the Gospel, not a part of the kingdom of God, but a command of the angry God, an order for the preservation of the world in the light of Christ. International peace is therefore no ideal state, but an order which is directed towards something else and is not valid in itself.[60]

This "something else" is the forgiveness of sins, Bonhoeffer explains in typically Lutheran fashion.

There is a community of peace for Christians only because one will forgive the other his sins. The forgiveness of sins still remains the sole ground of all peace, even where the order of external peace remains preserved in truth and justice. It is therefore also the ultimate ground on which all ecumenical work rests, precisely where the cleavage appears hopeless.[61]

During August of 1932 Bonhoeffer attended an ecumenical youth conference at Gland, Switzerland, where he delivered an address entitled, "The

56 *Ibid.*, pp. 161–162.
57 *Ibid.*, p. 164.
58 *Ibid.*, p. 162.
59 *Ibid.*, p. 163.
60 *Ibid.*, p. 168.
61 *Ibid.*, p. 169.

Church Is Dead." Dead is the old, dogmatic, divisive, irrelevant church; the future belongs to the ecumenical church of the living Christ. "Faith in the living church of Christ," Bonhoeffer states,

> only breaks through where one sees most clearly the dying of the church in the world, the process of ever new collapse, where one knows that the world, if it is honest, cannot say anything but "The church is dead," that the world cannot understand our action here as anything but the funeral preparations—and where, in spite of, contrary to, against everything, one hears how the New Testament proclaims life to the dying and how death and life come into contact in the cross of Christ and how life conquers death—only where one sees that does one believe in the church under the cross. One can only believe with a clear vision of reality, without any illusion about our morals and our culture. The believer can be neither a pessimist nor an optimist. To be either is illusory. The believer sees reality not in a certain light, but he sees it as it is and believes *only in God* and his power toward all and over all that he sees. He does not believe in the world, not even in the world that is capable of development and improvement, he does not believe in his power to improve the world and its good will, he does not believe in men, even in the good in men which must eventually prevail, he does not even believe in the church in its human power. The believer believes only in God, who makes and does the impossible, who makes life from death and who has called the dying church to life against and despite us and through us, though he alone does it.[62]

Bonhoeffer believed that ecumenical theology needed a strong emphasis on the living God as the basis of ecumenical thought and life in the church. Without ecumenical renewal through the Spirit of the living God the church was, and would remain dead in the contemporary world.

Bonhoeffer, the resistance fighter. Bonhoeffer the ecumenist had grown spiritually in many contacts with Christians across denominational lines. The ecumenical movement had given him a keen sense of international Christian responsibility. When Hitler seized power in Germany and plunged the world into the most destructive war of history, Bonhoeffer's sense of ecumenical responsibility not only for Germany, but for Christendom as a whole, impelled him to join the resistance movement against Hitler.

In keeping with his predilection for concrete commands and decisions, Bonhoeffer began to pray and work for the defeat of his own nation. He opposed Hitler as an "unnatural" perversion of God's created order of the natural life of man in society. It is not surprising that in his *Ethics,* which Bonhoeffer began while a member of the German resistance against Hitler, he sought to recover the concept of "the natural" for Protestant theological ethics. He wrote:

[62] *Ibid.,* pp. 183–184.

The concept of the natural has fallen into discredit in Protestant ethics. For some it was completely lost to sight in the darkness of general sinfulness, while for others, conversely, it was lighted up by the brilliance of absolute historicity. In both cases this was a disastrous mistake, for its consequence was that the concept of the natural no longer had a place in Protestant thought but was entirely abandoned to Catholic ethics. Now this meant a serious and substantial loss to Protestant thought, for it was now more or less deprived of the means of orientation in dealing with the practical questions of natural life. The significance of the natural for the gospel was obscured, and the Protestant Church was no longer able to return a clear word of direction in answer to the burning questions of natural life. She thus left countless human beings unanswered and unassisted in the midst of vitally important decisions, and confined herself more and more to an (orthodoxly static) apology for the divine grace. Before the light of grace everything human and natural sank into the night of sin, and now no one dared to consider the relative differences within the human and natural, for fear that by their so doing grace might be diminished. It was its treatment of the concept of the natural that demonstrated most clearly that this Protestant thought was no longer conscious of the true relation of the ultimate to the penultimate. The consequences of this loss were grave and far-reaching. If there were no longer any relative distinctions to be made within the fallen creation, then the way was open for every kind of arbitrariness and disorder, and natural life, with its concrete decisions and orders, was no longer subject to responsibility to God. The sole antithesis to the natural was the word of God; the natural was no longer contrasted with the unnatural. For in the presence of the word of God both the natural and the unnatural were equally damned. And this meant complete disruption in the domain of natural life.[63]

Bonhoeffer therefore made a radical departure from traditional Protestant thought and declared: "the concept of the natural must . . . be recovered on the basis of the gospel."[64] His active role in the resistance, for which he was hanged by the Nazis, was a concrete expression of his attempt to restore an evangelical understanding of the Christian responsibility for the natural. Although he loved Germany very much, he prayed and worked for the defeat of his own people in the name of the gospel of Christ. This is how he concretely understood Christ's call to discipleship, the call to suffer as Christ himself had suffered. "It is immensely easier to suffer in obedience to a human command," he said,

> than to suffer in the freedom of one's own responsible deed. It is immensely easier to suffer with others than to suffer alone. It is immensely easier to suffer openly and honorably than apart and in shame. It is immensely easier

[63] Dietrich Bonhoeffer, *Ethics*, trans. N. H. Smith (New York: Macmillan, 1965), pp. 143–144.
[64] *Ibid.*, p. 144.

to suffer through commitment of the physical life than in the spirit. Christ suffered in freedom, alone, apart and in shame, in body and spirit, and since then many Christians have so suffered with him.[65]

In the fellowship of suffering Bonhoeffer was united with men who stood completely outside the church and Christianity. But he recognized that they had important things in common with him. They had a right sense for God's order of the natural life of man. "The Christian rejoices," Bonhoeffer notes in his exposition of "The First Table of the Ten Commandments," written in 1944 while he was imprisoned as a member of the resistance,

> that he holds so many important things in common with other men. He is ready to work and to struggle alongside these men, where it is a matter of the realization of common goals. It does not surprise him that men in every age have come to [an] understanding of life that agrees extensively with the Ten Commandments, because the Giver of the Commandments is indeed the Creator and Preserver of life. Still, the Christian never forgets the decisive difference that exists between these laws of life and the Commandments of God. In the former, reason speaks; in the latter, God.[66]

But in Christ God has ceased to be merely the idea of a Supreme Being, or the ultimate order of value, or the limit and projection of the most exalted human possibilities. In Christ, Bonhoeffer insists, God has entered into man and his world. Therefore it is worthwhile to risk even one's own life out of a sense of responsibility for the world.

This is what Bonhoeffer did in the resistance movement. At great risk to his own life and safety he travelled to Geneva, Switzerland, in 1941, in order to plead with the Allies for a military truce while Hitler was being overthrown in Germany.[67] Bonhoeffer, together with W.A. Visser 't Hooft, who later became the first Secretary General of the World Council of Churches, composed a memorandum to British friends pleading for a military truce or pause to help the work of the resistance. But the names of Bonhoeffer and Visser 't Hooft did not mean enough in British ecclesiastical circles to initiate political action. Hence no specific answer came back from England to the waiting Bonhoeffer in Switzerland.[68]

Again in 1942 Bonhoeffer obtained courier identification from the Foreign Ministry through the influence of Admiral Canaris. He went to Sweden to give Bishop Bell of Chichester a message for the British govern-

---

[65] Dietrich Bonhoeffer, *I Loved This People*, trans. K. C. Crim (Richmond, Va.: John Knox Press, 1965), pp. 34–35.

[66] Dietrich Bonhoeffer, "The First Table of the Ten Commandments," in John D. Godsey, *Preface to Bonhoeffer* (Philadelphia: Fortress Press, 1965), p. 51.

[67] Eberhard Bethge, "Aus Bonhoeffers konspirativen Reisen," *Die mündige Welt* (Munich: Chr. Kaiser Verlag, 1959–1963), IV, p. 116.

[68] *Ibid.*, p. 117.

ment. It had two points: first, the British government must be assured that the resistance against Hitler is composed of peaceful men who had to disguise themselves in public in order to be able to show their true colors when it really counted. Second, the British government was asked to give the anti-Nazi revolution time to eliminate Hitler and to establish itself.[69] Although no encouraging reply came from England, Bonhoeffer continued to work for the resistance in the name of Christ. For his faith that works despite all discouragement and disappointment he was martyred in a Nazi concentration camp.

Bonhoeffer, the theological radical. It is not too difficult to understand that the extraordinary demands of Bonhoeffer's participation in the resistance initiated a radical development of his theological outlook. The surrender to Nazism on the part of many German Christians, and the escape into religious piety on the part of the anti-Nazi Confessing Church, left Bonhoeffer deeply disappointed and disturbed by the quietism and political inaction of evangelical as well as catholic Christianity in Germany.

In an attempt to rescue the church from irrelevance or sell-out surrender, Bonhoeffer developed three important emphases which radically departed from traditional Protestant theology. These revolutionary theological emphases have made his *Ethics* and *Letters and Papers from Prison* famous in the contemporary world of Christian thought.

The first of these is his concept of the natural. By means of this concept Bonhoeffer sought to rescue the church from contemporary social and ethical irrelevance by demanding from it concrete guidance in all questions of human life. He also broke through the traditional Protestant overemphasis on the cross of Christ and pointed to the incarnation. In the incarnation "Christ Himself entered into the natural life, and it is only through the incarnation of Christ that the natural life becomes the penultimate which is directed towards the ultimate. Only through the incarnation of Christ do we have the right to call others to the natural life and to live the natural life ourselves."[70]

Second, Bonhoeffer has revolutionized modern theology with his notion of "the world come of age." The radical "God is dead" theologians Altizer, Hamilton, and Van Buren have seized upon this theme in Bonhoeffer the theological radical. They have declared "the death of God" and proclaimed "the secular meaning of the gospel" with quotes from Bonhoeffer's prison letters. Many other theologians have also been stimulated by Bonhoeffer's idea of a world come of age, but they have received less publicity. Among these especially worthy of note are the theologians behind the Iron Curtain: Hanfried Müller of East Berlin's Humboldt University, J. M. Lochmann

---

[69] *Ibid.*, p. 125.
[70] Bonhoeffer, *Ethics*, p. 145.

of Comenius Theological Seminary in Prague, Czechoslovakia, and others. They have found in Bonhoeffer's idea of a world come of age, that is, a world which can get along very well without God, a new way to bridge the gap between Christianity and atheistic communism, thus enabling Christian theologians to find "a positive orientation of the church toward a socialist society."[71]

According to Bonhoeffer, modern man no longer needs God in order to explain reality or to account for the universe. The world has come of age and shed the tutelage of God. In the autonomous secular world there is no room for God. As Christians in this situation

> the only way to be honest is to recognize that we have to live in the world as if there were no God. And this is just what we do see—before God! So our coming of age forces us to a true recognition of our situation before God. God is teaching us that we must live as men who can get along very well without him. The God who is with us is the God who forsakes us (Mark 15:34). The God who makes us live in this world without using him as a working hypothesis is the God before whom we are ever standing. Before God and with him we live without God.[72]

In the world come of age, the secular godless world of contemporary society,

> God allows himself to be edged out of the world and on to the cross. God is weak and powerless in the world, and that is exactly the way, the only way, in which he can be with us and help us. Matt 8:17 makes it crystal clear that it is not by his omnipotence that Christ helps us, but by his weakness and suffering.[73]

Weakness and suffering are the marks of Christianity in a world come of age. "The world come of age is the world in which men have learned 'to solve every important question on their own, without the benefit of the working hypothesis God.' "[74]

The important theological implications follow from Bonhoeffer's idea of a world come of age. First,

> with the recognition of the world come of age Bonhoeffer proclaims the freedom of the Christian for understanding, affirming, and transforming the world. With this the traditional Christian agnosticism, pessimism, and quietism is overcome, and no more obstacles are put in the way of continued

[71] J. M. Lochmann, "From the Church to the World," New Theology No. 1, ed. M. E. Marty and D. G. Peerman (New York: Macmillan, 1964), p. 180.
[72] Dietrich Bonhoeffer, Letters and Papers from Prison, trans. R. H. Fuller (New York: Macmillan, 1962), p. 219.
[73] Ibid., pp. 219–220.
[74] Hanfried Müller, Von der Kirche zur Welt (Leipzig: Koehler & Amelang, 1961), p. 367.

progress. In every way the world is given to the Christian: "All is yours, but you are Christ's." This is the foundation of the future development of theology which Bonhoeffer has laid bare with his affirmation of "the world come of age."[75]

Second, genuine worldliness and the rule of Christ are interchangeable concepts. Now the world can really be the world. Christ has taken upon himself the sins of the world. Now man can truly and fully come of age and be human. There is no longer any need for man to play either God or Satan.[76]

The third of Bonhoeffer's theological ideas that has shaken the theological world to its very foundations is his vision of a "religionless Christianity." This vision was inspired by his profound search for a relevant Christianity and an authentically contemporary understanding of Christ. From his prison cell Bonhoeffer wrote:

> The thing that keeps coming back to me is, what *is* Christianity, and indeed what *is* Christ, for us today? The time when men could be told everything by means of words, whether theological or simply pious, is over, and so is the time of inwardness and conscience, which is to say the time of religion as such. We are proceeding towards a time of no religion at all: men as they are now simply cannot be religious any more. Even those who honestly describe themselves as "religious" do not in the least act up to it, and so when they say "religious" they evidently mean something quite different. Our whole nineteen-hundred-year-old Christian preaching and theology rests upon the "religious premise" of man. What we call Christianity has always been a pattern—perhaps a true pattern—of religion. But if one day it becomes apparent that this *a priori* "premise" simply does not exist, but was an historical and temporary form of human self-expression, i.e. if we reach the stage of being radically without religion—. . . what does that mean for "Christianity?"[77]

Bonhoeffer is well aware that it means a radical transformation of traditional Christianity.

> It means that the linchpin is removed from the whole structure of our Christianity to date, and the only people left for us to light on in the way of "religion" are a few "last survivals of the age of chivalry," or else one or two who are intellectually dishonest. Would they be the chosen few? Is it on this dubious group and none other that we are to pounce, in fervour, pique, or indignation, in order to sell them the goods we have to offer? Are we to fall upon one or two unhappy people in their weakest moment and force upon them a sort of religious coercion?[78]

[75] *Ibid.*
[76] Jürgen Moltmann, *Herrschaft Christi und soziale Wirklichkeit nach Dietrich Bonhoeffer* (Munich: Chr. Kaiser, Verlag, 1959), pp. 39–40.
[77] Bonhoeffer, *Letters and Papers from Prison*, pp. 162–163.
[78] *Ibid.*, p. 163.

appreciation of the value of the concrete and sensuous in religion and religious experience, which other humanists, philosophers, and theologians have viewed as a feminine aspect of their heritage, is largely lacking in Whitehead's religious development. To him the religious vision and feeling expressed in an "Ave Maria" was ultimately incomprehensible. His religion was that of the mystical flight of disembodied spirit into the ever elusive and abstract metaphysical realms of the cosmic mind of God. Whitehead's religion belonged to the type which Söderblom, the Swedish historian of religions and ecumenical churchman and theologian, termed "mysticism of infinity," and is akin to "the flight of the alone to the Alone" (Plotinus). "Religion is what the individual does with his own solitariness,"[2] Whitehead said. Later, in the years following his marriage to Evelyn Willoughby Wade in 1890, the hitherto recessive feminine aspects of Whitehead's personality were brought into considerable prominence in his humanistic appreciation of aesthetics and what he called "beauty." But until that time, his austerely abstract and mystically masculine mind dominated his conception of value.

In 1875, at the age of fourteen, he entered school and studied Latin, Greek, and mathematics. "I was excused," he recalled later, "in the composition of Latin Verse and the reading of some Latin poetry, in order to give more time for mathematics."[3] Mathematics became Whitehead's chosen field also later at Trinity College, Cambridge University, which he entered in 1880. He wrote that "during my whole undergraduate period at Trinity, all my lectures were on mathematics, pure and applied. I never went inside another lecture room."[4] Whitehead had a brilliant career as student in mathematics at Trinity College. He received his Bachelor's degree in 1884, his Master's degree in 1887, and the degree of Doctor of Science in 1905. From 1885 on he was Fellow and Senior Fellow of Trinity College, and Lecturer and later Senior Lecturer in mathematics and logic. For thirty years, from 1880 until 1910, Whitehead continued his residence at the University of Cambridge.

During the formative years of his life Whitehead's interests covered history and poetry in addition to mathematics. During his years of pre-university training "poetry, more especially Wordsworth and Shelley, became a major interest, and also history."[5] Wordsworth's mystical pantheism no doubt appealed to Whitehead's own religious sensitivities. Whitehead's religious vision tended strongly toward that type of religion which Arch-

---

[2] Alfred North Whitehead, *Religion in the Making* (New York: Macmillan Co., 1926), p. 16.
[3] Whitehead, *Science and Philosophy*, p. 12.
[4] *Ibid.*, p. 13.
[5] *Ibid.*, p. 12.

bishop Nathan Söderblom of the Church of Sweden termed "nature religion" or "culture religion." At its highest stage of development religion of this type tends to dissolve the religious concept of God in abstract, philosophical speculation. Whitehead was very concerned with the actual and concrete in his concept of nature. In his religious longings, however, he avoided to a large extent references to the particular and historically concrete revelation of God in the history of Israel and Jesus Christ. Infinity and abstraction are the marks of Whiteheadian religion, which is not to deny the fact that he was in some respects a man of extraordinary religious sensitivity.

Nevertheless, the abstract and elusive nature of Whitehead's religious vision has led students of Whitehead like Stephen Lee Ely to question "the religious availability of Whitehead's God."[6] From the point of view of a narrowly defined, supernaturalist, Western piety this question had to arise and be answered as Ely did when he concluded that

> the God that Whitehead derives from metaphysical analysis is not the God of religions. Whatever religious value Whitehead's God may have depends on aspects of God that lie beyond reason—aspects that Whitehead either intuits, guesses at, or has faith in. And if this is the upshot, why should not religionists intuit, or guess at, or have faith in a God who is more of a God? For what sort of a person is Whitehead's God intended? Both mystic and man in the street will refuse to undergo a long metaphysical agony which does not attain a usable God until supplemented by intuition or religious experience; they will point out that a metaphysically demonstrable God has never been a religious necessity. The philosopher, on the other hand, may not care to rely on intuition, guesswork, and faith. As for those who desire to see the problem of God's existence made clear and precise—these will be either confused or discouraged.[7]

The concept of God is the capstone of Whitehead's mature philosophy and religion. The God of Whiteheadian philosophy is at once the God of science and of religion, of the secular as well as of the religious worlds. It is here that Whitehead's real significance lies, so far as his contribution to a restatement and reconstruction of Christian theology appropriate to the atomic and space age is concerned. In one of his later and most mature works, *Process and Reality* (1929), Whitehead insisted that "the concept of God is certainly one essential element in religious feeling. But the converse is not true; the concept of religious feeling is not an essential element in the concept of God's function in the uni-

[6] Stephen Lee Ely, *The Religious Availability of Whitehead's God* (Madison: University of Wisconsin Press, 1942).
[7] *Ibid.*, p. 57.

verse."[8] Whitehead believed that "in this respect religious literature has been sadly misleading to philosophic theory, partly by attraction and partly by repulsion."[9] The specifically Christian religious vision of Whitehead centered in "the brief Galilean vision of humility."[10]

It dwells upon the tender elements in the world, which slowly and in quietness operate by love; and it finds purpose in the present immediacy of a kingdom not of this world. Love neither rules, nor is it unmoved; also it is a little oblivious as to morals. It does not look to the future; for it finds its own reward in the immediate present.[11]

During his residence at the University of Cambridge, Whitehead supplemented his lectures in mathematical and symbolic logic with extracurricular discussions and reading. "We discussed everything," he wrote later,

—politics, religion, philosophy, literature—with a bias toward literature. This experience led to a large amount of miscellaneous reading. For example, by the time that I gained my fellowship in 1885 I nearly knew by heart parts of Kant's *Critique of Pure Reason*. Now I have forgotten it, because I was early disenchanted. I have never been able to read Hegel: I initiated my attempt by studying some remarks of his on mathematics which struck me as complete nonsense.[12]

Nonetheless, Whitehead admitted later:

it is true that I was influenced by Hegel. I was an intimate friend of McTaggart almost from the very first day he came to the University, and saw him for a few minutes almost daily, and I had many a chat with Lord Haldane with his Hegelian point of view, and I have read books about Hegel. But lack of first-hand acquaintance is a very good reason for not endeavoring in print to display any knowledge of Hegel.

But, . . . I admit a very close affiliation with Bradley [i.e., Francis Herbert Bradley, the greatest of English Hegelians (1846–1924)] except that I differ from Bradley where Bradley agrees with almost all the philosophers of his school and with Plato, insofar as Plato was a Hegelian.[13]

An event of great significance for Whitehead's later philosophical work was his marriage to Evelyn W. Wade (1890), who bore him three children. "The effect of my wife," he said, "upon my outlook on the world has

---

[8] Alfred North Whitehead, *Process and Reality* (New York: Harper & Brothers 1960), pp. 315–316.
[9] *Ibid.*, p. 316.
[10] *Ibid.*, p. 520.
[11] *Ibid.*, pp. 520–521.
[12] Whitehead, *Science and Philosophy*, pp. 13–14.
[13] From a speech by Alfred North Whitehead recorded in the *Symposium In Honor of the Seventieth Birthday of Alfred North Whitehead* (Cambridge, Mass.: Harvard University Press, 1932), p. 25.

been so fundamental that it must be mentioned as an essential factor in my philosophic output."[14]

My wife's background is completely different, namely military and diplomatic. Her vivid life has taught me that beauty, moral and aesthetic, is the aim of existence; and that kindness and love, and artistic satisfaction are among its modes of attainment. Logic and Science are the disclosure of relevant patterns, and also procure the avoidance of irrelevancies.

This outlook somewhat shifts the ordinary philosophic emphasis upon the past. It directs attention to the periods of great art and literature, as best expressing the essential values of life. The summit of human attainment does not wait for the emergence of systematized doctrine, though system has its essential functions in the rise of civilization. It provides the gradual upgrowth of a stabilized social system.[15]

The effect of the influence of Whitehead's wife became noticeable in his later works, when he moved from a concern with mathematics, logic, and the philosophy of science to a more humanistic, aesthetic, and religious philosophical position.

In 1898, Whitehead published his first book, entitled *A Treatise on Universal Algebra,* which led to his election to the Royal Society in 1903. The ideas of the *Universal Algebra,* according to Whitehead,

were largely founded on Hermann Grassmann's two books, the *Ausdehnungslehre* of 1844, and the *Ausdehnungslehre* of 1862. The earlier of the two books is by far the most fundamental. Unfortunately when it was published no one understood it; he was a century ahead of his time. Also Sir William Rowan Hamilton's *Quaternions* of 1853; and a preliminary paper in 1844, and Boole's *Symbolic Logic* of 1859, were almost equally influential on my thoughts. My whole subsequent work on Mathematical Logic is derived from these sources.[16]

From 1898 to 1903, Whitehead worked on a second volume of *Universal Algebra* which he did not publish. When Bertrand Russell, one of his former students, and later his colleague and friend, published *The Principles of Mathematics* (1903), Whitehead discovered that Russell's projected second volume was to deal with practically the identical topics which he wanted to treat in his second volume of *Universal Algebra.* Consequently, the two men decided to collaborate in the production of a joint work. The result of their efforts was the three-volume *Principia Mathematica,* published between 1910 and 1913.

In 1910, Whitehead left Cambridge and moved to London, where

[14] Whitehead, *Science and Philosophy,* pp. 14–15.
[15] *Ibid.,* p. 15.
[16] *Ibid.,* p. 16.

he became associated with the University of London. He taught at University College, London, from 1911 until 1914, and at Imperial College of Science and Technology, in Kensington, from 1914 until 1924. For several years he was Dean of the Faculty of Science of London University and participated in the administration and supervision of higher education in London. In 1911 he published his *Introduction to Mathematics* in the Home University Library.

The year of 1918 marked, according to Whitehead,[17] the beginning of his work in the field of philosophy—a work which earned him the fellowship of the British Academy in 1931. In his works on the *Principles of Natural Knowledge* (1919) and *The Concept of Nature* (1920) there is a gradual shift of interest from mathematics and logic to problems of the philosophy of science. A few essays on education, which appeared during his years at London, are the first signs of Whitehead's awakening humanistic interest.

Some Whiteheadian scholars trace his early period of predominant interest in mathematics, symbolic logic, and philosophy of science until the year 1922.[18] In his philosophy of science of the early period, Whitehead had tried to maintain a strict separation between the human observer on the one hand, and the world of nature on the other. He hoped thereby to further the objectivity of human knowledge. But during the years 1925 to 1927, he began to place the knower into the world of natural reality. "The result is a position quite different from both the idealism and the naturalism current at that time, or indeed at any time. This new vision, of idealistic naturalism or naturalistic idealism, is given its full exposition in the final period."[19]

In 1924, during the transition period from a narrowly defined mathematical-scientific position to a wider humanistic and religious stance, Whitehead accepted an appointment as professor of philosophy at Harvard University, Cambridge, Massachusetts. In the U.S. Whitehead finally came into his own as a philosopher. After seven years in the U.S. he remarked on the occasion of his seventieth birthday: "I do feel that if a man is going to do his best he ought to live in America, because there the treatment of any effort is such that it stimulates everything that is eager in one."[20] All of Whitehead's mature and best known philosophical works were written in the U.S.A. He thrived on the American character and way

---

[17] Cf. *ibid.*, p. 17.

[18] Cf. William W. Hammerschmidt, *Whitehead's Philosophy of Time* (New York: King's Crown Press, 1947), p. 7; Nathaniel Lawrence, *Whitehead's Philosophical Development* (Berkeley: University of California Press, 1956), p. xix.

[19] John B. Cobb, Jr., *A Christian Natural Theology* (Philadelphia: Westminster Press, 1965), p. 136.

[20] Whitehead in *Symposium*, p. 24.

of life. "Americans are always warm-hearted," he said, "always apprecia-
tive, always helpful, but they are always shrewd; and that is what makes
for me the continual delight of living in America; and it is why when I meet
an American I always expect to like him, because of that always delightful
mixture of shrewdness and warm-heartedness."[21]

While teaching at Harvard University, Whitehead published three books
which reflect a transition from preoccupation with mathematics, logic, and
science, to wider humanistic, aesthetic, and religious concerns: *Science and
the Modern World* (1925), *Religion in the Making* (1926), and *Symbol-
ism* (1927). Following this period of extraordinary creativity during the
sixty-fourth through the sixty-sixth years of his life is the final period.
Whitehead was in his late sixties and early seventies when he reached the
height of his achievement in philosophy. His greatest work, *Process and
Reality,* appeared in 1929, when he was sixty-eight years old.

Process and Reality has the subtitle, *An Essay in Cosmology.* It reflects
Whitehead's attraction toward the areas of value and religion (particularly
the doctrine of God), while at the same time attempting to construct an
all-inclusive cosmology on the basis of scientific, mathematical, and logical
thought. He said that

> almost all of *Process and Reality* can be read as an attempt to analyze per-
> ishing on the same level as Aristotle's analysis of becoming. The notion of
> the prehension of the past means that the past is an element which perishes
> and thereby remains an element in the state beyond, and thus is objectified.
> That is the whole notion. If you get a general notion of what is meant by
> perishing, you will have accomplished an apprehension of what you mean by
> memory and causality, what you mean when you feel that what we are is
> of infinite importance, because as we perish we are immortal. That is the
> one key thought around which the whole development of *Process and Reality*
> is woven, and in many ways I find that I am in complete agreement with
> Bradley [i.e., Francis Herbert Bradley, the English Hegelian].[22]

Process and Reality shows the influence of the Hegelianism of Bradley
as well as the influence of the French philosopher Henri Bergson (1859–
1941). With the latter the notion of process is basic, while with the former
it is a sort of objective idealism which postulates the existence of a central
mind in a systematically ordered universe. Both of these ideas underlie the
entire cosmological scheme which Whitehead proposes in *Process and
Reality.* In his attempt to indicate where he differs from Bergson and
Bradley, Whitehead pointed out that

> there are these two prevalent alternative doctrines respecting the process
> apparent in the external world: one, which is Bergson's view, is that the

---

[21] *Ibid.,* p. 22.
[22] *Ibid.,* pp. 26–27.

intellect in order to report upon experienced intuition must necessarily introduce an apparatus of concepts which falsify the intuition; the other is that process is a somewhat superficial, illusory element in our experience of the eternally real, the essentially permanent. The latter is Bradley's standpoint, if I read him correctly. I think that it is at times Plato's view also. It is exactly on these points that I differ from Bergson on the one side, and from Bradley on the other.[23]

Together with *Adventures of Ideas,* which Whitehead published in 1933, *Process and Reality* is the most important work of the final period in the development of his humanistic and religious ideas. Reality, according to Whitehead, is one universal process systematically governed, according to certain laws, by cosmic mind, or God. In this process,

God and the World stand over against each other, expressing the final metaphysical truth that appetitive vision and physical enjoyment have equal claim to priority in creation. But no two actualities can be torn apart: each is all in all. Thus each temporal occasion embodies God, and is embodied in God. In God's nature, permanence is primordial and flux is derivative from the World: in the World's nature, flux is primordial and permanence is derivative from God. Also the World's nature is a primordial datum for God; and God's nature is a primordial datum for the World. Creation achieves the reconciliation of permanence and flux when it has reached its final term which is everlastingness––the Apotheosis of the World.[24]

Human life is a tiny but significant incident in the vast process of reality. Human life exists in the context of society. The highest aim of society is to be civilized, i.e. to be a society "whose members participate in the five qualities—Truth, Beauty, Adventure, Art, Peace."[25] In the mature statement of Whitehead's religious views, science and religion, Christianity and humanism, idealism and naturalism have been woven into the fabric of his mystical religious vision to form a new and creative whole.

In 1934 Whitehead published *Nature and Life,* and in 1938 appeared *Modes of Thought,* the last of his books belonging to his mature works of the final period. In these two books he continued to expound the major doctrines presented in *Process and Reality.* The great period of his mature creativity, however, was over. In 1937, at the age of seventy-six, he became Professor Emeritus which he remained until his death at Cambridge, Massachusetts, on December 30, 1947, at the age of eighty-six years. Looking back on his years at Cambridge, Whitehead said: "To-day in America, there is a zeal for knowledge which is reminiscent of the great periods of Greece and the Renaissance. But above all, there is in all sections of

23 *Ibid.,* pp. 25–26.
24 Whitehead, *Process and Reality,* p. 529.
25 Whitehead, *Adventures of Ideas,* p. 283.

the population a warm-hearted kindness which is unsurpassed in any large social system."[26]

Whitehead remained a British subject until his death, but he found himself so much at home with American thought and feeling that he lived happily in the U.S.A. with no feeling of being in exile during the twenty-three years of war and rapid social, political, and cultural change which he lived through in America. The years following Whitehead's death have been, to some degree, an illustration of the relevance and adequacy of his perceptive doctrine of objective immortality. "From knowledge gained through the years of the personalities who in our day have affected American university life," wrote Justice Felix Frankfurter, "I have for some time been convinced that no single figure has had such a pervasive influence as the late Professor Alfred North Whitehead."[27]

It is very probable that Whitehead will become much more influential in the years ahead than he is now. This applies especially to Christian theology. What Platonism was to Augustine, and Aristotelianism to Thomas Aquinas, and Kant to modern philosophy and Protestant theology since Schleiermacher, that Whitehead may become for the philosophy and theology of the future, ecumenical church. "In recent years there has been a marked renewal of interest in his work," a Whiteheadian scholar recently observed,

and we may expect that the days of his greatest influence lie in the future. Cf. Lowe, *Understanding Whitehead*, p. v; and Lowe, "Whitehead's Philosophical Development," Schilpp, ed., *The Philosophy of Alfred North Whitehead,* p. 124. The objective evidence for the claim of probable increase in the influence of Whitehead lies in the increased volume of published work about his thought and the growing number of dissertations being written about him. The recent belated recognition of the great importance also of the work of Charles Hartshorne is closely connected with this. See Schubert Ogden, "Theology and Philosophy: A New Phase of the Discussion," *The Journal of Religion,* Jan., 1964, pp. 1–16. More subjective is the judgment that the approaches to both philosophy and theology that have been dominant in recent decades and that have militated against attention to the work of both Whitehead and Hartshorne are running dry and that new vitality can be attained best in both disciplines by serious dialogue with Whitehead. Still more subjective is my opinion that even in the physical sciences there is a dawning awareness of the need to wrestle again with the questions on which Whitehead cast so much light. This is suggested by the work of Milic Capek, *The Philosophical Impact of Contemporary Physics*

[26] Whitehead, *Science and Philosophy,* p. 21.
[27] Felix Frankfurter, "Alfred North Whitehead," in Alfred North Whitehead, *The Aims of Education* (New York: The New American Library, 1963), p. vii.

(D. Van Nostrand Co., Inc., 1961), and Adolf Grunbaum, *Philosophical Problems of Space and Time* (Alfred A. Knopf, Inc., 1963).[28]

Cobb may very well be correct in his prediction of a Whiteheadian revolution of philosophy and natural theology. The following lend support to this contention.

(1) The substitution of the dynamic categories of process for the old static notions based on a philosophy of unchanging substance and the fixity of the species. Process thought enables modern philosophy and theology to contribute to a better understanding of the most basic reality that impresses itself on modern man: the reality of change and transition.

(2) The discovery of the interrelatedness of all aspects of reality. The serene vision of wholeness permits modern ecumenical theology to demonstrate convincingly that the movement toward Christian unity is in harmony with the ultimate forces that give meaning and coherence to the entire universe.

(3) The inclusion of God in the process of reality. The integration of God into the totality of everything that is can help theology to prove, or at least to show, that God is not some irrelevant, static, unmoved Absolute outside of cosmic reality as we know it. God is in the midst of life, change, creativity, and advance into novelty. He is an integral part of the system of process, not an entity outside or beyond or above everything that is real.

(4) The achievement of a comprehensive synthesis of human knowledge. Whitehead included in his categorical scheme the insights of modern cosmology, ontology, anthropology, philosophy of science, epistemology, logic and mathematics. Protestant-Anglican-Orthdox and Roman Catholic ecumenism needs, and in fact presupposes, this kind of a synthetic vision of integral coherence.

(5) The specification of reality under God. Whitehead conceived of God as judge (the "static vision" of God's "primordial nature") and redeemer (God's "consequent nature") in such a way that God's action becomes inseparable from a vast, universal historical and natural process moving toward its appointed end in God.

(6) The philosophical analysis of a cosmology of process. Whitehead's analysis has the great advantage over its contemporary competitors that it is able to do justice to the insights of modern science and at the same time to overcome its nihilistic tendencies by opening up new ways of understanding the relation of God to man and man to God within the all-pervasive context of creativity.

(7) The frank recognition of the historical relativity of all philosophy,

[28] Cobb, *op. cit.*, pp. 15–16.

including the Whiteheadian scheme. In Whitehead's thought this manifests itself in openness to other truth-claims, philosophical humility, and intellectual caution.

(8) The patient insistence on seeing every issue in the broadest possible perspective. Whitehead betrays here his Anglican background and concern for catholicity and inclusiveness rather than a narrow, sectarian exclusiveness. He expressed the hope that his own comprehensive synthesis would soon be considered too narrow and fragmentary, and be superseded by something more adequate.

(9) The affirmation of both the objective reality and the relativity of values. Whitehead is able to overcome nihilism and skepticism by showing that the appetition which seeks the realization of all possible values is part of God's primordial vision.

(10) The incorporation of many points of contact for dialogue with non-Christian religions. Whitehead sets the stage for a totally new approach to non-Christian religions by his doctrine of immanence and by the subordination of ethical to aesthetic categories. Thus he opens the door to a new concept of modern Christian missions structured with the aid of natural and philosophical categories congenial to those of Oriental religious philosophy. The fact and spirit of the *Declaration on the Relationship of the Church to Non-Christian Religions,* issued by the Second Vatican Council, is one among many indications that the spirit of ecumenism will issue into a new look at non-Christian religions. Whitehead offers to supply ecumenical theology with the theoretical framework into which the concrete religious realities can be built so as to give them intelligibility, coherence, and aesthetic harmony.

Chapter IV

Process Theology: Cobb and Ogden

John B. Cobb, Jr. belongs to the significant group of process theologians who promise to change the static and obsolete ways of theological substance thought. He was born in Kobe, Japan, the son of Christian missionaries. Cobb studied at Emory University, Atlanta, Georgia, a Methodist university where the radical "God is dead" theologian Thomas J. J. Altizer is presently teaching in the field of Bible and religion. Cobb also studied at the University of Michigan and at the Divinity School of the University of Chicago. John Cobb is an ordained Methodist minister. At the present time he is Associate Professor of Systematic Theology at Southern California School of Theology, Claremont, California.

Cobb explicitly acknowledges that "the philosophy by which I am myself grasped, and on the basis of which I propose to develop a Christian natural theology, is that of Alfred North Whitehead."[1] The philosophical

---

[1] John B. Cobb, Jr., *A Christian Natural Theology* (Priladelphia: Westminster Press, 1965), p. 15.

excellence of Whitehead is such that Cobb states: "For myself I am persuaded that he [Whitehead] ranks with Plato, Aristotle, and Kant as one of the greatest creative thinkers of all time."[2]

The reason for Cobb's profound admiration of Whiteheadian process thought is that in Whitehead's work

> there is a fully developed alternative to the nihilistic tendencies of most modern thought. No one else in the twentieth century has attempted so impressive a synthesis of that knowledge which forces itself upon the attention of the honest and open mind. In recent years there has been a marked renewal of interest in his work, and we may expect that the days of his greatest influence lie in the future.[3]

Cobb's recognition of Whitehead's process philosophy as a fertile ground for a Christian natural theology places him in the camp of process theologians. Naturally, there are other process theologians who do not explicitly recognize Whitehead as their philosophical father. The French priest-scientist Pierre Teilhard de Chardin was a process theologian who did not announce his dependence on Whitehead. Nevertheless, he was a contemporary of Whitehead and shared with him the fundamental vision of an all-inclusive process of reality.

Both Whitehead and Teilhard de Chardin were influenced by the process thought of the French philosopher Henri Bergson. Bergson's concept of duration, or true, inner time found systematic and scientific expression in Whitehead's idea of process. Similarly, there are interesting parallels between Whitehead's notion of creativity, Teilhard de Chardin's idea of energy in evolution, and Bergson's conception of the vital life force, *élan vital*.

Teilhard de Chardin is promising to revolutionize Roman Catholic theology by replacing the ancient Aristotelian idea of an unchanging substance undergoing accidental adventures with the notion of evolutionary processes.

Similarly Whitehead is reshaping our thinking by substituting process categories for those of the old philosophies of substance. The difference between Teilhard de Chardin and Whitehead is that Whitehead has a philosophically more adequate, coherent, and comprehensive system of process thought than the quasi-mystical utterances of Teilhard de Chardin can afford us.

All modern process thought goes back to Hegel, who did most of his creative work during the first third of the nineteenth century. Bergson's concept of process and creative evolution is a reflection of the Hegelian

[2] *Ibid.*, p. 16.
[3] *Ibid.*, p. 15.

notion of reality as a vast, universal, evolutionary process in which the Absolute Idea or the Absolute Spirit gradually realizes itself.

According to Hegel, the universe is never static, never finished, never complete. Reality is a constant movement of the dialectic of thesis, antithesis, and synthesis. The syntheses of the Hegelian system of process are stages of creative evolution, and never final, static, unchanging perfections. Reality, according to Hegel, is endless process and unceasing creative change. In this change the Absolute Idea realizes itself.

It is important to see Whiteheadian process theology in its wider context in Western philosophy and theology. To say that Teilhard de Chardin parallels some of the insights of Whitehead and that Whitehead is dependent to some degree on Bergson and Hegel does not in any way detract from the originality and momentous impact of Whitehead on modern process theology. Cobb and Ogden are good illustrations of process theologians who are well aware of Hegel and Bergson, but who find in Whitehead the most satisfactory and adequate statement of process thought.

In his book *Living Options in Protestant Theology* Cobb analyzed the theological presuppositions and assumptions of a number of recent theologies and found that all of them had assumptions and implications belonging to the area of natural theology. Cobb then argued that Whitehead's process philosophy furnishes us with the most adequate conceptual tools by means of which to construct a sorely needed Christian natural theology.

Having demonstrated the need for a natural theology, Cobb proposes to construct what he termed "a Christian natural theology" on the basis of Whiteheadian process thought. A word of explanation is needed for each one of these three terms, "Christian," "natural," and "theology."

(1) *Christian.* According to Cobb,

> any perspective is Christian when it includes the serious acknowledgement of Jesus as Lord. This acknowledgement is not the statement of a belief about Jesus' nature but the submission of ourselves to him. Even if we dislike the term "Lord" and prefer to describe our relationship to him in some other way, we may still be Christian. The acknowledgement of Jesus as Lord means that our lives and thoughts are opened to his positive influence as supremely worthy and important. Understanding Jesus' Lordship in this way, we may assert that its acknowledgement constitutes the invisible church.[4]

(2) *Natural.* The term "natural" refers primarily to modern cosmology. Cobb is convinced that the disintegration of meaningful discourse about God has occurred,

---

[4] John B. Cobb, Jr., *Varieties of Protestantism* (Philadelphia: Westminster Press, 1960), p. 245.

not as a function of that theology which is the expression or articulation of faith, but as a function of that cosmology which has destroyed the horizons within which early Christian, medieval, and early modern man understood his existence. For this reason it seems equally evident that the restoration of meaning to this term requires direct consideration of those forces which have destroyed it as well as the continuation of that proclamation and that theology which presuppose its meaningfulness. This means that natural theology in our generation is not to be seen as a dubious luxury of the systematician but as foundational to the proclamation and to the realization of faith as well.[5]

The word "natural" in Cobb's process theology represents his program for a return to a meaningful concept of God. The way to restore the central reality of Christian theology to its rightful place is by means of a natural theology based on the thought of Alfred North Whitehead. Cobb emphasizes "that natural theology is possible as well as needed presupposes that the destructive forces of modern cosmology are not rooted with any final necessity in the intellectual situation of modern man."[6] Cobb has demonstrated by his use of Whiteheadian process thought "that a cosmology lacking the destructive implications of much modern cosmological thought is not only possible but also more adequate to the modern situation than its competitors."[7]

(3) *Theology.* Cobb defines theology as "any coherent statement about matters of ultimate concern"[8] governed by the perspective of the community of faith. By making the community of faith an integral part of his definiton of theology Cobb places himself into the context of and the service of the church. Process theology is theology which makes extensive and explicit use of Whiteheadian philosophical categories in order to be in a better position to elucidate the message of the church. Thus Cobb recognizes that in our ecumenical age the church and process thought must be and remain allies if we are to have an adequate ecumenical theology for the future ecumenical church.

Cobb begins his "natural theology" with "an introduction to Whitehead's philosophy."[9] He argues that much of contemporary philosophy can be expressed in terms of a simple duality of physical and mental realities. Whitehead uses human experience as the key to an interpretation of the universe in terms of physical and mental poles which stand in mutual tension and in mutual requirement one of the other. Thus "Whitehead launched boldly forth on the speculative possibility that human experience

[5] Cobb, *A Christian Natural Theology,* p. 15.
[6] *Ibid.*
[7] *Ibid.*
[8] *Ibid.,* p. 252.
[9] *Ibid.,* pp. 23–46.

as such is a clue to the ultimate nature of things."[10] In his philosophical scheme electronic events, for instance, "are to be thought of as occasions of electronic experience. Their disconnectedness can be conceived as being like the disconnectedness of successive human experiences."[11] Experiences consist of discrete and indivisible units which Whitehead calls "occasions." These occasions follow upon each other so quickly that "the direct analysis of a single occasion of experience is impossible."[12] But with the exception of change, the individual occasions have the same qualities as the experience has on a much larger scale.

Actual occasions have physical and mental poles. "The physical pole of our experience can be analyzed into 'physical prehensions' or 'physical feelings.' Each physical prehension is the feeling by one momentary occasion for another momentary occasion."[13] In this connection Cobb stresses that "it is of utmost importance for the understanding of Whitehead's philosophy to note that the occasion that is felt is always in the past of the occasion that feels it. Cause always precedes effect. The relation of prehension is always asymmetrical. The earlier occasion has 'causal efficacy' for the later. The later occasion 'prehends' the earlier. These terms cannot be reversed. In other words, there is no causal relation between contemporary occasions."[14] Cobb here emphasizes that for his Christian natural theology

the deeply ingrained commonsense view that cause and effect are often, if not always, simultaneous is derived from experiences at the macrocosmic level and does not apply to the world of microcosmic entities. At the macrocosmic level it seems that the pressure I exert on the pen causes movement of the pen simultaneous with the exertion of pressure rather than subsequent to it. At this level Newtonian mechanics seems quite adequate. But the inability of models derived from our experience of objects like pens to deal with the microcosmic world is precisely the cause of the collapse of the old world views.[15]

The "mental pole" of an actual occasion introduces "originality of the occasion of experience which is not derivative from the thing experienced but is contributed by the experient. . . . This originality plays a role in sense experience . . . but it also plays a role in more primitive levels of experience. Its most striking role is in imaginative thought."[16]

10 *Ibid.*, p. 27.
11 *Ibid.*
12 *Ibid.*, p. 29.
13 *Ibid.*, pp. 30–31.
14 *Ibid.*, p. 31.
15 *Ibid.*
16 *Ibid.*, p. 33.

Also important for Cobb's Christian natural theology is the White-headian concept of eternal objects. Cobb explains that

> eternal objects are not actual entities like the occasions of experience. They are pure possibilities for realization in any experience at all, conceived quite apart from any such realization. Every actual occasion is that realization of some limited number of such possibilities. When we entertain such a possibility without reference to where it has been met in embodied form, we have an instance of what Whitehead calls a "conceptual prehension." A conceptual prehension is a prehension of an eternal object as such. Just as physical comprehensions comprise the physical pole of each actual occasion of experience, so conceptual prehensions constitute the mental pole.[17]

A Christian natural theology based on the thought of Whitehead must also take cognizance of the "subjective aim" in every occasion of experience. The subjective aim is the purpose present in any occasion. Finally, there is the process concept of "satisfaction." Cobb states that "the occasion of experience as a whole is a synthesis of syntheses of syntheses of the simple elements out of which it is composed. This final momentary synthesis Whitehead calls its 'satisfaction.' "[18]

Equipped with the rational tools of Whiteheadian process philosophy, Cobb then proceeds to discuss the human soul and immortality, man's freedom and the moral life, God as an actual entity in time and space, and religion. He points out that "Whitehead is remarkable among recent philosophers for his insistence that man has, or is, a soul. Furthermore, he is convinced that this doctrine has been of utmost value for Western civilization and that its recent weakening systematically undercuts the understanding of the worth of man."[19] Whitehead's process philosophy thus provides an excellent base for a Christian natural theology.

Traditionally, philosophers have thought of the soul as an unchanging, individual, actual entity. This view has been rendered unsatisfactory in view of the discoveries of modern psychology and science. Whitehead overcomes this difficulty by casting his view of the soul on a social model. Cobb stresses that in process thought

> individuals exist only momentarily. If we identified the soul with such an individual, there would be millions of souls during the lifetime of a single man. But when we speak in Platonic or Christian terms, we think of a single soul for a single man. If we hold fast to this usage, and Whitehead basically does so, then we must think of the soul as that society composed of all the momentary occasions of experience that make up the life history of the man.

17 *Ibid.*, p. 34.
18 *Ibid.*, p. 35.
19 *Ibid.*, p. 47.

The soul is not an underlying substance undergoing accidental adventures. It is nothing but the sequence of the experiences that constitute it.[20]

Cobb's Christian natural theology envisages the possibility that not only man, but also the higher animals have souls.

Wherever it is reasonable to posit a single center of experience playing a decisive role in the functioning of the organism as a whole, there it is reasonable to posit a soul. For the soul is nothing but such a center of experience in its continuity through time. The use of the term "soul" carries no connotation in Whitehead of preexistence or of life after death. There is no suggestion that the soul is some kind of supernatural element which in some way marks off man from nature and provides a special point of contact for divine activity. The soul is in every sense a part of nature, subject to the same conditions as all other natural entities.[21]

But while "in faithfulness to Whitehead it cannot be argued that there is" life after death, it can be shown that "the usual philosophical and commonsense arguments for the impossibility of life after death are removed by his philosophy."[22] Naturally, this makes Whitehead an ideal choice for a Christian natural theology.

Process thought views man as a responsible being with freedom and personal identity through time. Cobb notes that

if we are to understand human freedom in Whitehead's terms, we must begin by considering the kind of freedom that human experience shares with all the other occasions of experience. Whitehead believes that freedom is a universal or categorical feature of all actual entities whatsoever; so human freedom must be viewed as a special case in this wide context.[23]

We may now ask: Is it meaningful to speak of a stone or a book as having freedom? This question misses the point. A stone is a corpuscular society made up of many individual entities, and so is a book. Freedom can be attributed to these individual entities, not to the corpuscular societies which they compose. A book is very different in kind from the individual entities of which it is composed. The behavior of sub-atomic particles is quite different from that of the stone or the book they compose. Moreover,

when freedom is affirmed of these microscopic entities, it must be understood that this is freedom within limits—ordinarily very narrow limits. The notion of freedom as such, unqualified freedom, is nonsensical. Freedom must always be freedom within some settled conditions. These settled con-

20 *Ibid.*, pp. 47–48.
21 *Ibid.*, p. 48.
22 *Ibid.*, p. 65.
23 *Ibid.*, p. 94.

ditions are the totality of the world as it has been down to the moment of the becoming of the new occasion. The new occasion must occur in just that world and it must take some account of all that has occurred in that world. The causal efficacy of the past for the new occasion is just as important for Whitehead's view as is the freedom of the new occasion. The new occasion must take account of every occasion in its past. Its freedom lies in its own self-determination as to just how it will take account of all these occasions.[24]

From this very brief glimpse at a process view of freedom we move on to a consideration of the reality of God. Whitehead introduces God in order to complete his metaphysical system, not for religious purposes. He argues for the existence of God in "the traditional way from the order of the universe to a ground of order."[25]

> The strength and importance of Whitehead's argument for the existence of God, therefore, does not lie in some new and more penetrating structure of the argument. The argument is little more than a pointing to the need of a principle of limitation. The importance lies in the unusual thoroughness and adequacy of the description of the world from which the argument begins. If one is persuaded that Whitehead's account is indeed the most penetrating that now exists, that it does justice to the complexity of the phenomena of science and of history alike, then the fact it too leads, almost in spite of the author's apparent intention, to a doctrine of God as the source and ground of order is an important further confirmation of the inescapability for speculative reason of some kind of belief in God.[26]

Cobb maintains that even

> more important than the mere fact that Whitehead too could not understand the world apart from God, is the particular form that his doctrine of God takes. This, of course, is a function of the categories in which the description of the world is developed. If the world is viewed as a complex machine, then the correlative doctrine of God is likely to be that of a creator who stands outside of his creation. But if the world is viewed in organic terms, then the principle of life, order, and growth must be immanent to the organisms. That there *is* something which we may properly call God is sufficiently indicated by the kind of order that is visible to all. But what that "something" is, where it is, how it functions, these questions can be reflectively considered only in the light of the categories in terms of which the world is understood.[27]

Cobb concludes his Christian natural theology with the question of "the religious availability of Whitehead's God." He remarks that Whitehead ruled out the God of a narrow, supernaturalistic piety. He also excluded

[24] *Ibid.*, p. 95.
[25] *Ibid.*, p. 169.
[26] *Ibid.*, pp. 172–73.
[27] *Ibid.*, p. 173.

the notion of a transcendent creator God who by an act of the will called all things into being out of nothing and continues to govern omnipotently from outside his creation. . . . But from the very first introduction of thought about God into his system of philosophical ideas, Whitehead affirmed that that of which he wrote was which had inspired the worship of the ages.[28]

Cobb's concern for the contemporary relevance of the church's gospel to the modern world animates also the work of another well-known process theologian, *Schubert Miles Ogden*. Born on March 2, 1928, at Cincinnati, Ohio, Ogden an ordained Methodist minister, studied at Ohio Wesleyan University and the University of Chicago.

Ogden began his theological career as a disciple of the German biblical scholar and existentialist theologian, Rudolf Bultmann. In 1960 Ogden edited and translated a number of Bultmann's shorter writings under the title of *Existence and Faith*. From 1962 to 1963 he was a Fulbright research professor and Guggenheim fellow at the University of Marburg, where Bultmann was professor of New Testament and Theology.

Ogden's first book, *Christ Without Myth*, published in 1961, bears the stamp of the Christological emphasis of the early Ogden. The subtitle of the work, "A Study Based on the Theology of Rudolf Bultmann," shows Odgen's attempt to gain a theological foothold in the Bultmannian camp. He does this in a critical and constructive manner.

In the critical part Ogden reduces Bultmann's theology to two basic propositions:

> (1) Christian faith is to be interpreted exhaustively and without remainder as man's original possibility of authentic, historical (*geschichtlich*) existence as this is more or less adequately clarified and conceptualized by an appropriate philosophical analysis. (2) Christian faith is actually realizable, or is a "possibility in fact," only because of the particular historical (*historisch*) event of Jesus of Nazareth, which is the originative event of the church and its distinctive word and sacraments.[29]

In the critical sections of his book Ogden seeks to demonstrate that "these two propositions are mutually incompatible."[30] Their incompatibility may be demonstrated by the following example: "When Bultmann affirms that authentic historical existence is factually possible *only* as faith in Jesus Christ . . . he cannot but pay the price of surrendering all serious talk of man's freedom and responsibility."[31] Bultmann, however, strongly affirms the freedom and responsibility of the individual for his own life and his relations to other men.

28 *Ibid.*, p. 215.
29 Schubert M. Ogden, *Christ Without Myth* (New York: Harper, 1961), p. 112.
30 *Ibid.*
31 *Ibid.*, p. 119.

The constructive part of Ogden's book on *Christ Without Myth* addresses itself to the problem of the gospel and its proclamation to modern man. The contemporary Protestant theologian, Ogden states, "must by all means do his work in obedience to the New Testament proclamation and with a critical loyalty to the entire theological tradition; and yet he can do this responsibly only by also embracing the criticism of that tradition which arises with necessity out of modern man's picture of himself and his world."[32] In other words, only those elements of traditional Christianity that are still admitted to be valid by the modern criticism of the tradition can be admitted to theological discourse in Ogden's vision of it.

Central to the contemporary theological task is thus the doctrine of Christ, for he is the focus of the New Testament proclamation. Ogden stresses that

> the *sine qua non* for a more adequate christology is to observe the important distinction between "knowledge about" and "knowledge of" or, in Bultmann's terms, *existential* and *existentiell* understanding. The statement that Jesus is the decisive representation of the truth of man's existence can be appropriately clarified only when it is recognized that "truth" here is not the timeless truth of "knowledge about," but the *existentiell* truth of "knowledge of." What confronts us in Jesus is not, in its first intention, a "worldview" addressed to our intellects, but a possibility of self-understanding that requires of us a personal decision.[33]

Ogden concludes from this distinction between general truth and personal truth that, "while we may hesitate . . . to say that Jesus is mankind's 'teacher,' we may confidently affirm that he is its 'preacher.' "[34] Ogden's aim is to make clear that

> to say that Jesus is the preacher of mankind in the sense of the decisive historical manifestation of the essential God-man relationship is to say something quite different than that he is an accidental occasion through which some timeless and impersonal truth can be appropriated by the intellect. Indeed, it is to say nothing less, though also nothing more, than that in him the eternal Existence or Thou in whom all truth is grounded is himself personally present.[35]

From the emphasis on the person and work of Christ Ogden gradually moves toward a stronger interest in the significance of philosophy for the completion and supplementation of Bultmann's theological program. Bultmann had used the existential philosophy of the twentieth-century German philosopher Martin Heidegger as the philosophical framework of his

[32] *Ibid.,* p. 17.
[33] *Ibid.,* p. 162.
[34] *Ibid.*
[35] *Ibid.,* p. 163.

theology. Ogden is critical of this "questionable theological foundation." At the same time he stresses that

> the genius of Bultmann's view is that he attempts to apply also to the realm of knowledge, and thus to the problem of theological method, the Pauline-Lutheran doctrine of righteousness by faith alone without the works of the law. Therefore, what is ultimately at stake in his insistence on the dialectical relation between theology and faith is the general dialectic of works and faith and, beyond this, the "infinite qualitative difference" between time and eternity that is Bultmann's overriding major premise.[36]

Unlike theologians like Karl Barth, Ogden's attitude is "essentially positive" toward the idea of "a genuine discussion between Christian theology and secular philosophy,"[37] and thus appears to be in basic agreement with Bultmann. However, Ogden objects to Bultmann's reliance on the early Heidegger, and especially on the latter's famous work, *Being and Time,* first published in 1927. Ogden believes that the early Heidegger "can be too easily misinterpreted as an atheistic existentialist. The result is that Bultmann's theology is restrictively existentialist, in the sense that . . . Bultmann cannot speak of God directly, but only indirectly by speaking of man and his possibilities of existential self-understanding."[38]

Ogden wants to speak directly about God. His center of interest is shifting from the person of Christ to the doctrine of God. Therefore he can say: "My enthusiasm for the later Heidegger is not . . . unrestrained . . . since I see in the work of process philosophers like Alfred North Whitehead and Charles Hartshorne even more significant resources for completing and supplementing Bultmann's basic theological program."[39] Ogden has now come to the point where he realizes that the most powerful philosophical weapon in the battle for a meaningful doctrine of God is process theology and process philosophy. Where Bultmann has to be silent about God, process thought can speak about God because it has the conceptual tools and the philosophical vision necessary to relate God to every aspect of reality.

In an article of 1964 on "The Temporality of God,"[40] Ogden further emphasizes the contemporary significance of process thought for the development of a genuinely modern idea of God. He takes as his starting point a footnote of Heidegger's book, *Being and Time,* which reads:

[36] Schubert M. Ogden, "The Understanding of Theology in Ott and Bultmann," *The Later Heidegger and Theology,* ed. J. M. Robinson and J. B. Cobb, Jr. (New York: Harper & Row, 1963), p. 172.

[37] *Ibid.,* p. 157.

[38] *Ibid.,* p. 158.

[39] *Ibid.,* p. 159.

[40] Schubert M. Ogden, "The Temporality of God," *Zeit und Geschichte: Dankesgabe an Rudolf Bultmann zum 80. Geburstag,* ed. Erich Dinkler (Tübingen: Mohr, 1964), pp. 381–398.

It requires no extensive discussion to show that the traditional concept of eternity in the sense of the "stationary now" (*nunc stans*), is drawn from the vulgar understanding of time and is limited by an orientation to the idea of "constant" presence-on-hand. If the eternity of God would admit of being "construed" philosophically, then it could be understood only as a more primal and "infinite" temporality. Whether the *via negationis et eminentiae* could offer a possible way to this goal would remain uncertain.[41]

Ogden then goes on to say that Heidegger's "fundamental insight that God is essentially temporal and related to others . . . is no mere concession to the modern temper, but the restatement in formal ontological terms of the understanding of God implicit in Holy Scripture."[42] Unfortunately Heidegger never develops this immensely significant thought. But "there are other contemporary philosophers"[43]—and here Ogden is thinking primarily of the process philosophers Whitehead and Hartshorne—"for whom such a view is not confined to a footnote, but is carefully expounded in the setting of a fully developed neoclassical metaphysics."[44]

"Neoclassical" is Ogden's term for the process thought of Whiteheadian metaphysics. God is a metaphysical necessity for the system of process philosophy. He forms an integral part of the totality of concrete reality, guiding the process of the evolution of the universe by the wisdom of his primordial vision of the order of the world.

This conception of God as a factor in the process of the universe is given even greater emphasis in Ogden's latest book entitled, *The Reality of God*. The introduction of the lead essay of this work opens with the observation that while the Protestant theologians of the last generation were occupied with subjects other than God, in contemporary Protestant theology "the reality of God has now become the central theological problem."[45]

This reality, Ogden argues, must be approached with the equipment of process philosophy, as opposed to the obsolete concepts of classical thought. The supernaturalism of classical philosophy cannot give us a conceptually adequate Christian doctrine of God which could demand the respect and allegiance of modern men, for whom an absolute and static God in a relative and changing world is incredible, incomprehensible, and irrelevant. But in the process thought of Whitehead

Protestant theology now has at its disposal just the conceptual resources which make a relatively more adequate Christian theism possible. Among the

[41] *Ibid.*, p. 382.
[42] *Ibid.*, p. 397.
[43] *Ibid.*, p. 398.
[44] *Ibid.*
[45] Schubert M. Ogden, *The Reality of God and Other Essays* (New York: Harper & Row, 1966), p. 1.

most significant intellectual achievements of the twentieth century has been the creation at last of a neo-classical alternative to the metaphysics and philosophical theology of our classical tradition. Especially through the work of Alfred North Whitehead and, in the area usually designated "natural theology," of Charles Hartshorne, the ancient problems of philosophy have received a new, thoroughly modern treatment, which in its scope and depth easily rivals the so-called *philosophia perennis*. It is my belief that the conceptuality provided by this new philosophy enables us so to conceive the reality of God that we may respect all that is legitimate in modern secularity, while also fully respecting the distinctive claims of Christian faith itself.[46]

How do we begin to change our thinking about God after the manner of process philosophy? Ogden suggests that

the starting-point for a genuinely new theistic conception is what Whitehead speaks of as "the reformed subjectivist principle." According to this principle, we can give an adequate answer to the metaphysical question of the meaning of "reality" only by imaginatively generalizing "elements disclosed in the analysis of the experiences of subjects." In other words, the principle requires that we take as the experiential basis of all our most fundamental concepts the primal phenomenon of our own existence as experiencing subjects or selves.[47]

In addition to this existential base of our experience of reality there is the necessity laid upon us to find a better understanding of the nature of the self. Classical philosophy and philosophical theology had conceived of the human self as an unchanging substance. Whiteheadian ideas replace the old notion of the self as static substance by the concept of the self as a process of growth and change. Process theologians like Ogden insist that

whatever else the self is, it is hardly a substance which, in Descartes' phrase, "requires nothing but itself in order to exist," nor is it altogether without intrinsic temporal structure. To the contrary, the very being of the self is relational or social; and it is nothing if not a process of change involving the distinct modes of present, past, and future.[48]

The revolution of philosophy which is brought about by process thought promises to overcome the inadequacies of classical philosophical theologies like that of Aquinas. Ogden gives the following illustration of how Whitehead's neo-classical process philosophy is able to furnish us with better and more adequate expressions of truth of the Christian faith.

Aquinas' use of the *analogia entis,* or analogy of being "rests on the premise that God can be in no sense really relative or temporal." But

[46] *Ibid.,* pp. 56–57.
[47] *Ibid.,* p. 57.
[48] *Ibid.*

granted that premise, Aquinas "can say that he [God] 'knows' or 'loves' only by contradicting the meaning of those words as we otherwise use them."[49] All human knowledge is relative and conditioned by time. Likewise human love is something very relative and temporal. And when we use the term "knowledge" or "love" we mean to include this relativity and temporality in the meaning of these terms for us. Ogden is here stressing the point that absolute, changeless knowledge and impassible, unmoved love are contradictions in terms for modern men.

Ogden holds that on Whitehead's neo-classical premises of process thought,

> this difficulty, along with innumerable others, is at last removed. God is now conceived as precisely the unique and in all ways perfect instance of creative becoming, and so as the one reality which is eminently social and temporal. Instead of being merely the barren Absolute, which by definition can be really related to nothing, God is in truth related to everything, and that through an immediate sympathetic participation of which our own relation to our bodies is but an image. Similarly, God is no longer thought of as utterly unchangeable and empty of all temporal distinctions. Rather, he, too, is understood to be continually in process of self-creation, synthesizing in each new moment of his experience the whole of achieved actuality with the plenitude of possibility as yet unrealized.[50]

This, in brief, is the magnificent vision of God in modern process philosophy and theology. It is more adequate and more coherent than anything that the classical tradition of philosophical theology from Origen to St. Thomas has to offer. It is a concept of God which is dynamically related and vitally relevant to the mind and need of modern man.

[49] *Ibid.*, p. 59.
[50] *Ibid.*

Chapter V

Process Theology: Teilhard de Chardin

The ecumenical movement has taught Christians everywhere that the most effective witness for Christ and the Gospel is a united spirit of understanding and cooperation between all of the separated denominations of Christianity. The same spirit of interdependence and continuity must permeate the relations between religion and science. This basic conviction characterizes the astonishingly bold "meta-synthesis" of the French priest-scientist Pierre Teilhard de Chardin. His entire life and thought was devoted to uniting these two most powerful forces of man's spiritual life in the space age.

The most general characteristics of the theology of Teilhard de Chardin place him squarely in the camp of modern process thought. The work of Teilhard bears the imprint of Darwin and Bergson, and their ideas of evolution, process, and intuitive awareness. Teilhard de Chardin was in a sense a prophet and seer with a vast and magnificent vision of the entire process of reality both human and divine. Sometimes his prophetic utterances border on scientific and religious mysticism. But it is just this almost mystical awareness of the relatedness of the universe and the cosmic Christ which has made Teilhard de Chardin the most influential modern representative of process thought in the Roman Catholic world, and his influence on current Protestant theology is marked.

Teilhard de Chardin was born on May Day, 1881, at Sarcenat near Orcines, Puy-de-Dome, in a France that was in deep spiritual unrest over the conflict between the traditional claims of religion and the new claims of the rising science. The interests of the Christian religion were represented in France by the Ultramontanists; i.e., "beyond the mountains" (of the Alps from the point of view of France and northern and western Europe, that is, Italian). The Ultramontanists were religious traditionalists dedicated to the exaltation of the papacy, and prescientific religious life. Their Protestant equivalent would have been the worship of the "paper pope," an obscurantist fundamentalism in matters of Christian faith, and a militantly anti-scientific biblical literalism.

Science tended to be atheistic or anti-religious, because shortsighted and narrow-minded religious people opposed almost every scientific discovery or advance. The discovery that the earth was much older than six thousand years, and had evolved over hundreds of millions of years in a manner unknown to the biblical writers, was denounced as false and rejected by countless Roman Catholic and Protestant Christians. (The idea that the earth was less than 6,000 years old was commonly accepted as biblical truth by Christians from the seventeenth century on. One of its most influential propagators was the Anglican Archbishop of Armagh and primate of Ireland, James Ussher [1581–1656]. He proposed a chronology derived from the Bible according to which the creation of the world took place in 4004 B.C. This chronology was later inserted in the margin of the King James Version of the Bible, and thus became widely accepted as infallible scriptural truth.)

The great discoveries of geology were followed by the scientific revolution of biology. Here again Darwin's theory of evolution was bitterly attacked by Roman Catholics and Protestants alike as contrary to the Bible (as people in the nineteenth century thought), degrading man to the level of apes, and blaspheming God who had made man in his image.

Modernist theologians like Alfred de Loisy of France, George Tyrrell of England, and Hermann Schell of Germany sought to mediate in this conflict between science and religion. Loisy and Tyrrell were excommunicated, but their sacrifice and example of courage helped pave the way for our contemporary attitude of openness toward the great contributions which science and religion can make to the happiness and well-being of man.

During his childhood Teilhard learned from his father how to observe natural phenomena keenly and scientifically. Thus he developed an interest in geology. Geology and Darwinian biology had brought the idea of evolution to the foreground of the battle of science with religion. The Christian was faced with the decision between religious belief in the fixity of the human species and evolution, between the constructions of substance philosophy and the literal meaning of the Genesis account of creation six thousand years ago, and a universe in process for billions of years. Already as a student in the Jesuit College of Mongre, Teilhard was convinced that science and religion need one another if each of them was to fulfill its highest goal.

In 1898 Teilhard was a Jesuit novice in the south of France. Two years later the Jesuits were expelled from France. He continued his studies in Jersey, England. The years from 1905 to 1908 he spent teaching in Cairo, Egypt. During these years he discovered that without the religious impulse the scientist cannot muster the courage and faith necessary for bold and patient scientific research. At the same time Teilhard realized that science has helped religion to free itself from sentimentalism, activism, superficiality, and superstition. For modern man science has opened up the endless mysteries of the universe and thus deepened his understanding of the marvelous power of God in the intricacies of the atom and the vast movements of the galaxies. Science can help us to become more fully aware of the living God who is most hidden and yet most near, the God who guides all things by the loving power of his infinite wisdom to "the supreme and universal focus Omega," when Christ will be all in all.

Having been ordained to the priesthood, Teilhard studied paleontology at Paris. During World War I he refused the post of chaplain in the armed services in order to serve as stretcher-bearer in the battles of Ypres, Verdun, Chemin des Dames and several of the most destructive battles of the First World War. Teilhard believed that his Christian witness as a stretcher-bearer would be more appropriate and effective than the military chaplaincy. Binding up wounds and saving lives appeared to him as a Christian alternative to the blessing of arms by chaplains and bishops on both sides of the front. Teilhard's protest against the powerlessness of traditional Christianity in the face of the great crisis of Western Christendom, and his practical Christian concern for the lives of men, are reminiscent of Archbishop Nathan Söderblom's practical Christian work for peace through the ecumenically united witness of the separated churches.

Following the war Teilhard taught at the Institute Catholique for some years. During this time his concern for relevant Christianity, which had matured rapidly during the terrors of World War I, found expression in his important book, *The Divine Milieu* (1926–27). The main idea of this work was that of the service of God through the activities of daily life. The artificial separation between science and religion, between life in the material world and the spiritual life of the earnest Christian believer, and between matter and mind, abstracted what properly and naturally belonged together and thus threatened to paralyze the creative Christian effort in the world. Acutely aware of the Marxist criticism of the narcotic effects of religion, Teilhard sought to emphasize "the spirituality of matter."

Inspired by the vision of the Incarnation he insisted on the material world as the place where we encounter God and Christ in the midst of our life and work. God is present to us in the soil that the plough furrows, the divine milieu surrounds the tip of our pen, the key of the typewriter, the wheel on the machine. Spiritual energy permeates the material and is capable of divinizing all our human activities, not just the religious ones. The redemption which appeared through Jesus' incarnation points to a vast cosmic process in which nothing of value will be lost. Both the spiritual and the material are united in this process, so that contact with God is not limited to a few precious hours of Sunday worship and private prayer, but extends to every sphere and every second of our lives if we would only become aware of the divine milieu all around and within us. The divine milieu is that in which we live and move and have our being, it is closer to us than our own breathing, it is that which has its ultimate fullness, or *pleroma,* in Jesus Christ. The unnatural separation of divine providence and human action, of the spirituality of religion from scientific naturalism, denies the reality of the incarnation in its fulness of the divine milieu serving the spiritual through the material and the religious through the scientific.

Teilhard was animated by the firm belief that scientific research into the secrets of the origin and development of the world and man would be of great value for the demonstration of Christ as the universal center of unification.[1] To this center everything moves and at its focus everything converges in a process which aims at God's being all in everything and to everyone. This unshakable conviction inspired Teilhard's scientific researches and explorations into the origins of life on earth. The 1920's brought frequent visits to China on scientific expeditions. In 1929 an important specimen of Sinanthropus was discovered and evaluated with the aid of Teilhard, whose interest in relating the theory of evolution to the Christian understanding of creation was one of the driving forces behind these important scientific discoveries. Scientific research trips led him to Sinkiang province in China, the Gobi desert, the Kashmir area, Thailand, and the island of Java.

[1] Pierre Teilhard de Chardin, *The Phenomenon of Man* (2nd ed. New York: Harper & Row, 1965), p. 294.

The Japanese invasion of China held Teilhard in semicaptivity at Peking, from 1939 until 1946. During this time he wrote his most significant theological work, *The Phenomenon of Man,* in which he combined a natural, evolutionary optimism with the Christian idea of universal redemption through the recapitulation of all things in Christ. After his release from China he made scientific research trips to Africa (in 1951 and 1953) continuing his paleontological researches into the evolution of life on earth. In 1951 he came to the United States where he spent the rest of his life working with research teams. He died on April 10, 1955, in New York.

During the last years of his life, Teilhard returned to the vision of the divine milieu that had guided him throughout his life as a scientist and religious man, and which sustained him to the end. It was inspired by the Pauline prophecy of a process through which all things would be subjected to and governed by Christ in order "that God may be everything to everyone" (1 Cor 15:28). While he acknowledged that the individual Christian could experience already in this present life a foretaste of the glory of a human life for which, through Christ, God is everything, Teilhard held that the full realization of God's kingdom lay in the future of the human race. God's way of leading mankind to his kingdom was the way of evolution, Teilhard believed. Scientific research could tell us much more about the origin and destiny of man than we know today. Thus science would bring out more clearly the meaning of the truth and prophetic utterances of the Holy Scriptures and the Christian religion.

Many answers have been given to this profound question so forcefully raised by Psalm 8. "Man is a rational animal," "man is a tool-making animal," "man is a linguistic animal," "man is a political animal." Teilhard said, "Man is evolution."[2] Only this evolutionary answer, he thought, gave adequate expression to the entire phenomenon of man as an essentially incomplete process of development from humble and mysterious beginnings to an eternal destiny. The other traditional answers gave a false impression of the fixity of the human species which appeared to be going nowhere and to have no redemptive goal or destiny.

The idea of evolution had been proposed by Darwin and refined by his successors. The concept of process as the essential nature of man had been philosophically stated by the French philosopher Henri Bergson. The influence of Bergsonism is apparent in Teilhard's thought. Bergson's revolution consisted in the substitution of temporal values of motion and change for non-temporal, static values. Where the French philosopher Descartes had asserted, "I think, therefore I am," Bergson substituted "I continue (*je dure*), therefore I am." Thus he moved from the static aspect of eternity to the process view of duration.

[2] *Ibid.,* p. 221.

In one important aspect, however, Teilhard differed from Bergson. Bergson held that, apart from the general idea of duration and change, philosophy can make progress only if it limits itself to detailed problems and refuses to espouse general theories and universal systems. Reality could only be grasped by intuition, he believed, and not by scientific research and critical rational investigation, because the solution of a particular philosophical problem by means of a certain method does not necessarily mean that an analogous solution of the other problems of philosophy is possible.

Teilhard was certain that a vast and bold "mega-synthesis" is necessary if we are to affirm the meaningfulness of life.[3] Science cannot progress if it loses itself in fine details, and religion cannot abandon its claim to illumine every aspect of life. Both must unite in a universal, unifying vision of the ultimate coherence and purposefulness of things. The mode of thought that permits modern men to affirm this vision is the evolutionary process view of reality—a view in which everything is related, interdependent, in continual change, and undergoing continuous development.

Christ at the Omega Point

In his significant book on *The Phenomenon of Man* Teilhard gave a detailed outline of the religious and scientific import of evolution. Evolution is the ascent of reflection and consciousness which exhibits a trend toward "a synthesis based on love."[4] Biogenesis, or the development of life, points in the same direction toward which the movement of the Christian religion would direct the hearts and minds of all men.

For Christian faith the "spiritual and transcendent pole of universal convergence" is Jesus Christ, exhibiting the redemptive process of the living God "by whom and through whom and to whom are all things." The point where all the lines of evolution converge and take on their maximum coherence and meaning is "Omega," a transcendent focus and redemptive pole which makes irreversible the universal involution of thought. Thought evolves through the involution upon itself of the material of the universe.[5]

The guarantee that the process of human development, or hominization, will lead to the successful achievement of the goal of cosmic involution is the incarnation of God in his creation. However, freedom and the possibility of a setback are not denied thereby. But the tendency of the universe to exploit favorable cases for the advancement of the dialectical process of evolution and involution makes setbacks increasingly improbable once "the biological synthesis of reflection" has begun to direct all the energies of the

---

[3] *Ibid.*, p. 244.
[4] *Ibid.*, p. 298.
[5] *Ibid.*, p. 298.

universe toward their converging unification at the Omega Point revealed in the Incarnate Son of God, Jesus Christ.

In contrast to pantheism (where God becomes everything) Teilhard's understanding of the Omega Point of God in Christ is that God then will be all in everyone, he will be in the hearts and minds of all men, "the Alpha and the Omega, the First and the Last, the Beginning and the End."[6] The communicating activity of love makes the believer to be at one with God without identifying him with God.

The value of the spirit in relation to the material increases as the evolution of mankind continues to progress toward the fullness of God in Christ. Once man has broken through the psychic barrier into the realm of thought, the Spirit of God and the spirit of man begin to cooperate in their joint control over, and guidance of, the material (from which human thought emerged) by the spiritual. Later on, when mankind will have crossed the threshold of "collective reflection," the focus of spirit and consciousness will modify the divergent tendencies of the space-time process so as to make them converge toward the universal Omega Point where spirit is focused by the differentiating action of love.[7]

The profound Pauline insight into the place of evil in a universe whose Lord is ultimately Jesus Christ, "Do not be overcome by evil, but overcome evil with good" (Rom 12:21), informed the Teilhardian understanding of the evolving destiny of the human race. The function of evil in a God-directed world continually in process provided an everlasting challenge to Teilhard's view of the cosmic drama of evolution. He found the key to the solution of the problem of evil in the Cross. In his strongly Christocentric perspective Jesus Christ illumines the inner meaning of the evolution of the noosphere (the sphere of thought) with its sufferings and failures. The amount and power of evil diffused everywhere in the world is so excessive and inexplicable that, if there were not the redemptive power of God incarnate in the world, the extraordinary effect of the primeval catastrophe of the deviation of the Fall would have immolated long ago the evolutionary process on the altar of self-destruction.[8]

Teilhard distinguishes four kinds of evil[9] and shows how each kind is the by-product of a vast evolutionary process largely beyond direct and conscious human control. Evil is very seldom a conscious and deliberate act of the human will. The course of evolution means progress only at great risks and with enormous efforts. Evil appears necessarily through the very structure of the process of the universe. The increasingly complex

---

6 Rev 21:6.
7 Teilhard de Chardin, *op. cit.*, p. 309.
8 *Ibid.*, p. 313.
9 *Ibid.*, pp. 311–313.

interiorization and involution of the universe is achieved only at the cost of hard labor, excruciating suffering, and universal sin.

There is the evil of growth, symbolized by the pangs of childbirth. Work and effort are required by every movement and effort toward greater unity, not only in the highest realms of spiritual life, but also in the humblest chemical syntheses.

Then, secondly, there is the evil of disorder and failure. The groping universe, which often operates by the law of chance, requires many failures for one success, uncounted days of misery for a moment of joy, countless sins for one saint. In the vast play of huge numbers evil forms and reforms itself at every stage of the evolutionary process—from physical disorder, pain and suffering, wickedness and sin, up to the highest level of the spirit tormented by critical self-analysis and the inescapable need to make choices. From the chaos of sub-atomic particles to the agony of Gethsemane the evil of disorder and failure relentlessly asserts itself in the process of the universe.

Third, there is the evil of decomposition which pervades every aspect of the universe. Corruption, sickness, death, and decay are the inevitable by-products of evolution. For mankind death is the condition of the replacement of one individual by another one succeeding him. Death is the essential requisite of the evolutionary structure of plant, animal, and human life.

Fourth and finally, there is an evil peculiar to man: the evil of anxiety and loneliness. Man becomes conscious of his insecure position in a dark and cold universe which he does not comprehend either in its demands upon him or in the inner coherence of its workings.

It is well to emphasize in conclusion the Teilhardian conviction that no human effort alone can guarantee the cosmic security that would give peace and rest to the human soul. "Thou hast created us for thyself, and our hearts are restless until they rest in Thee." These famous words of St. Augustine, the great Church Father beloved of Luther and the Reformers, express powerfully the interior meaning of the Teilhardian vision of the function and place of evil and its eventual and continual transmutation into greater good. Evil generates in part that restlessness which spurs us on toward the great future point of universal convergence, the point at which all things take on their maximum coherence through the uniting power of love. This point is man's ultimate and eternal destiny, the Omega Point of the Second Coming of Christ as Lord and glorious Saviour of all.

CHAPTER VI

RADICAL THEOLOGY: ALTIZER, HAMILTON, AND VAN BUREN

In a collection of essays and articles of the two Protestant theologians Altizer and Hamilton, published under the title of *Radical Theology and the Death of God,* the two men define radical theology as "an attempt to set an atheist point of view within the spectrum of Christian possibilities."[1] This "attempt" is "a contemporary development within Protestantism—with some Jewish, Roman Catholic and non-religious response and participation already forming—which is carrying the careful openness of the older theologies toward atheism a step further."[2] It is the attempt to demonstrate that it is possible to be a Christian and an atheist at the same time.

Thomas J. J. Altizer is a native of Charleston, West Virginia. He attended St. John's College, Annapolis, Maryland, and received the degrees of A.B., A.M., and Ph.D. at the University of Chicago. Altizer is a member

---

[1] Thomas J. J. Altizer and William Hamilton, *Radical Theology and the Death of God* (Indianapolis: Bobbs-Merrill, 1966), p. ix.
[2] *Ibid.*

of the Protestant Episcopal Church and teaches Bible and religion at Emory University, Atlanta, Georgia.

Altizer is profoundly impressed by the crisis of traditional meanings and values in the religion and culture of our time. He believes that we are living in a time when "all traditional meaning and value have been profoundly challenged, and when theology is moving in circles."[3] Since under these circumstances Christian thought is not getting anywhere, "it would seem all too obvious that the moment has arrived to engage in a radical quest for a new mode of religious understanding."[4]

Two things are necessary if this quest is to be successful. According to Altizer,

> the first requirement of such a quest is a forthright confession of the death of the God of Christendom, a full acknowledgment that the era of Christian civilization has come to an end, with the result that all cognitive meaning and all moral values that were once historically associated with the Christian God have collapsed.[5]

Second, the death of God is an event which has occurred in our history and time. It is of fundamental importance to Altizer's objective of a new religious understanding that we recognize

> that the death of God is a historical event: God has died in *our* time, in *our* history, in *our* existence. Insofar as we live in our destiny, we can know neither a trace of God's presence nor an image of his reality. We must acknowledge, therefore, that if God has died in our history, then insofar as the church has become Christendom, insofar as the church has entered history, it has become a corpse . . . and *all* traditional theological meaning, *all* our inherited religious meaning, is in process either of dissolution or of transformation.[6]

In support of his observation of the evaporation of all traditional moral and religious meanings Altizer points to the distinction which modern theologians have made between faith and religion. He states that

> one of the most fascinating developments of the twentieth century rebirth of theology has been the contemporary theologian's insistence that the Christian faith transcends religion. Faith is now conceived of as being directed against "religion," against piety, against the interior religious life of the church itself. While this doctrine has its roots in the ancient prophet's protest against the priestly religion of Israel, it goes beyond this protest insofar as it challenges the *religious* meaning of faith. But we must ask why it is that

[3] Thomas J. J. Altizer, *Mircea Eliade and the Dialectic of the Sacred* (Philadelphia: Westminster Press, 1963), p. 13.
[4] *Ibid.*
[5] *Ibid.*
[6] *Ibid.*

the theologian in our time is forced to dissociate faith and religion. Surely one answer lies in the gradual evaporation of the religious life of the historic church.[7]

Another answer may lie in the "subtle yet devastating effects of the death of God"[8] on contemporary theology which as a result, "has lost all real contact with the sacred."[9] Altizer proposes that "the study of non-Christian religions can be conceived as a mode of reentry into the world of the holy."[10] He realizes that

> we can know these alien manifestations of the sacred only through a modern Western mode of understanding—which means a way of knowing that is itself a product of the death of God; yet fortunately we have not ourselves been immersed in the historical process of secularizing these religious forms, and thus they can speak to us most forcefully when they are most alien to our own interior lives.[11]

The conclusion of Altizer's search for a way to the sacred through an exposure to non-Christian ideas of holiness is the affirmation of the present as "the holy place." "No longer can we dream that the path to the sacred is *backwards,* nor can we live in the vain hope that the true path is only *forwards:* the Center is everywhere, eternity begins in every Now."[12]

The rebirth of theology must therefore come out of a resolute living in the present. In his article on "America and the Future of Theology," written in 1963, Altizer suggests that

> there is some evidence to suggest the possibility that American theology is now living in the present. First of all, there is very little theology in America today: dogmatic theology has virtually disappeared, biblical scholarship is largely archeological and philological, church history barely maintains its existence as a discipline; and, in terms of German influences, Bultmann has replaced Barth as the guiding light of the younger theologians.[13]

Secondly, Altizer recognizes a resurgence of theological liberalism, in the process of which

> the American theologian is now opening himself to the logician and the philosopher, the psychiatrist and the psychoanalyst, the literary critic and the social scientist. Older theologians are dismayed as they see the traditional forms of faith gradually transformed by this process, but the one conviction

[7] *Ibid.,* p. 14.
[8] *Ibid.*
[9] *Ibid.*
[10] *Ibid.*
[11] *Ibid.,* pp. 14–15.
[12] *Ibid.,* p. 200.
[13] Thomas J. J. Altizer, "America and the Future of Theology," *Radical Theology and the Death of God,* p. 17.

that would seem to be shared by all who are actively engaged in American theology today is that these older forms of faith have no relevance to the present. Unquestionably American theology is in a process of transition. . . .[14]

Altizer asserts that if American theology is to be true to the American genius, it must focus its attention on the present and work toward a better future. The present poverty of contemporary American theology is a sign that theologians have ceased trying to unite the present with the past traditions of Christianity. Altizer holds that quite possibly

the poverty of contemporary American theology is witness to theology's acceptance of its vocation of silence, that at last theology has accepted its sentence of death and is preparing itself for a true renewal. The new formula for theology may well reverse the old: not the goal of converging the present and the past, but rather that of seeking a convergence of the present and the future.[15]

What is this "vocation of silence" to which theology, according to Altizer's analysis, is called in contemporary America? It is a vocation of silence in the presence of which

theology must cultivate the silence of death. To be sure, the death to which theology is called is the death of God. Nor will it suffice for theology to merely accept the death of God. If theology is truly to die, it must *will* the death of God, must *will* the death of Christendom, must freely choose the destiny before it, and therefore must cease to be itself. Everything that theology has thus far become must now be negated; and negated not simply because it is dead, but rather because theology cannot be reborn unless it passes through and freely wills, its own death and dissolution.[16]

In Altizer's view, the contemporary theologian must negate the past in order to be open to the present. Theology in America today must creatively utilize the death of God in order to find its way into "our profane present."[17] It must live completely in the present. Only if it does so can the time come when "the horizon of our present will open into a future epiphany of faith that will draw *all* things into itself."[18]

The vision of this "future epiphany of faith" inspired Altizer's book of 1966, entitled *The Gospel of Christian Atheism*. This *Gospel* is the manifesto of the "radical Christian." Altizer says that

the radical Christian must not be thought of as a reformer; he believes that the ecclesiastical tradition has ceased to be Christian, and is now alive only

[14] *Ibid.*
[15] *Ibid.,* p. 18.
[16] *Ibid.,* p. 15.
[17] *Ibid.,* p. 20.
[18] *Ibid.*

in a demonic and repressive form. No, the radical Christian is a revolutionary, he is given to a total transformation of Christianity, a rebirth of the Christian Word in a new and final form.[19]

The primary sources of Altizer's *Gospel of Christian Atheism* are the writings of the English poet William Blake, and some of the books of the German philosophers Hegel and Nietzsche, both of whom lived and worked in the nineteenth century. With the aid of some aspects of their thoughts, Altizer attempts to construct the kind of godless theology to which a "radical" Christian could subscribe. The radical Christian is a man who

> wagers upon the Christ who is totally profane. He bets upon the Christ who is the totality of the moment before us, the Christ who draws us into the fullness of life and the world. Finally, radical faith calls us to give ourselves totally to the world, to affirm the fullness and the immediacy of the present moment as the life and the energy of Christ. Thus, ultimately the wager of the radical Christian is simply a wager upon the full and actual presence of the Christ who is a totally incarnate love.[20]

The meaning of "a totally incarnate love" in the context of Altizer's Christian atheism is that of an immersion in the fullness of the world and the actuality of time and flesh. It is a total living in the present and for the actual and immediate. In this situation "every nostalgic yearning for innocence, all dependence upon a sovereign other, and every attachment to a transcendent beyond, stand here revealed as flights from the world, as assaults upon life and energy, and as reversals of the full embodiment of love."[21]

Love, life, and energy are Altizer's synonyms for Jesus and for God. "Jesus is the name of the love of God, a love that eternally dies for man."[22] The result of the death of God is that the traditional picture of Jesus becomes totally altered until it becomes identified with every actual manifestation of energy and life. "As the God who *is* Jesus becomes ever more deeply incarnate in the body of humanity, he loses every semblance of his former visage, until he appears wherever there is energy and life."[23] *The Gospel of Christian Atheism,* according to Altizer, is the gospel of the God who is Jesus, who in Jesus achieved the "total union of God and man, even if that union should finally obliterate the God of a former faith."[24]

---

[19] Thomas J. J. Altizer, *The Gospel of Christian Atheism* (Philadelphia: Westminster Press, 1966), p. 26.
[20] *Ibid.,* pp. 156–157.
[21] *Ibid.,* p. 156.
[22] *Ibid.,* p. 75.
[23] *Ibid.,* pp. 74–75.
[24] *Ibid.,* p. 74.

The incarnation of "the God who is Jesus" as a historical process spells the death of God and the re-emergence of God wherever there is love, life, and energy. To live in the fullness of love, life, and energy is to be in the presence of God.

William Hamilton became an exponent of radical theology and the death of God after having been an American Baptist minister. He is presently the William Newton Clarke Professor of Christian Theology and Ethics at Colgate Rochester Divinity School in Rochester, New York. His main concern is to set forth "the new essence of Christianity"[25] which is to provide men with an appropriate form of "belief in a time of the death of God."[26]

Under the impact of the problem of evil, which according to Hamilton, has caused the collapse of the "traditional and correct portrait of God,"[27] it becomes necessary for radical theology to redefine the meaning of divinity. "If there is divinity apart from Jesus," Hamilton contends,

> it is a form of divinity that Jesus as suffering Lord corrects, destroys, transforms. In Jesus the Lord we see for the first time what Christian "divinity" must be taken to be: it is God withdrawing from all claims to power and authority and sovereignty, and consenting to become himself the victim and subject of all that the world can do . . . Divinity in Jesus is not withdrawal from the world: it is a full consent to abide in the world, and to allow the world to have its way with it.[28]

And the world did have its way with the divinity of Jesus with the result that, in the case of William Hamilton, God was lost in the event of the death of God. The same thing happened to such other theologians as Altizer. Having the same mind, they banded together to form a group of

> the death of God radical theologians . . . men without God who do not anticipate his return. But it is not a simple not-having, for there is an experience of loss. Painful for some, not so for others, it is loss nonetheless. The loss is not of the idols, or of the God of theism, but of the God of the Christian tradition. And this group persists, in the face of both bewilderment and fury, in calling itself Christian. It persists in making use of the phrase "death of God," in spite of its rhetorical color, partly because it is a phrase that cannot be adapted to traditional use by the theologians today.[29]

With the loss of God goes the loss of the community of faith, the church. Hamilton quite frankly states: "I do not see how preaching, wor-

[25] William Hamilton, *The New Essence of Christianity* (New York: Association Press, 1961).
[26] *Ibid.*, p. 35.
[27] *Ibid.*, p. 44.
[28] *Ibid.*, pp. 90–91.
[29] William Hamilton, "American Theology, Radicalism, and the Death of God," *Radical Theology and the Death of God*, p. 6.

ship, prayer, ordination, the sacraments can be taken seriously by the radical theologian."[30] Nevertheless, there is neither regret nor retreat for the radical theologian. He must clearly recognize that

> the death of God must be affirmed; the confidence with which we thought we could speak of God is gone, and our faith, belief, experience of him are very poor things indeed. Along with this goes a sharp attack on religion which we have defined as any system using God to meet a need or to solve a problem, even the problem of not having a God. Our waiting for God, our godlessness, is partly a search for a language and a style by which we might be enabled to stand before him once again, delighting in his presence.[31]

The death of God is a necessary condition for the search for a new style of the godless Christian life. Now that God is dead, a person can really be a Christian, because now everything that stands between the person and suffering is taken away. An example of this new view of the Christian life is the notion of sin. The great American theologians, Reinhold Niebuhr, for instance, in the first volume of his *Nature and Destiny of Man,* said that sin was always ultimately sin against God. The same view is adopted by the ecumenical consensus as represented by Barth and Brunner. This concept of sin is, however, no longer possible for the radical theology in which the function of God has been taken over by the human community. Sin now becomes laziness or indifference to the suffering of man in the human community.

Niebuhr also traces sin to pride. The same is done by Barth, Brunner, and the general ecumenical consensus. Their doctrine of sin was shaped during the era of Hitler and Stalin. Hamilton argues that today the sin of the church is not so much pride as it is sloth, sensuality, and sluggishness. Redemption from sin is, according to radical theology, Christological and ethical.

The union of Christology and ethics characterizes the work of Hamilton. He insists that now that it is known that God is dead, radical theologians must begin to develop a new Christology which will be characterized by three things: first a new optimism with regard to the historical reliability of the New Testament record of the life of Christ; second, a profound agreement with the Italian novelist Ignazio Silone that in the twentieth century Jesus Christ is hidden under the mask of the struggle for justice; third, the transformation of the *imitatio Christi* tradition into a substitute for the old doctrine of the two natures of Christ. *Imitatio* means that Christ is present as we become Christ or Christ-like.

The belief that men can to a substantial degree become Christ-like is an

[30] *Ibid.,* p. 7.
[31] William Hamilton, "The Death of God Theologies Today," *Radical Theology and the Death of God,* p. 41.

expression of Hamilton's new optimism with respect to the perfectability of the conditions of human life. His optimism

> is not an optimism of grace, but a worldly optimism. . . . It faces despair not with the conviction that out of it God can bring hope, but with the conviction that the human conditions that created it can be overcome, whether those conditions be poverty, discrimination, or mental illness. It faces death not with the hope of immortality, but with the human confidence that man may befriend death and live with it as a possibility always alongside.[32]

Hamilton thinks "that the new optimism is both a cause and a consequence of the basic theological experience which we today call the death of God."[33]

It may well be asked exactly what constituted this "basic theological experience" of the death of God which led Hamilton down the path of radical theology. This experience can be described in three stages.

During the first stage, Hamilton followed certain thoughts of Dietrich Bonhoeffer's prison letters. In his thoughts about the possibility of having a Christianity without religion Bonhoeffer had called for the disappearance of God as *Deus ex machina* problem solver and need fulfiller. The religious *a priori,* which Reinhold Seeberg had taught Bonhoeffer, was found to be no longer universally valid in the contemporary world. From the religious church men must move into the world. The world and its structures must be ordered to meet the needs of man. If the world cannot fulfill the needs of man, God cannot do it either. Hamilton notes that the protest against religion, which runs through Bonhoeffer's *Letters and Papers from Prison,* find a related emphasis in the second part of the first volume of Karl Barth's *Church Dogmatics,* where Barth bluntly states that religion is unbelief.

During the second stage of Hamilton's development toward the position of radical theology he was forced to acknowledge the death of God as he confronted the problem of suffering. Unmerited suffering, as we find it in the story of Job, for instance, poses a problem for the doctrine of God. In the work of Albert Camus the problem of evil and suffering is unveiled as the insurmountable barrier to Christianity, and almost proof that God is dead. Hamilton finds the neo-orthodox theology of Barth, Brunner, and Niebuhr poorest in its treatment of the problem of suffering and of the doctrine of providence.

During the third and final stage of his evolution toward the God-is-dead position Hamilton stood before the problem of revelation and had to conclude that God was dead. The doctrine of revelation made him realize that

---

[32] William Hamilton, "The New Optimism—from Prufrock to Ringo," *Radical Theology and the Death of God,* p. 169.
[33] *Ibid.*

his personal experience was that of a real loss of transcendence as defined by Barth, fundamentalism, and the neo-orthodox ecumenical consensus. He found it impossible to accept Barth's idea that we cannot know God, but that he has made himself known to us in Christ. Radical theology cannot accept this kind of revelation as necessary. All it can do is say that man cannot know God nor can he experience the transcendent God of the Christian tradition as being manifested in Christ.

Paul Tillich, in his preface to *The Protestant Era* declares that he who denies God affirms him, and that the experience of doubt is the form of modern man's relationship to God. Similarly Blaise Pascal, in his *Pensées,* says, "Thou wouldst not seek me hadst thou not found me." Both men, Hamilton maintains, are trying to convince us that not-having is having. This paradoxical way of affirming revelation is no longer possible for radical theology. For the radical theologian there is only the complete, irretrievable loss of God and transcendence.

Paul M. van Buren's theology exhibits the same trend of a loss of the sense of divine transcendence which characterizes the work of the radical theologians Altizer and Hamilton. Van Buren is a priest of the Protestant Episcopal Church in the U.S.A. Before becoming associate professor of theology at the Episcopal Theological Seminary of the Southwest in Austin, Texas, he was theological adviser to the Detroit Industrial Mission.

Radical theologians like William Hamilton openly recognize van Buren to be one of their number. In a survey of contemporary "death of God theologies" Hamilton observes that

> the work of Paul van Buren says something about the rather strange sense of community that one finds in the death of God group that two such different personalities as van Buren and Altizer could have a common theological vocation. Altizer is all *élan,* wildness, excessive generalization, brimming with colorful, flamboyant, and emotive language. Van Buren is ordered, precise, cool. While he has certainly moved beyond the position of his book, it is in fact, *The Secular Meaning of the Gospel,* that has placed him firmly in the death of God camp. . . .[34]

The Secular Meaning of the Gospel was written as an answer to the question: "How may a Christian who is himself a secular man understand the Gospel in a secular way?"[35] By the term "secular" van Buren means "certain empirical attitudes"[36] characterized by "a deep interest in questions of human life this side of the 'beyond,' and a corresponding lack of interest

34 Hamilton, "The Death of God Theologies Today," *Radical Theology and the Death of God* (New York and Indianapolis: Bobbs-Merrill, 1966), pp. 31–32.
35 Paul M. van Buren, *The Secular Meaning of the Gospel* (New York: Macmillan, 1963), p. xiv.
36 *Ibid.,* pp. xiii-xiv.

in what were once felt to be great metaphysical questions."[37] i.e., questions about God, immortality, and the soul.

Van Buren opens his book with a quote from Bonhoeffer which reads:

Honesty demands that we recognize that we must live in the world as if there were no God. And this is just what we do recognize—before God! God himself drives us to this realization.—God makes us know that we must live as men who can get along without Him. The God who is with us is the God who forsakes us (Mark 15:34)! We stand continually in the presence of the God who makes us live in the world without the God-hypothesis[38]

Taking these lines as his motto, van Buren then proceeds to use the tools of British linguistic analysis in order to distill the meaning of the gospel for a world which lives as if there were no God. He relies especially on the British language philosophers R. B. Braithwaite and R. M. Hare.

Following very closely the approach of Braithwaite, van Buren argues that when the gospels speak about God and make assertions about him and his actions, these biblical utterances are in actuality expressions of a particular human perspective. R. M. Hare interpreted biblical statements about God and his works as expressions of a "blik," or viewpoint. R. B. Braithwaite held that they communicate "an intention to behave in a certain way."[39] Van Buren is very close to Hare and Braithwaite in interpreting scriptural utterances as not really assertions at all but as indications of a perspective on life.

Van Buren connects the human historical perspective represented in the Bible with the story of the life, death, and resurrection of Jesus of Nazareth. The connection with Jesus is a necessary one for van Buren. He stresses that

when the language of the Gospel is analyzed so as to reveal its logical meaning or function, the history of Jesus of Nazareth proves to be indispensable to it: if this history is pushed into the background, faith may be a perspective, but it is either not historical at all, or it is grounded in some other piece of history.[40]

The effect that the story of Jesus has on other men is a liberating one. According to van Buren, "the man who says, 'Jesus is Lord,' is saying that the history of Jesus and of what happened on Easter has exercised a liberating effect upon him, and that he has been so grasped by it that it has become the historical norm of his perspective upon life."[41]

[37] *Ibid.,* p. xiv.
[38] *Ibid.,* p. 1.
[39] *Ibid.,* p. 145.
[40] *Ibid.,* p. 196.
[41] *Ibid.,* p. 141.

The way in which the freedom of Jesus grasps other men is analogous to the way one catches a contagious disease. The believer

speaks in part of a piece of history, which is certainly past. It is the history of a free man and the peculiar character of his freedom. But the Gospel goes on to speak of the moment in which this freedom became contagious in the Easter event, and the speaker, by his very speaking and by the way in which he does it, indicates that this contagious freedom has also touched him. All this constitutes an invitation to the listener to share this discernment and commitment. Perhaps (but also perhaps not) the listener will "see" for the first time, or he will see again, or he will see more clearly than he has in the past. The light will dawn; he will be possessed of a new way of seeing himself, the world, and all things, and he will "catch" something of the contagious freedom of Jesus.[42]

Van Buren argues that the chief aim of the New Testament is to communicate the contagious freedom of Jesus and the discernment and commitment that go with it. The new perspective of freedom was already "objectively" there, even before the new convert discerned it.

It belongs to the language of a discernment situation that we speak of that situation as containing already ("objectively"), prior to its becoming the occasion of discernment, what was only "seen" at a later time. As the lover might say to his beloved, "I must have passed you a thousand times and spoken to you a hundred, and there you were, the most beautiful girl in the world, and I did not see you. And then, that night, all of a sudden I realized. . . ." She did not become the most beautiful girl in the world for him only "that night." He will insist that she always was that, and that he, poor fool, woke up only later to the fact.[43] Such is the language of the "objective" liberation of mankind in the death and resurrection of Jesus. To insist that this is incorrect and that the actual liberation takes place in the moment of believing, which is perfectly true in a psychological sense, is to misunderstand the language appropriate to a situation of discernment which leads one to a commitment embracing all of life.[44]

In a sense van Buren's gospel of secular Christianity is a work of translation. However, as van Buren correctly realizes, "in throwing light on certain major questions, it goes beyond the work of translation, for it involves a decision about the location of the center of theology."[45] He finds this center in a secular doctrine of Jesus Christ. Van Buren's treatment

---

[42] *Ibid.,* pp. 152–153.
[43] "The case of 'love at first sight' is a compressed variation. The 'prior acqaintance' . . . would in this case be prior acquaintance with other people and prior knowledge of the fact of 'falling in love,' together with at least the first impression of the beloved as a person distinct from these other people."
[44] *Ibid.,* p. 153.
[45] *Ibid.,* p. 196.

of the doctrine of Christ appears to reduce theology to ethics. Hence his "decision to interpret the Gospel as a secular Christology . . . raises an obvious question: Although traditional theology does have a historical, intentional, and ethical dimension, does it not include a good deal more?"[46]

Van Buren's reply to this perfectly legitimate question is another intriguing question: "In a secular age, what would that 'more' be?"[47] He then goes on to make the characteristically empirical and secular observation that

> it is our inability to find any empirical linguistic anchorage for that "more" that has led to our interpretation. If this is a reduction in the content of theology, it is the sort of reduction which has been made by modern culture in many fields. Astrology has been "reduced" to astronomy, for example; we have excluded from the study of the stars a cosmological or metaphysical theory about their effect on human life. Alchemy was "reduced" to chemistry by the rigorous application of an empirical method. During the Renaissance, the metaphysical ideas and purposes of medieval painting were excluded, leaving "only" the work of art. In almost every field of human learning, the metaphysical and cosmological aspect has disappeared and the subject matter has been "limited" to the human, the historical, the empirical.[48]

The conclusion to which van Buren is driven is that "theology cannot escape this tendency if it is to be a serious mode of contemporary thought, and such a 'reduction' of content need no more be regretted in theology than in astronomy, chemistry, or painting."[49] This means that the traditional Christian idea of God, as well as any other concept of God, belongs to the prescientific age and therefore must be reduced to an empirically verifiable historical perspective or the expression of the intent to act in a certain way. In the radical theology of van Buren God is part of a cosmological or metaphysical theory which became obsolete with the advent of science and must be reduced to nothing. God is irrelevant or dead as far as the secular age of empirically minded men is concerned.

[46] *Ibid.,* p. 197.
[47] *Ibid.,* p. 198.
[48] *Ibid.*
[49] *Ibid.*

Chapter VII

Neo-Orthodox Theology: Barth, Brunner, and Niebuhr

Neo-orthodox theology was born of a protest and reaction against the dominant liberalism of the nineteenth and early twentieth century. *Karl Barth's* commentary on *The Epistle to the Romans,* published in 1919 and in revised edition in 1922, was the trumpet call of dialectical theology which subsequently became the new or neo-orthodoxy.

It is significant that Barth's famous commentary on Romans was a product of the crisis of World War I. The liberal theological vision of the social gospel, the building of the kingdom of God on earth, the progress of culture united with Christianity—this great vision collapsed as the Christian nations of Europe, the flower of world culture, plunged the world into its most destructive war thus far in history. The synthesis of Christianity and culture and the optimistic belief in human progress and the continued perfectibility of human society was, as the result of World War I, partially or totally discredited in the eyes of Christendom and the Western world. It was denounced as unrealistic, blind to the reality of sin and evil, and lax about the truth of the Christian faith.

Neo-orthodoxy sought to rescue Christianity from the general dissolution of Western culture by going behind the era of nineteenth-century liberalism to the Reformation of the sixteenth century and the period of Protestant orthodoxy in the seventeenth and eighteenth centuries. Hence the name "neo-orthodoxy." The period of Protestant orthodoxy had been the favorite object of liberal theological criticism. Therefore, neo-orthodox theologians found it to be a helpful weapon in their struggle against liberalism. And by claiming to be the true heirs of Martin Luther, John Calvin, and the Reformation, neo-orthodox thinkers sought to brand liberalism as a dangerous innovation and a disastrous deviation from the biblical faith of the Reformation.

The great work of neo-orthodox theology is Karl Barth's monumental *Church Dogmatics*. It has been compared with the *Summa Theologiae* of St. Thomas with respect to the comprehensiveness of its treatment of the great issues of theology. After an initial period of theological criticism, Barth began, in the 1930's, the constructive period of his theological creativity. The product was the *Church Dogmatics* which Barth never completed.

The literal meaning of theology is reasoning about God. If theology speaks about matters other than God, it does so only in order to point out their relationship to God. The question now arises: On what basis can a theologian claim to speak about God? What is the source of this knowledge about God? Barth's answer is that man can know about God only because God has revealed himself. Apart from this self-revelation of God there is no true knowledge of God.

The question now presents itself: What is this self-revelation of God and where can it be found? Barth answers that

> the revelation of God, in which man's fulfillment of the true knowledge of God takes place, is the disposition of God in which He acts towards us as the same triune God that He is in Himself, and in such a way that, although we are men and not God, we receive a share in the truth of His knowledge of Himself. Certainly it is the share which He thinks proper and which is therefore suitable for us. But in this share we have the reality of the true knowledge of Himself. This share is given as God unveils Himself to us in that other, second objectivity, that is to say, in the objectivity of His works and signs in our creaturely sphere, before the eyes and ears and in the hearts which as such and of themselves alone are quite incapable of knowing Him. But the heart of it all is that it is He Himself, the one, supreme and true Lord, who thus unveils Himself to us; that in revelation we have to do with His action as the triune God, and therefore with Himself in every creaturely work and sign that He uses. On this basis and only on this basis can there be real knowledge of God.[1]

[1] Karl Barth, *Church Dogmatics* (Edinburgh: T. & T. Clark, 1958), II/1, p. 51.

From this quotation alone emerges a number of the characteristics of Barth's theology: the emphasis on the sovereignty and freedom of God; the radical separation of God and man, the creature; the total dependence of man on God's grace and revelation.

Barth's insistence on revelation as the only source of man's knowledge of God prompts him to take issue with man's two traditional ways of claiming to know God—the way of religion and the way of philosophy. His polemics against religion have been very influential on contemporary theology. Barth begins his attack upon religion "by stating that religion is unbelief. It is a concern, indeed, we must say that it is the one great concern, of godless man."[2]

Why does Barth equate religion with unbelief? It is because in his view religion

> is a feeble but defiant, an arrogant but hopeless, attempt to create something which man could do, but cannot do, or can do only because and if God Himself creates it for him: the knowledge of the truth, the knowledge of God. We cannot, therefore, interpret the attempt as a harmonious cooperating of man with the revelation of God, as though religion were a kind of outstretched hand which is filled by God in His revelation. Again, we cannot say of the evident religious capacity of man that it is, so to speak, the general form of human knowledge, which acquires its true and proper content in the shape of revelation. On the contrary, we have here an exclusive contradiction. In religion man bolts and bars himself against revelation by providing a substitute, by taking away in advance the very thing which has to be given by God.[3]

Man has, according to Barth, the power to do this.

> But what he achieves and acquires in virtue of this power is never the knowledge of God as Lord and God. It is never the truth. It is a complete fiction, which has not only little but no relation to God. It is an anti-God who has first to be known as such and discarded when the truth comes to him. But it can be known as such as a fiction, only as the truth does come to him.[4]

The truth concerning God comes to man; it is inaccessible to human reflection in philosophy or to human religious sensibilities. This basic and characteristic assertion of Barthian theology is at the root of Barth's denunciation of philosophy as the handmaiden of theology. Philosophy knows nothing about God's self-revelation, which is the Word of God, or Jesus Christ. Therefore it can know nothing about God and his grace. Hence philosophy is utterly useless and misleading to theology.

"Apart from and without Jesus Christ," Barth maintains,

2 *Ibid.*, I/2, p. 299.
3 *Ibid.*, I/2, p. 303.
4 *Ibid.*

we can say nothing at all about God and man and their relationship one with another. Least of all can we say that their relationship can be presupposed as that of a covenant of grace. Just because it is a covenant of grace, it cannot be discovered by man, nor can it be demonstrated by man. As the covenant of grace it is not amenable to any kind of human reflection or to any questions asked by man concerning the meaning and basis of the cosmos or history. Grace is inaccessible to us: how else can it be grace? Grace can only make itself accessible. Grace can never be recalled. To remember grace is itself the work of grace. The perception of grace is itself grace.[5]

If we can say nothing about God and man except as we look in the direction of Jesus Christ, where are we to find the authoritative statement of the meaning and significance of Jesus Christ? Barth replies: In the apostolic and catholic church which exists on the basis of the Bible. According to him

the Church is apostolic and therefore catholic when it exists on the basis of Scripture and in conformity with it, i.e., in the orientation which it accepts when it looks only in the direction indicated by the witness which speaks to it in Scripture, with no glances aside in any other direction. . . . And the direction in which it looks is to the living Jesus Christ. As Scripture stirs up and invites and summons and impels the Church to look in this same direction there takes place the work of the Spirit of Scripture who is the Holy Spirit.[6]

Philosophy, which exists outside of the Bible, can only lead theology astray.

Barth's negative and hostile attitude toward philosophical theology has been so widely influential in our century that a critical evaluation of this theology from the point of view of philosophical theology is much needed. For among the theologians of the contemporary period no one has more consistently and self-consciously denied the relevance of philosophy to theology than Karl Barth. He insisted that only principles of interpretation derived from the revelation of God in the Bible may be used by the theologian. Yet he himself went through a period of existentialist philosophy in his exegesis. Later in his development, in the *Church Dogmatics,* he rejected philosophy as an ally of theology and built what he considered a pure biblical theology, a theology which criticizes the church's proclamation only by the standard of Holy Scripture, and not by a philosophical or cultural norm outside of the Bible.

The main target of Barth's attack upon the use of philosophy by theology was the work of the German theologian and churchman, Friedrich Schleiermacher (1768–1834). Schleiermacher had created a fascinating

[5] *Ibid.,* IV/1, p. 45.
[6] *Ibid.,* IV/1, pp. 722–723.

synthesis between philosophy and theology, religion and science, faith and culture. Probably no one since St. Thomas Aquinas had been so successful and influential in wedding philosophical and theological interests together into a creative synthesis. Barth considered Schleiermacher as one of the greatest and most influential theologians of all time. In his judgment "the first place in a history of theology of the most recent times belongs and will always belong to Schleiermacher, and he has no rival."[7] His admiration for Schleiermacher did not prevent Barth from severely criticizing him. He suspected that Schleiermacher did not only want to be a modern man,

> but he wanted to see in Christianity the basis and guiding spirit of modern humanity. If this suspicion is justified, then the tragic guilt or the apostasy of his theology is: (1) that he ultimately was interested in Christianity only for the sake of culture (a viewpoint with which everything was already lost), (2) that he permitted himself to be pushed into the fundamentally unworthy position of an apologete, and that from this viewpoint and for the sake of apologetics he reflected upon Christianity and set up his propositions regarding its nature, (3) . . . that he let himself be manoeuvered into the mystical-naturalistic corner, where the historical dimension of Christianity could only play a very problematic role.[8]

From Barth's point of view Schleiermacher's apologetic "culture Protestantism" moved theology close to the brink of its "impending metamorphosis into a philosophy,"[9] and he saw this development consummated when his contemporary, the famous theologian Ernst Troeltsch, moved from the department of theology in order to teach in the department of philosophy. Barth protested that if Christian theology were permitted to become identified with liberal or philosophical theology, then the dissolution and apostasy of theology would be imminent. This nightmare of the doom of theology as a consequence of its alliance with philosophy and culture aroused violent protest from Barth, who saw at the bottom of this development the disastrous violation of the Calvinistic principle that "the finite is not capable of the infinite" (*finitum non capax infiniti*).[10] It has been well said that

> just because to Schleiermacher human culture as such was holy, not sin-pervaded, he was blind in principle to the positive truth that, under God, culture is a parable full of promise. In short—and in theology this is the

---

[7] Karl Barth, *Protestant Thought: From Rousseau to Ritschl* (New York: Harper & Bros., 1959), p. 306.
[8] Karl Barth, "Schleiermacher," *Die Theologie und die Kirche* (Munich: Chr. Kaiser Verlag, 1928), pp. 188–189.
[9] Barth, *Protestant Thought*, p. 312.
[10] Cf. Karl Barth, "Ludwig Feuerbach," *Die Theologie und die Kirche*, p. 230.

unpardonable sin—he makes only what may be called a quantitative difference between man and God, thereby suggesting that the revelation of God in Christ is merely a more excellent way than others, instead of proclaiming that it is the true and only way, all other ways being dross and illusion. Nothing, Barth finds, is more characteristic of Schleiermacher's ultimate attitude than his tendency to make a fetish of "continuity," and therefore to gloss over man's worst troubles with a veneer of immanentism.[11]

From a Barthian perspective

the dogma of continuity might be called the real foundation of the more recent European pantheism, consisting as it does in the assertion of the homogeneity and the continuous connexion between all parts of the universe. In the last resort, there is an unbroken line of development from matter to life, from life to mind, from man to God. Thus in religion the measure of all things is man, not the sovereign God who has spoken His Word.[12]

In order to provide a totally different approach to theology in the twentieth century, Barth chose God's revelation of Himself as the starting-point for his church dogmatics. He argues that the choice of this starting-point is the proper one for Christian theology, because theology cannot start with man's ascent to heaven (this was, in Barth's view, the cardinal error of liberalism), but must begin with God's descent to earth, where he reveals himself in his Word. When the world and the Christianity of liberal Cultural Protestantism collapsed in World War I, Barth proclaimed the Word of God as the truth which calls all other truths, all faith in the progress of mankind, into question.[13] In his famous *Commentary on Romans* (*Der Römerbrief*) he outlined a dialectical method for his "theology of crisis" in the sense of a judgment which the sovereign God passes upon sinful and arrogant modern man.

In line with his repudiation of the liberal Protestant doctrine of continuity between human and divine reality, Barth denounces the Thomistic use of the analogy of being (*analogia entis*) as "the invention of the Anti-Christ,"[14] because he believes it will lead theology back to the bankrupt liberalism of Friedrich Schleiermacher, Albrecht Ritschl, and Wilhelm Herrmann—the three great lights in Protestant nineteenth-century theology. Barth proposes to replace the analogy of being with a new, biblical "analogy of faith" (*analogia fidei*). He finds this analogy of faith outlined in Rom 12:6, according to which man's knowledge of God must be reversed into God's knowledge of man. Man's religion, though it

[11] H. R. Mackintosh, *Types of Modern Theology* (London: Nisbet, 1954), p. 271.
[12] *Ibid.*
[13] Karl Barth, *Der Römerbrief* (5th ed.; Zürich: EVZ Verlag, 1954), p. 11.
[14] Karl Barth, *Die kirchliche Dogmatik*, I, Part I (Munich: Chr. Kaiser Verlag, 1932), p. viii.

may be the highest achievement of the human spirit, and man's claim to have knowledge of God are sinful pride. God's knowledge of man is truth revealed in Holy Scripture and in the Word of God, Jesus Christ.

Barth defines theology as a function of the church, which arises out of the need of the church to be self-critical. Theology is to be done only in the church, for the church, and by the church.[15] From the 1919 edition of *Romans,* to the *Christian Dogmatics* of 1927 and the *Church Dogmatics* of 1932, Barth has moved increasingly toward a dogmatic stance grounded in a positive "orthodoxy" modelled along Calvinistic lines, but with an amazing openness to dialogue with Roman Catholic and Lutheran theologians, and especially with the father of modern theology, Schleiermacher. The Barthian form of "neo-orthodoxy" owes so much to the spiritual heritage of Schleiermacher that orthodox Calvinists have condemned Barth as a "modernist."[16]

Generally speaking, however, Barth endeavors methodically to go behind liberal theology, not only to undercut Cultural Protestantism, but also because he finds the orthodox mind as represented by the Calvinistic and Lutheran scholastics of the seventeenth century, as well as St. Augustine, St. Anselm, and St. Thomas Aquinas, more instructive and helpful than the liberal theologies against which he reacted.[17]

Barth completely rejected philosophy as the handmaiden of theology. In the first edition of his *Commentary on Romans* (1919) and in the *Christian Dogmatics* of 1927 he had used existentialist philosophical categories in the course of his explication of his "theology of crisis." But in the second edition of the *Commentary on Romans* (1921) philosophical language was purged and replaced by biblical terminology. Likewise the *Christian Dogmatics* was reworked completely, following Barth's study of St. Anselm. The fruit of this study was published in 1930 under the title of *Fides Quaerens Intellectum, Faith that Challenges the Intellect.*

The Swiss theologian found in the medieval theology of St. Anselm the inspiration for his monumental *Church Dogmatics,* of which the first volume appeared in 1932. St. Anselm had defined God as "He than whom none greater can be conceived." This definition of God immediately appealed to Barth, who had always endeavored to exalt the sovereignty of God and his free, incomprehensible grace. Furthermore, Anselm had argued that reason does not precede faith, but rather follows it. Faith determines the material and the perspective of theology. Reason, with the

[15]*Ibid.,* p. 1.

[16] Cornelius van Til, *The New Modernism* (Philadelphia: Presbyterian and Reformed Publishing Co., 1947).

[17] Karl Barth, *Anselm: Fides Quaerens Intellectum,* trans. Ian W. Robertson (London: SCM Press, 1960), p. 9.

aid of prayer and grace, then seeks to explicate what faith already knows. For faith seeks understanding with the aid of reason but not on the basis of reason. Faith can only be understood on the basis of faith. At the same time, no faith is adequate which does not try to break through to understanding. In this sense, *fides quaerens intellectum,* faith challenges the intellect. But it is always faith that comes first; for Barth believes in order that he may understand; he does not seek understanding in order to be able to believe. The constant danger which accompanies such a viewpoint is that of irrationalism.

Barth had learned from Schleiermacher that faith requires experience, and from St. Anselm that the relationship of faith and reason is that of *credo ut intellegam,* I believe in order that I may understand. Reflecting on St. Anselm's theology, Barth concluded in profound agreement that St. Anselm

> "assumed" neither the Church's *Credo* nor his own *credere* [believing], but he prayed and the Church's *Credo* and his own *credere* were assumed. God gave Himself to him to know and he was able to know God. On this foundation, comparable to no philosophical presupposition and inconceivable for all systematic theology, he has come to know and has probed the Existence of God. For this reason his last word must be gratitude.[18]

With St. Anselm Barth insists that faith and prayer are integral parts of any adequate theological method.

> All restlessness of faith is indeed conquered in prayer, but precisely the prayer of faith is its profound unrest. As prayer as well as restlessness is expectation, expectation of its Object. . . . But this Object is the free God. . . . He must *teach* man to seek Him, and He must *show* Himself to man, in order that he may find Him.[19]

The objectivity of God, the Subject, is the life of faith and the starting point of dogmatic theology as well as its final end.

For Barth the foundation of faith is the Word of revelation addressed to man—not philosophy, the history of religions, or historical criticism. "God's Word is God Himself in His revelation. For God reveals Himself as the Lord. . . ."[20] i.e., as the central point of reference and the supreme and exclusive authority of theology. Scripture and the doctrine of the Trinity are therefore inescapable authorities, and no theology can be considered adequate which does not continually go back to these two pillars of faith.

God's Word of revelation is for Barth not something abstract. It became

18 *Ibid.,* p. 170.
19 Barth, *Die kirchliche Dogmatik,* I/1, p. 243–244.
20 *Ibid.,* p. 311.

incarnate in a human being, Jesus Christ. It comes to us in the church through Holy Scripture. Biblical exegesis, therefore, takes a prominent place in Barthian theology. He maintains that "God's Word is God Himself in the Holy Scriptures."[21] Theology must be biblical, and consequently must proceed as the Bible does: from God's revelation to man, not *vice versa* from man's need to a theological answer. The ultimate criterion of theology is for Barth not the authoritative tradition of the church, but the person and work of Jesus Christ. As theology becomes "subservient" to Christ, it gains "from Him its freedom from every other authority."[22]

A final critical remark must be made, in conclusion, regarding Barth's effort to do exclusively biblical theology without any use of philosophy. The Roman Catholic theologian, Hans Küng, made a study of Barth's doctrine of justification which ended with the conclusion that there is a substantial agreement between Barth and the canons and decrees of the Council of Trent as far as the concept of justification is concerned. Küng argued in that study that "the easiest approach to Barth is via Holy Scripture."[23] No doubt Barth's "discoverey" of the "new world" in the Bible not only launched him on his theological voyage, but also has had an enormous impact on his theological method. Already in the Commentary on Romans he contended that his dialectical method grew out of the inner dialectic of biblical theology. Throughout the *Church Dogmatics,* the Bible is the one certain place of encounter between God's self-revelation and man.

Barth's insistence on the text of Holy Scripture would seem to indicate that revelation is immanent in the Bible. But the way in which he unfolds his doctrine of God makes the biblical revelation appear as "just an active and transient moment exclusively dependent on the real free act of God."[24] Perhaps this is an inevitable tension in Barthian thought, but it actually appears as a contradiction between the authoritative value of the Bible in Barth's theology on the one hand, and the "sovereignty" of God, for whom the Bible is "a transient moment," on the other.

A further source of difficulty for Barth is the existence of internal contradictions in the Bible (for instance, Colossians 1:20 versus Mark 9:43, 46, 48). To reconcile these would require the effective presence of an independent principle, a norm other than the Bible.

Since this external norm cannot be a wordless revelation, for a wordless revelation cannot give us the necessary information, it must be secular

---

[21] *Ibid.,* I/2, p. 505.
[22] Mackintosh, *op. cit.,* p. 276.
[23] Hans Küng, *Rechtfertigung* (Einsiedeln: Johannes Verlag, 1957), p. 22.
[24] Sebastian A. Matczak, *Karl Barth on God* (New York: St. Paul Publications, 1962), p. 325.

science, history, or anthropology. . . . A norm other than Scripture is something Barth does not want at all. But the construction of his system has not enabled him to escape it. The result is that Barth's theology.is self-contradictory. He operates on the basis of incompatible axioms and against his hope and aims arrives at an untenable or irrational position.[25]

Thus the great question which Barth's theology puts before us is: Is Christianity ultimately irrational and self-contradictory, or is it fundamentally reasonable and therefore rationally explicable with the aid of philosophy?

Emil Brunner, like Karl Barth was a Swiss theologian. Initially Brunner thought of himself as sharing completely the theological views of Barth. Barth later issued his famous *No!* to Brunner's theology and dissociated himself from Brunner, who taught systematic and practical theology at the University of Zürich, Switzerland, while Barth taught at Basle, also in Switzerland.

The starting point for Brunner's theology is the church. The church is the context in which, and for which, theology is being carried on. More than that,

the question of the nature of the Church is the decisive question for theology, and also for every system of theological ethics. The view we hold of the nature of the Church reveals most plainly where we stand in relation to faith; and it is through this belief in the Church that faith is able to influence world history at any particular time.[26]

The nature of the church is defined by Brunner in terms of God and Christ. "The sole foundation of the Church is the will and the choice of God; God, not man, is the *auctor ecclesiae.*"[27] This strongly theocentric emphasis is one of the characteristics of neo-orthodox theology. Another common trait of neo-orthodoxy is its emphasis on the central significance of the person and work of Christ. Brunner states that "where Christ is, there is the Church, and nowhere else. And the Church is wherever Jesus Christ is; for it is the fact of His Presence among men which creates community in faith and love."[28]

The reality of the church is that of a community of faith and love. For a better understanding of the central emphases of Brunner's theology it is important to have a clear conception of what he means by "faith" and "love."

For Brunner faith is not the possession of doctrinal truths. He defines

[25] Gordon H. Clark, *Karl Barth's Theological Method* (Philadelphia: Presbyterian and Reformed Publishing Co., 1963), p. 224.

[26] Emil Brunner, *The Divine Imperative,* trans. Olive Wyon (Philadelphia: Westminster Press, 1947), p. 523.

[27] *Ibid.,* p. 524.

[28] *Ibid.,* pp. 525–526.

faith in terms of expectation and hope. "To have faith—really have it, means to be a man on the watch. For what faith possesses—really possesses—is the promise of that which as yet it does not possess."[29] In the light of this promise Christian faith is able to differentiate between the truth of faith, or of divine revelation, and the truths of philosophy. "We must not," Brunner insists,

> say that the philosophical, rational Logos idea is the idea of the divine Logos of which faith speaks; for the idea of the Logos of which faith speaks is always the idea of a Person, the idea of the Son, in whom God loves the world from everlasting to everlasting, and who in Jesus Christ became flesh. Apart from this, His revelation, we do not know the Logos of God; the philosophical Logos idea is only its abstract substitute in abstract thinking.[30]

Brunner's point is that faith and truth and revelation are something intensely personal, something that "became flesh," not something general or abstract.

The emphasis on truth as encounter with a person in faith and in love leads Brunner to reject the traditional proofs of God as incompatible with the standpoint of faith.

> From the standpoint of the Christian faith there are two things to be said about the proofs for the existence of God in general. First, faith has no interest in them. The way in which the divine revelation produces the certainty of faith is quite different from that of proof, and it is completely independent of the success or failure of the process of proof. Secondly, the content of the knowledge "secured" by these proofs is something quite different from the content of the knowledge of faith. The "God" of the proofs for the existence of God is not the Living God of faith, but an intellectual abstraction, an "Idea," an "Absolute," a "Highest," or "necessary Being," the "unconditioned Value," et cetera, an entity whose concept may perhaps be brought into agreement with the God of faith, but which never evokes it.[31]

Brunner here agrees with Barth that the philosophical proofs of God are incapable of evoking faith, but, unlike Barth, Brunner believes that they can be brought into harmony with the God of biblical faith. Here Brunner has a much more positive and open-minded attitude toward philosophy and its constructive use in theology.

Faith is very closely related to love in the theology of Emil Brunner. He is convinced that "faith must be active in love. The community of worship

[29] Emil Brunner, *The Philosophy of Religion,* trans. A. J. D. Farrer and B. L. Woolf (New York: Scribner's, 1937), p. 191.

[30] Emil Brunner, *Revelation and Reason,* trans. Olive Wyon (Philadelphia: Westminster Press, 1946), p. 318.

[31] *Ibid.,* pp. 340–341.

must become a community of life."[32] Life and love belong together in Brunner's thought. To live, really live, is for him to love, and to love means really to live. Hence it is not surprising that he locates the original and "real" being of man in the love of God, and the alienation of fallen and sinful man in the wrath of God. "As the original being of man is existence in the love of God, so also the existence of fallen man is existence in the wrath of God. Man never escapes God, not even in hell. Indeed, this is the very essence of hell—that one would like to be free from God at last, and it is impossible."[33]

The church is the true humanity, because it is built on faith and love in which the contradictions of sin are, at least in principle and by way of promise, overcome. Therefore, if we wish to know where man can live in a way that is true to himself, we must turn to the all-sufficient love of the triune God. "Only where this love—which no longer knows any contradiction—realizes itself, is the meaning, the truth of man, realized."[34]

The realization of love is a process of inwardness carried out by the power of the Holy Spirit. It is not in man's power to realize the love which will bring to light the truth of his innermost being. The truth of each individual man is not his own, but that of the Holy Spirit who works truth by love. Hence, "even a Christian can say that subjectivity is truth (Kierkegaard), but he knows that it is a subjectivity that is no longer his own. . . . The doctrine of the Holy Spirit is the Christian answer to the truth in subjectivism, the doctrine of that inwardness which is not in the least degree our own."[35]

But Brunner warns that the saving significance of the work of love in man must not blind us to the reality of the wrath of God. It was the justice, the wrath, the "alien work" of God which brought Christ to the cross and made the atonement absolutely necessary for man's salvation. God's wrath is just as real as his love, and he will not renounce the one for the sake of the other. "God cannot and will not contradict Himself. Even as the God of love He cannot deny his wrath. His activity in the world, His law, and the *opera aliena* are all really, and not apparently, His work. This He will not renounce."[36]

But while God is both the God of wrath and the God of love, Brunner tends to subordinate justice to love. He declares that "love is greater than

[32] Brunner, *The Divine Imperative,* p. 534.

[33] Emil Brunner, *Man in Revolt,* trans. Olive Wyon (Philadelphia: Westminster Press, 1947), p. 163.

[34] *Ibid.,* p. 493.

[35] Brunner, *The Philosophy of Religion,* pp. 112–113.

[36] Emil Brunner, *The Mediator,* trans. Olive Wyon (Philadelphia: Westminster Press, 1947), p. 520.

justice—that love which is God himself. Justice can be taught and learned, but not love. Love can only be given by Him who is Himself the source of all love."[37] The greatness of the love of God becomes manifest in Jesus Christ. In him the justice of the wrath of God is taken into the love of God. In our Lord the justice of God is the love of God. Brunner holds that "the Gospel of Jesus Christ is the Gospel of this justice which is identical with love. Hence it is the message of that which lies beyond all earthly institutions."[38] In other words, the church as an earthly institution can never completely convey the full meaning and power of the love and justice of God. It can only point to them as a witness and herald of the good news of Jesus Christ. And since love is the clue to the being of man, and this love has become visible in our Lord, Brunner can say that "only in the Mediator Jesus Christ do we know ourselves as we really are."[39]

Man can know himself as he really is only in Jesus of Nazareth because only he is the revelation of the love of God and the justice of God. For Brunner this revealed knowledge is accessible only to faith, for "the true God can be known only by His coming down to us, in the revelation of Christ which is disclosed to faith."[40] Thus with the introduction of the concept of revelation we have come to the great divide in Brunner's thought. For him, "revelation means that God speaks and man is silent. God Himself acts, God alone acts, we merely receive, we merely endure. God Himself steps on the stage, and we retire."[41]

This stress on the sole activity of God in revelation and on the corresponding passive attitude of man runs counter to the self-confidence and activism of modern man. Hence it is not surprising that the Christian church, with its insistence on revelation, finds itself an alien in our modern world. Brunner points out that the case was exactly opposite in the world in which Christianity was born. "In the ancient world, in which the Christian Church first arose, the idea of revelation, and the belief that there was such a thing as revelation, was something that belonged to life as such; it was taken for granted."[42]

This situation prevailed through the Middle Ages and into the early Renaissance. It was in the later Renaissance that men began to question from every side the truth of the proclamations of the church based upon the divine revelation in the Scripture. These questionings and criticisms

---

[37] Emil Brunner, *Justice and the Social Order,* trans. Mary Hottinger (New York: Harper, 1945), p. 261.
[38] *Ibid.*
[39] Brunner, *The Mediator,* p. 600 (italics omitted).
[40] Brunner, *Revelation and Reason,* p. 319.
[41] Brunner, *The Mediator,* p. 520.
[42] Brunner, *Revelation and Reason,* p. 4.

came largely as a result of "complete preoccupation with the things of this world, and an immanental philosophy."[43] In these characteristics of the Renaissance were the seeds of science and irreligion.

The church itself is responsible for at least part of the opposition to revelation. For centuries the church taught certain "revealed" truths as final which were later proved erroneous through scientific research. As a result, the church waged a losing battle against scientific research. Further, the church backed up its teachings by a connection with the state. This made it possible for it to punish severely all those who would not accept revealed truth as heretics. This strategy proved to be of great detriment to the church. Though many are willing to forget the past and forgive the church for its mistakes, there remains a large group who fear the element of the irrational in the claim of revelation. Brunner puts this problem very clearly when he notes

> what a torrent of nonsense, superstition, delusions, and emotional phantasies have at all times poured into the life of humanity under the cover of the claim to "revelation"! Who can assure us that the Christian claim to be "revelation" is not something of the same sort? What means are there to ensure that once the rational criteria have been removed, there is a distinction between sense and nonsense, delusion and truth?[44]

The modern scientific spirit and the attacks from without are not the only threat to the church. What threatens its very life lies within its own walls. This threat appears in the form of certain static doctrinal and dogmatic formulations. The greatest error in this area affects the idea of revelation. Very little really comprehensive thought was given to the nature of revelation in the early church. In fact, it was not until the Reformation that the essence of revelation was clarified. Before this time there was a dangerous identification between the church's doctrine of the Bible and its doctrine of revelation. Instead of revelation meaning "the whole of the divine activity for the salvation of the world,"[45] it was defined as a book, a doctrine. Revelation then became "the infallible doctrine, divinely 'given' in the Bible, and clearly stated and formulated in the system of Christian dogma."[46] Just as revelation became a formal instrument, so faith was not properly understood. Faith, instead of being what Brunner terms "knowledge as encounter,"[47] that is, personal truth personally understood, came to be regarded as doctrinal belief. Under the impact of the idea

[43] *Ibid.*, p. 5.
[44] *Ibid.*, p. 6.
[45] *Ibid.*, p. 8.
[46] *Ibid.*, p. 9
[47] *Ibid.*

of faith as doctrinal belief, the written word of the Bible and doctrinal formulations became absolutely authoritative.

The doctrine of the verbal inspiration of the Scriptures followed as a logical consequence of the idea that the written Scriptures were the source of infallible and divinely revealed truth. Moreover, "once this view of the Scriptures was accepted, of necessity the idea of revelation was narrowed down to the idea of the inspiration of the Scriptures." Here then we have the answer to the question, "why has the theology of the Church been developed within the narrow limits of the doctrine of the authority of the Bible?"[48]

In contrast to the prevailing popular Catholic view during the Middle Ages, at the time of the Reformation faith was again defined as "personal encounter with the God who meets us personally in Jesus Christ" and revelation "was again understood as God's action in Jesus Christ."[49] However, this Reformation insight was destined to be choked and to remain ineffective until it was again brought to light by the neo-Reformation theology and neo-orthodoxy of Brunner. The Reformation church, in casting about for a tractable norm by which to judge both the Roman Catholics and the fanatical sects, hit upon the idea of written scriptures as the source and guarantee of infallible doctrine. The price of this move was the loss of the real essence of the Reformation, according to Brunner. Instead of the Pope in Rome, the "paper-Pope" became the supreme authority. "The absolute authority of the Church had been replaced by the absolute authority of the Book."[50]

The idea of an absolutely authoritative Scripture based on verbal inspiration was destined to break down, for it could not stand the attacks of historical science and natural science. Had the church only known, it would probably have been more conservative in its claims regarding the authority and infallibility of Scripture. Little did the church realize that the stage was being set for a violent reaction against the neat structure of orthodox doctrine. The reaction came in great waves of Enlightenment, rationalism, romantic idealism, naturalism, and humanism. The lively questioning of authority set in, and the prerogative of Scripture was shattered. However, in the midst of this breakdown, a fresh stirring of thought took place. This resulted in a new interest in the scriptural idea of revelation, and in fact in the whole history of revelation. No longer were the "orthodox-confessional theories" or the "orthodox traditional view of Scripture" taken as the final word.[51]

---

48 *Ibid.*
49 *Ibid.*, p. 10.
50 *Ibid.*, p. 11.
51 *Ibid.*

Thus the problem of revelation came to the fore and took precedence over the problem of the Bible as the inspired word of God. It is significant to note here that finally a clear distinction is made between revelation and the Scriptures. Formerly, Scripture was *the* revelation, and revelation was *the* Scripture. Certainly these two are vitally connected but making them identical leads to sheer objectivism and the letter which killeth.

Brunner insists that the written Scriptures find their proper place as only one among three which bear witness to the unique historical revelation of God in Jesus Christ. These three are the Bible, the church, and the Holy Spirit. Each must be considered in relation to the other. To make Scripture or church exclusively authoritative leads to a false heteronomy. To hold that the Holy Spirit is the sole authority would lead to theological and spiritual anarchy. In Brunner's thought these three which bear testimony to *the* revelation in Jesus Christ (which is both historical and eternal)[52] must be kept in dynamic balance, for each is integrally bound up with the other.

Brunner insists that the written Scripture and the fact of revelation must be distinguished. It is necessary that they should be connected, but to make them identical is the mistake of orthodoxy.[53] The connection, to be sure, is a vital one but the "identity between Scriptural word and God's Word is indirect rather than direct."[54] The Scriptures have an authoritative claim on us only to the extent that they bring to us the original historical, and authoritative revelation of the living Word, Jesus Christ himself.[55] Thus the authority of the Bible is definitely a derived or secondary authority.

Brunner's theology thus recognizes a living process of revelation wherein the word comes from God to man. The emphasis on the God-man direction, rather than on the movement of the soul upward to God, is typical of neo-orthodox theology. The word descending from God to man takes three main forms. First, there is the living word of God made flesh in Jesus Christ. Second, we have the spoken word of the apostle and preacher who share the message of the revealed event. Third, there is the written word. Together these three constitute the threefold form of the revelation of God.

The stress of Brunner's doctrine of revelation lies on the activity of God who reveals himself to man from beyond himself. A similar emphasis can be found in the thought of the greatest of contemporary American neo-orthodox theologians, Reinhold Niebuhr.[56]

Reinhold Niebuhr is probably the most influential contemporary American theologian of our century. He was born at Wright City, Missouri, in

52 *Ibid.*, p. 119.
53 Brunner, *The Mediator*, p. 34.
54 Brunner, *The Philosophy of Religion*, p. 32.
55 Brunner, *The Mediator*, p. 241.
56 Reinhold Niebuhr, *The Nature and Destiny of Man* (New York: Scribner's, 1964), I, 17.

1892. Having studied at Eden Theological Seminary and Yale Divinity School, he served as Evangelical and Reformed pastor in Detroit for thirteen years. In 1928 he joined the faculty of Union Theological Seminary in New York as Professor of Christian Ethics, and remained there until he retired in 1960. His great work is *The Nature and Destiny of Man,* which gives the best statement of Niebuhrian neo-orthodoxy.

It is characteristic of Niebuhr's basic ethical and practical interest that he devotes his *magnum opus* to the clarification of the problem of the nature and destiny of man, rather than to "the Word of God" or "church dogmatics." His aim is to demonstrate "that the two main emphases of Western culture, namely the sense of individuality and the sense of a meaningful history, were rooted in the faith of the Bible and had primarily Hebraic roots."[57] Let us look at each of these two chief emphases in turn.

Traditional Christian thought, influenced by Plato or Aristotle, had seen man as a "rational animal," distinguished from all other beings by his capacity for forming and analyzing concepts. In modern times, the philosophies of idealism had continued this rationalistic tradition by indentifying man with his universal reason. Modern naturalism had opposed this autonomous view of human nature, and made man dependent on the blind and purposeless forces of nature.

In contrast to both idealism and naturalism, Niebuhr stresses that

> individual selfhood is expressed in the self's capacity for self-transcendence and not in its rational capacity for conceptual and analytic procedures. Thus a consistent idealism and a consistent naturalism both obscure the dimension of selfhood, the former by equating the self with universal reason (as in Plato and Hegel) and the latter by reducing the self to an unfree nature not capable of viewing itself and the world from the position transcending the flow of events, causes and sequences.[58]

Man's ability to lift himself above his own reason as well as above the forces of nature to which he is subject is the source of his individual worth.

What gives meaning and significance to the Western view of the value of the individual is the biblical-Hebraic emphasis about human self-hood. The Western appreciation of the individual has derived much of its power and significance from the biblical stress on

> the unity of the self in its body, mind and spirit, in its freedom from natural necessity and in its involvement as creature in all these necessities. This unity was obscured in all forms of dualism, of which that of Descartes is a convenient example, which cut the self in two entities, body and mind, or

---

[57] *Ibid.,* p. vii.
[58] *Ibid.*

body and spirit. The unity of the self can only be expressed in poetic, religious and metaphorical symbols.[59]

The Bible, when it speaks of man as being made in the image of God, is using poetic, religious and metaphorical language in order to express the reality of the human self. Likewise the New Testament seeks to express the evolutionary destiny of the self when it says that God has predestined man "to be conformed to the image of his Son, in order that he might be the first-born among many brethren."[60] Jesus Christ is the "Omega-Point," as Pierre Teilhard de Chardin said, where all the lines traversed by the evolutionary development of man converge into one magnificent unity.

The moral nature of the human self is what gives the individual in Western culture his abiding and inalienable freedom. Against those who see the source of human evil in the passions of man's emotional and irrational nature. Niebuhr puts forth the doctrine of the Fall and of original sin. And against those who attribute the problems of human selfhood to ignorance Niebuhr likewise argues "that human evil, primarily expressed in undue self-concern, is a corruption of its [i.e. human selfhood's] essential freedom and grows with its freedom."[61] More education will not eradicate sin and evil; neither will greater freedom. Rather, the opportunities for evil, as well as for good, increase with more freedom and better education.

Niebuhr declares that the biblical symbols of the Christ and his adversary, the anti-Christ, are "symbols of the fact that both good and evil grow in history, and that evil has no separate history, but that a greater evil is always a corruption of a greater good."[62] Greater freedom is a greater good, but also a greater opportunity for evil. Better and more education enlarges the possibilities for evil, which is a corruption of the enrichment and enhancement of life which education can bring. "Therefore," Niebuhr observes, "every effort to equate evil purely with the ignorance of the mind and with the passions of the body is confusing and erroneous."[63]

The equation of evil with ignorance or uncontrolled passion permits modern man to falsify the reality and power of evil and to make light of it. Niebuhr notes that

the final certainty of modern anthropology is its optimistic treatment of the problem of evil. Modern man has an essentially easy conscience; and nothing gives the diverse and discordant notes of modern culture so much harmony as the unanimous opposition of modern man to Christian conceptions of the sinfulness of man. The idea that man is sinful at the very centre of his per-

59 *Ibid.*, pp. vii–viii.
60 Rom 8:29.
61 Niebuhr, p. viii.
62 *Ibid.*, p. ix; cf. II, pp. 316–319.
63 *Ibid.*, p. viii.

sonality, that is in his will, is universally rejected. It is this rejection which has seemed to make the Christian gospel simply irrelevant to modern man, a fact which is of much more importance than any conviction about its incredibility.[64]

Modern man may think that he cannot believe in God or in Christ because the scientific world-view has made such belief impossible. But the real reason for disbelief in the Christian message is that modern man's easy conscience would be sorely troubled if he shared the Christian view of the essential and inescapable sinfulness of human nature.

Following St. Augustine, Niebuhr sees man's basic sin in pride. Human pride includes "the idolatrous pursuit of false securities and redemptions in life and history."[65] Because of man's pride, he refuses to see some of the obvious facts of human history.

> It is obvious that man does not have the power to extricate himself from flux and finiteness, as idealists and mystics of the ancient and the modern world believed. It is equally obvious that history does not solve the basic problems of human existence but reveals them on progressively new levels. The belief that man could solve his problem either by an escape from history or by the historical process itself is a mistake which is partly prompted by the most universal of all "ideological" taints: the pride, not of particular men and cultures, but of man as man.[66]

A biblical understanding of man can help us to see the limitations of human knowledge and power. Niebuhr believes that the scriptural concept of man is truer to reality than any other, because it has acknowledged pride as man's ineradicable sin. "For this reason it is possible to make a truer analysis of human destiny upon the basis of a religious faith which has disavowed human pride in principle, though it must not be assumed that any particular Christian analysis will not exhibit in fact what it has disavowed in principle."[67]

The great practical value of a Christian understanding of the nature and destiny of man is, according to Niebuhr, that it frees men from the vain attempt to achieve a perfect life or a premature end of history. Christian faith understands the meaning of history, and therefore can accept suffering and historical responsibility without claiming to possess the proud certainty of knowledge. Niebuhr holds that

> if the Christian faith really finds its ultimate security beyond all the securities and insecurities of history; if it is really "persuaded that neither death,

---

[64] *Ibid.*, I, p. 23.
[65] *Ibid.*, II, p. 321.
[66] *Ibid.*, II, p. 320.
[67] *Ibid.*

nor life, nor angels, nor principalities, nor powers, nor things present, nor things to come, nor height, nor depth, nor any other creature, shall be able to separate us from the love of God, which is in Christ Jesus our Lord," it may dissuade men from the idolatrous pursuit of false securities and redemptions in life and history. By its confidence in an eternal ground of existence which is, nevertheless, involved in man's historical striving to the very point of suffering with and for him, this faith can prompt men to accept their historical responsibilities gladly. From the standpoint of such a faith history is not meaningless because it cannot complete itself; though it cannot be denied that it is tragic because men always seek prematurely to complete it.[68]

As a neo-orthodox theologian Niebuhr closes his analysis of the nature and destiny of man with a strong reliance upon grace and faith. He concludes that

wisdom about our destiny is dependent upon a humble recognition of the limits of our knowledge and our power. Our most reliable understanding is the fruit of "grace" in which faith completes our ignorance without pretending to possess its certainties as knowledge; and in which contrition mitigates our pride without destroying our hope.[69]

Here again are found the characteristically neo-orthodox themes of faith, grace, and the sin of man, who is unable to save himself either by knowledge or by living a good life.

In conclusion we can say that the work of neo-orthodox theology was a temporary relief in the crisis of theology in the twentieth century. The theological fate of Brunner, who today is almost forgotten, shows that the compromise of Reformation orthodoxy and modern liberalism which he represented was too inadequate and unstable to be of lasting value. Reinhold Niebuhr's social and political interests give him a better chance for survival. He still has power and revelance for American theology concerned with the struggle for social justice and world peace. But his defeatist attitude toward culture is out of step with the current cautious optimism in theology. Hence his theology, which was shaped by the depression of the 1930's, is increasingly found to be lacking in contemporary relevance.

[68] *Ibid.,* II, pp. 320–321.
[69] *Ibid.,* II, p. 321.

CHAPTER VIII

CHRISTIANITY AND JUDAISM: BUBER

With Martin Buber we move from the world of Christian theology into the wider sphere of Judaic-Christian thought. Although Jewish thinkers may consider Franz Rosenzweig (1886–1929) the greatest and most profound and authentic Jewish philosopher and theologian of the twentieth century,[1] for contemporary Christian thought Martin Buber's influence has been incomparably greater than that of any other modern Hebrew religious thinker.

In order to facilitate a better understanding of Buber's thought a few biographical remarks are in order. Martin Buber was born in 1878 and attended a Polish high school at Lemberg, Poland. In 1896 he enrolled as a student of philosophy at the university of Vienna, Austria. He studied the thought of mystics like Jacob Boehme, Meister Eckhart, and Nicholas of Cusa.[2] The vitalist philosophy of Friedrich Nietzsche attracted Buber espe-

[1] Arthur A. Cohen, *Martin Buber* (New York: Hillary House, 1957), p. 21.
[2] *Ibid.*, p. 31.

cially during the early years as a student. Ironically, Nietzsche later became very popular with Hitler and the National Socialists in Germany and Austria.

However, it was not in Vienna, but in Berlin that Buber encountered the two trends of thought which were to provide the focus of his future thinking. In the summer of 1898 he met there

> the two men who were to influence him decisively: Simmel, whose lectures he attended, while also attending those of Dilthey; and Theodor Herzl, an attractive personality, who was one of the originators of the Zionist movement that was to mean so much in Buber's life. Those were to be the formative influences in his intellectual development; both his thought and his life were in fact largely determined by Simmel's "Philosophy of Life," and by the dynamism of the Zionist movement.[3]

In 1901, Buber joined the staff of the Zionist periodical *Die Welt,* and in 1904 he and Chaim Weizmann, later to become the first President of the State of Israel, projected in Berlin a Zionist monthly called *Der Jude.* 1904 was an important year for the then twenty-six-year-old Buber:

> he happened to read a statement by Rabbi Israel ben Eliezer (1700–1760), the so-named *Baal Shem Tov,* founder of the Hasidic movement, [in] which the Baal Shem describes the intensity and depth of the daily renewal expected of each Hasid. In this description Buber recognized within himself precisely this quality of intensity and return. As a result of this experience and its consequences, Buber retired from his journalistic and Zionist activities and engaged for a period of five years in close study of Hasidic texts. The fruit of these years was a series of works which constitute a veritable history of the literature of the Hasidic movement. With painstaking attention and devotion he succeeded in reconstructing and publishing versions of the traditions and teachings of many of the greatest mystics the world has ever known.[4]

In 1916 Buber founded and edited the Zionist journal *Der Jude,* which he had planned and projected with Weizmann twelve years earlier. The journal, which appeared for the next eight years, emphasized the sanctification of the Jewish community. Into this period falls the publication of the book *I and Thou* in 1923. "It is a great book; perhaps one of the rare and sustained works of universal meaning written in our time."[5] The theological impact of this work on Christian thought has been enormous. It discloses the genius of Buber's method, which is

---

[3] Hans Urs von Balthasar, *Martin Buber and Christianity,* trans. Alexander Dru (London: Harvill Press, 1961), p. 31.

[4] Cohen, *op. cit.,* p. 31.

[5] *Ibid.,* pp. 46–47.

one of ruthless simplification and clarification in which everything super-fluous or inessential is mercilessly swept aside—everything that had accu-mulated during the centuries, everything decadent and distorted: a method of *reduction*, reducing everything to essentials, and which does not falter on the threshold of the Old Testament, but makes use of the whole apparatus of modern biblical scholarship to break through to the kernel and to uncover the source, in order to display it alone as the driving power and inspira-tion of the whole.[6]

During the 1920's Buber, together with Franz Rosenzweig, established a program of cultural and educational activities in the Free Jewish Aca-demy of Frankfort-on-Main. While engaged in a translation of most books of the Hebrew Bible into German, Buber and Rosenzweig offered open seminars on Jewish religious history, theology, Bible, language, and litera-ture. From 1923 to 1933 Buber was also professor of Jewish theology and later of the history of religions at the University of Frankfort-on-Main. From the lectures and writings of this period it emerges quite clearly that to Buber "Judaism is coincident with a vital prophetic tradition. That is the simple and basic theme of all his sometimes minute interpretations of Scripture. Even the founder Abraham—the visionary, the man of prayer who intercedes for others—must be understood in that light."[7] "Buber conceived of the Bible as the meeting-place of God and man. God is the eternal *I* in quest of a *Thou* to whom he can speak, and man is the *I* who can return to God the address of *Thou*."[8]

In 1938 the sixty-year-old Buber went to Israel to become professor of social philosophy at the Hebrew University, Jerusalem. He died in the holy city on June 13, 1965, at the age of 87 years. During his lifetime "Buber's considerable affection for the person and teaching of Jesus has been a source of consternation to the Jewish community and delight to Christians who see in Buber's appreciation of Jesus a modification of classic Jewish obduracy."[9] However, Buber was self-consciously committed to Judaism and its God-given task in the world. This task he believed Christianity could never fulfill in the way in which Judaism could.

There are many reasons, according to Buber, why Christianity can never give itself unreservedly to the worldly task as Judaism sees it. For one thing it is to a certain extent heir to the late Jewish, or to be more precise, Iranian apocalyptic religious ideas which, by rigidly fixing the ultimate his-torical decision in the future, clips its own wings. There is also the concep-tion of "the fulness of time" which, from the start, outstrips and so rules

---

6 Balthasar, *op. cit.*, p. 32.
7 *Ibid.*, p. 36.
8 Cohen, *op. cit.*, p. 62.
9 *Ibid.*, p. 65.

out a completely free future, with the result that the Christian does not really face an open future but simply has to wait in expectation for what has already happened, the return of the saviour who worked the salvation of the whole world and everything in it.[10]

Buber's philosophy of I *and* Thou. It has been suggested by some students of Buber's thought that his work

> is divided rather clearly into three major areas of concentration: the primary problem of being ([treated in his books] *I and Thou, Dialogue, Daniel, The Question of the Single One*); the literature of Biblical, Hasidic, and Jewish exegesis which historically exemplifies his insight into the problem of being ([dealt with in books like] *Moses, The Prophetic Faith, The Legend of the Baal Shem, The Tales of Rabbi Nacman, For the Sake of Heaven, Two Types of Faith*); and his efforts to make concrete his primary insight and explore its implications for modern man.[11]

For the purposes of this concise exposition of Buber's thought the following triadic division has been adopted: (1) Buber's philosophy of the *I* and *Thou,* (2) Hasidism, and (3) Zionism.

The classical formulation of Buber's philosophy of the "inter-personal" (*das Zwischenmenschliche*) reality of human existence occurs in his book of 1923, entitled *I and Thou*. The mystical and poetic vision of his book *Daniel,* published in 1913, was refined and clarified into the concept of the *I* and the *Thou*. In *Daniel* Buber wrote: "all reality is fulfilled unification. Nothing individual is real in itself; everything individual is only preparation. The creative hours, acting and beholding, forming and thinking, are the unifying hours. The hero and the wise man, the poet and the prophet are unifying men."[12] But the reality of "fulfilled unification" is not a static state; it is rather a process of becoming. Buber holds that "the polarity which man experiences in himself wills unity. And unity is not now or ever something which 'is there'; unity is that which eternally becomes. Not out of the world: out of our action comes unity."[13]

As we move from the existential discussion of the subject-object problem in *Daniel* to the dialogic of *I and Thou* we hear Buber speaking of two basic attitudes which a man can take toward the world. These two fundamental relations to the universe can be described by two "primary words." "The one primary word is the combination *I-Thou*. The other primary word is the combination *I-It;* . . ."[14] The "I" in each one of these two

10 Balthasar, op. cit. p. 56.

11 Cohen, *op. cit.,* p. 85.

12 Martin Buber, *Daniel,* trans. Maurice Friedman (New York: Holt, Rinehart and Winston, 1964), p. 72.

13 *Ibid.,* p. 124.

14 Martin Buber, *I and Thou,* trans. R. G. Smith (2d. ed.; New York: Scribner's, 1958), p. 3.

basic combinations is different from that in the other. The precise nature of this difference will become clear as we consider what each one of the two primary words signifies.

According to Buber's philosophy of interpersonal dialogic "primary words do not signify things, but they intimate relations. Primary words do not describe something that might exist independently of them, but being spoken they bring about existence."[15] They bring about existence because they are derived from, and communicate, being. "If *Thou* is said, the *I* of the combination *I-Thou* is said along with it. If *It* is said, the *I* of the combination *I-It* is said along with it."[16] But the two *I*'s of these two combinations are different. "The primary word *I-Thou* can only be spoken with the whole being. The primary word *I-It* can never be spoken with the whole being."[17]

For Buber the *I* does not exist as a self-sufficient entity. Protesting against nineteenth-century individualism he stresses that "there is no *I* taken in itself, but only the *I* of the primary word *I-Thou* and the *I* of the primary word *I-It*."[18] For "when a primary word is spoken the speaker enters the word and takes his stand in it,"[19] which means that he commits himself to participation in the realm of the interpersonal, of relatedness between *I* and *Thou*.

The distinction between *It,* the thing, and the *Thou,* which is no thing, is important. "When *Thou* is spoken, the speaker has no *thing;* he has indeed nothing. But he takes his stand in relation."[20] It is different when we enter the sphere of *It.* "For where there is a thing there is another thing. Every *It* is bounded by others; *It* exists only through being bounded by others. But when *Thou* is spoken, there is no thing. *Thou* has no bounds."[21]

Thou is not even an *experience* or a secret mystical ecstasy between persons which could be described and analyzed. Let us say, for instance, that

I experience something.—If we add "secret" to "open" experiences, nothing in the situation is changed. How self-confident is that wisdom which perceives a closed compartment in things, reserved for the initiate and manipulated only with the key. O secrecy without a secret! O accumulation of information! *It,* always *It!*[22]

15 *Ibid.*
16 *Ibid.*
17 *Ibid.*
18 *Ibid.*, p. 4.
19 *Ibid.*
20 *Ibid.*
21 *Ibid.*
22 *Ibid.*, p. 5.

Buber distinguishes three spheres of reality in which we encounter the *Thou.*

First, our life with nature. There the relation sways in gloom, beneath the level of speech. Creatures live and move over against us, but cannot come to us, and when we address them as *Thou,* our words cling to the threshold of speech.

Second, our life with men. There the relation is open and in the form of speech. We can give and accept the *Thou.*

Third, our life with spiritual beings. There the relation is clouded, yet it discloses itself; it does not use speech, yet begets it. We perceive no *Thou,* but none the less we feel we are addressed and we answer—forming, thinking, acting. We speak the primary word with our being, though we cannot utter *Thou* with our lips.[23]

At this point the question presents itself: "with what right do we draw what lies outside speech into relation with the world of the primary word?"[24] The answer Buber gives is that "in every sphere in its own way, through each process of becoming that is present to us we look out toward the fringe of the eternal *Thou;* in each we are aware of a breath from the eternal *Thou;* in each *Thou* we address the eternal *Thou.*"[25] We may safely assume that Buber's eternal *Thou* is a name for God.

God, the eternal *Thou,* is the unifying center of the universe. Therefore to come to God means to go through the world of things and conditioned being, not to flee from it as from something evil. As a true son of the Judaic-Christian tradition Buber insists that

the primary word *I-It* is not of evil—as matter is not of evil. It is of evil— as matter is, which presumes to have the quality of present being. If a man lets it have the mastery, the continually growing world of *It* overruns him and robs him of the reality of his own *I.* . . .[26]

We need the world of things, but we must not let the world of things control us.

The world of *It* and the world of the temporal *Thou* are lines of relations traversed by the *I,* which depend on interpersonal relatedness for their very existence. Buber holds that

the extended lines of relations meet in the eternal *Thou.* Every particular *Thou* is a glimpse through to the eternal *Thou;* by means of every particular Thou the primary word addresses the eternal *Thou.* Through this mediation of the *Thou* of all beings fulfilment, and non-fulfilment, of relations comes

[23] *Ibid.,* p. 6.
[24] *Ibid.*
[25] *Ibid.*
[26] *Ibid.,* p. 46.

to them: the inborn *Thou* is realised in each relation and consummated in none. It is consummated only in the direct relation with the *Thou* that by its nature cannot become *It*.[27]

The mediation of temporal beings and things is necessary if we are to meet the living God. God is the nearest and the most distant *Thou* at the same time. He is related to every *It* and every *Thou* in the universe, and in this relatedness we meet him. In agreement with the teachings of Hasidim, Buber affirms that

> men do not find God if they stay in the world. They do not find Him if they leave the world. He who goes out with his whole being to meet his *Thou* and carries to it all being that is in the world, finds Him who cannot be sought.
>
> Of course, God is the "wholly Other"; but He is also the wholly Same, the wholly Present. Of course He is the Mysterium Tremendum that appears and overthrows; but He is also the mystery of the self-evident, nearer to me than my I.
>
> If you explore the life of things and of conditioned being, you come to the unfathomable, if you deny the life of things and of conditioned being you stand before nothingness, if you hallow this life you meet the living God.[28]

The living God is, in Buber's view, utterly indescribable. He cannot be presented in terms of things, nor can he be understood by means of the negation of things, as the *via negativa* attempts to do. God can also not be controlled or predicted as things can be controlled or as the behavior of "mass man" or "the consumer" can be predicted by political machines and advertising agencies, because "the eternal *Thou* can by its nature not become *It;* for by its nature it cannot be established in measure and bounds, not even in the measure of the immeasurable, or the bounds of boundless being."[29] "And yet, in accordance with our nature, we are continually making the eternal *Thou* into *It,* into some thing—making God into a thing."[30]

To make God into *It,* into a thing among things, is to fail to recognize the personal structure of the living God. Buber states that

> as a Person God gives personal life, he makes us as persons become capable of meeting with him and with one another. But no limitation can come upon him as the absolute Person, either from us or from our relations with one another; in fact, we can dedicate to him not merely our persons but also our relations to one another. The man who turns to him therefore need not turn away from any other *I-Thou* relation; but he properly brings them to him, and lets them be fulfilled "in the face of God."[31]

[27] *Ibid.,* p. 75.
[28] *Ibid.,* p. 79.
[29] *Ibid.,* p. 112.
[30] *Ibid.*
[31] *Ibid.,* p. 136.

God "makes us as persons become capable of meeting with him and with one another." This basic assertion of Buber points to the fact that human life emerges out of authentic encounter. The question now arises: how is genuine meeting possible? Buber answers that

> the principle of human life is not simple but twofold, being built up in a twofold movement which is of such kind that the one movement is the presupposition of the other. I propose to call the first movement "the primal setting at a distance" and the second "entering into relation." That the first movement is the presupposition of the other is plain from the fact that one can enter into relation only with being which has been set at a distance, more precisely, has become an independent opposite. And it is only for man that an independent opposite exists.[32]

In other words, "distance provides the human situation; relation provides man's becoming in that situation."[33]

Of course, "man can set at a distance without coming into real relation with what has been set at a distance."[34] Man can refuse to accept values and points of view which differ from his own. But this would preclude his entering into any actual *I-Thou* relations, for "genuine conversation, and therefore every actual fulfillment of relation between men, means acceptance of otherness."[35] The most common opportunity of accepting otherness occurs in human speech, which Buber calls "the great characteristic of men's life with one another."[36] Acceptance of, and respect for, otherness in conversation and dialogue is the basis for human life at its best, which comes into being in genuine meetings. Opposed to the effort to enter into *I-Thou* relations through the medium of language "is the lust to make use of men by which the manipulator of 'propaganda' and 'suggestion' is possessed, in his relation to men remaining as in a relation to things, to things, moreover, with which he will never enter into relation, which he is indeed eager to rob of their distance and independence."[37]

Buber makes an important distinction between the social and the personal dimensions of human life. He points out that to belong to a group of people "means only that each individual existence is enclosed and contained in a group existence. It does not mean that between one member and another of the group there exists any kind of personal relation."[38] In

---

[32] Martin Buber, "Distance and Relation," trans. R. G. Smith, in Martin Buber, *The Knowledge of Man*, ed. and trans. M. Friedman and R. G. Smith (London: Allen & Unwin, 1965), p. 60.

[33] *Ibid.*, p. 64.

[34] *Ibid.*

[35] *Ibid.*, p. 69.

[36] *Ibid.*, p. 68.

[37] *Ibid.*, p. 69.

[38] Martin Buber, "Elements of the Interhuman"; *The Knowledge of Man*, p. 72.

fact, "in general it must be said that the leading elements in groups, especially in the later course of human history, have rather been inclined to suppress the personal relation in favour of the purely collective element."[39]

The personal element Buber describes in terms of the interpersonal or interhuman *I-Thou*. By interpersonal (*das Zwischenmenschliche*) or interhuman (*das Zwischenmenschliche*) he means "solely actual happenings between men, whether wholly mutual or tending to grow into mutual relations. For the participation of both partners is in principle indispensable. The sphere of the interhuman is one in which a person is confronted by the other. We call its unfolding the dialogical,"[40] because the most typical confrontation of *I* and *Thou* takes the form of a dialogue.

It may now be objected that Buber is here leaving the realm of the theological and philosophical and moving into psychology. He denies this, saying that

> it is basically erroneous to try to understand the interhuman phenomena as psychological. When two men converse together, the psychological is certainly an important part of the situation, as each listens and each prepares to speak. Yet this is only the hidden accompaniment to the conversation itself, the phonetic event fraught with meaning whose meaning is to be found neither in one of the two partners nor in both together, but only in their dialogue itself, in this "between" which they live together.[41]

Nothing is more destructive of interpersonal dialogue than semblance and untruth. Buber therefore emphasizes that "the essential problem of the sphere of the interhuman is the duality of being and seeming."[42] This duality has an important bearing on the meaning of truth. Buber stresses that "whatever the meaning of the word 'truth' may be in other realms, in the interhuman realm it means that men communicate themselves to one another as what they are,"[43] and not as they wish to appear before one another. In other words, "human truth is a verification by man's being true."[44] If it is the case that truth is a matter of one's true and whole being, then, as Buber says, "evil cannot be done with the whole soul; good can only be done with the whole soul."[45]

Hasidism is a popular form of Jewish communal mysticism which arose in Poland in the eighteenth century. Its founder was Rabbi Israel ben Eliezer (1700–1760), who became known as *Baal Shem Tov*. The basic

[39] *Ibid.*, p. 73.
[40] *Ibid.*, p. 75.
[41] *Ibid.*
[42] *Ibid.*
[43] *Ibid.*, p. 77.
[44] Martin Buber, *Images of Good and Evil*, trans. M. Bullock (London: Routledge & Kegan Paul, 1952), p. 56.
[45] *Ibid.*, p. 71.

emphasis of the Baal Shem Tov was on mystical communion with God through the hallowing of community and everyday life rather than through withdrawal from the world. Love of God and love of the world were thus inseparably related in the teaching of Hasidism. The Hasidic movement spread rapidly as a revolt against the cold and arid dogmatism of traditional Rabbinism, and soon included about half of Eastern European Jewry. It was often bitterly opposed by the official rabbinical interpreters of Judaism. The struggle between eighteenth-century pietism and Protestant orthodoxy provides a contemporary parallel to Hasidism.

Buber gives the following summary of Hasidism, of which he became an ardent admirer and disciple, and to the study of which he devoted some of the most productive years of his life:

> The name "hasidism" (in Hebrew hasidut, i.e., originally, "allegianc" and hence "piety") designates a mystical-religious movement which seized Eastern European Jewry about the middle of the eighteenth century and numbers many congregations to this day.
>
> In most systems of belief, the believer considers that he can achieve a perfect relationship to God by renouncing the world of the senses and overcoming his own natural being. Not so the hasid. Certainly, "cleaving" unto God is to him the highest aim of the human person, but to achieve it he is not required to abandon the external and internal reality of earthly being, but to affirm it in its true God-oriented essence and thus so to transform it that he can offer it up to God.[46]

To affirm every temporal entity as the dwelling place of the divine is a form of pansacramentalism. In this sense hasidism is an expression of religious pansacramentalism. But, as Buber points out,

> to hasidic pansacramentalism the holy in things is not, as it is to primitive pansacramentalism, a force which one takes possession of, a power which one can overpower, but it is laid in the things as sparks, and waits for its liberation and fulfilment through the human being who gives himself completely.[47]

The complete giving of the hasid to the divine spark in things is a passionate expression of the religious vision of wholeness and unity. Buber observes that

> the hasidic movement is usually taken to be a revolt of "feeling" against a religious rationalism which overintensified and rigidified the teaching of divine transcendence, and against a ritualism which made the practice of observing the commandments detached and shallow. But what acts in this

---

[46] Martin Buber, *The Way of Man According to the Teachings of Hasidism* (London: Routledge & Kegan Paul, 1950), p. 5.

[47] Martin Buber, *Hasidism* (New York: Philosophical Library, 1948), pp. 134–135.

antithesis cannot be understood by means of the conception of feeling; it is the soaring up of a true vision of unity, and of a passionate asking for wholeness.[48]

While Buber interprets hasidism in terms of pansacramentalism, he denies that it is a form of pantheism. Hasidism

> teaches the absolute transcendence of God, but as combined with his conditioned immanence. The world is an irradiation of God, but as it is endowed with an independence of existence and striving, it is apt, always and everywhere, to form a crust around itself. Thus, a divine spark lives in every thing and being, but each such spark is enclosed by an isolating shell. Only man can liberate it and re-join it with the Origin: by holding holy converse with the thing and using it in a holy manner, that is, so that his intention in doing so remains directed towards God's transcendence. Thus the divine immanence emerges from the exile of the "shells."[49]

The divine immanence is not confined to things, however. Buber insists that

> also in man, in every man, is a force divine. And in man far more than in all other beings it can pervert itself, can be misused by himself. This happens if he, instead of directing it towards its origin, allows it to run directionless and seize at everything that offers itself to it; instead of hallowing passion, he makes it evil. But here, too, a way to redemption is open: he who with the entire force of his being "turns" to God, lifts at this his point of the universe the divine immanence out of its debasement, which he has caused.[50]

Consequently, "the task of man, of every man, according to hasidic teaching, is to affirm for God's sake the world and himself and by this very means to transform both."[51] Buber maintains that "as God's cry of creation does not call to the soul, but to all things, as revelation does not take possession of and govern the soul, but all of the human being, so it is not the soul, but the whole of the world, which is to be redeemed in the redemption."[52] Of course, this is not an original insight of Hasidism. "In Chassidism I see only a movement of concentration," says Buber, "it is the concretion of all those elements which are to be found in a suspended form everywhere in Judaism at all times, also in Rabbinic Judaism."[53]
Hasidism is an example of that myth-bearing power from which

---

[48] Martin Buber, "Symbolical and Sacramental Existence in Judaism,' *Hasidism*, p. 135.
[49] Buber, *The Way of Man*, p. 6.
[50] *Ibid.*
[51] *Ibid.*
[52] Martin Buber, "The Faith of Judaism," *Mamre*, trans. Greta Hort (Melbourne: Melbourne University Press, 1946), p. 17.
[53] *Ibid.*, p. 1.

"Jewish religiousness has at all times received its inner life."[54] In the hasidic movement "mysticism and saga flowed together into a single stream."[55] According to Buber "the Hasidic legend . . . is the latest form of the Jewish myth that we know."[56] Its founder, Rabbi Israel ben Eliezer, who was called the Baal Shem Tov, or the master of God's name,

> spoke of the solitude of God and of God's presence that is exiled in the destiny of the imperfect world. He told how all creatures suffer in its separation and work toward its reunification. "It is," he said, "as if the mystery of eternity were already near and waiting to fulfill itself. But the demonic might that opposes the unification of heaven and earth has once again dispatched its messenger to hinder it. In luring darkness he moves through the world of men and seduces them through the false appearances of redemption."[57]

Buber held that the teachings of Baal Shem are important not because of their objective content, but because of "their character of pointing to a life."[58] By this Buber means that "what consitutes the uniqueness and the greatness of Hasidism is not a teaching, but a mode of life, a mode of life that shapes a community and that is consonant with community by its very nature."[59]

The life-oriented character of Hasidism becomes apparent in the legends which transmit its teaching in the community of faith. For instance,

> Rabbi Hanokh told this story:
> There was once a man who was very stupid. When he got up in the morning it was so hard for him to find his clothes that at night he almost hesitated to go to bed for thinking of the trouble he would have on waking. One evening he finally made a great effort, took paper and pencil and as he undressed noted down exactly where he put everything he had on. The next morning, very well pleased with himself, he took the slip of paper in his hand and read: "cap"—there it was, he set it on his head; "pants"—there they lay, he got into them; and so it went until he was fully dressed. "That's all very well, but now where am I myself?" he asked in great consternation. "Where in the world am I?" He looked and looked, but it was a vain search; he could not find himself. "And that is how it is with us," said the rabbi.[60]

The fact that Hasidism is essentially a mode of life rather than a teaching is also borne out by the following story.

---

[54] Martin Buber, *The Legend of the Baal-Shem*, trans. M. Friedman (New York: Harper, 1955), p. xi.
[55] *Ibid.*, p. xii.
[56] *Ibid.*, p. xiii.
[57] *Ibid.*, p. 207.
[58] Martin Buber, *The Origin and Meaning of Hasidism*, ed. and trans. M. Friedman (New York: Horizon Press, 1960), p. 25.
[59] *Ibid.*, p. 24
[60] Buber, *The Way of Man*, p. 33.

"Where is the dwelling of God?" This was the question with which the rabbi of Kotzk surprised a number of learned men who happened to be visiting him. They laughed at him: "What a thing to ask! Is not the whole world full of his glory!" Then he answered his own question: "God dwells wherever man lets him in."[61]

The emphasis on the hallowing of the joys and sorrows of daily life is apparent in the following story.

A man who was afflicted with a terrible disease complained to Rabbi Israel that his suffering interfered with his learning and praying. The rabbi put his hand on his shoulder and said: "How do you know, friend, what is more pleasing to God, your studying or your suffering?"[62]

The startling and thoughtful nature of many of the tales of the Hasidim endows them with a lasting freshness and relevance. Here are two examples. Rabbi Zalman "once . . . interrupted his prayers and said: 'I do not want your paradise. I do not want your coming world. I want You, and You only.' "[63] The point of the story is that the important things about the Kingdom of God are not the details but the central fact of the divine presence. Now the other example. "It is told that once, when the maggid [preacher] of Koznitz was praying, Adam, the first man came to him, and said: 'You have atoned for your share in my sin—now won't you atone for my share in it too?' "[64] The point of this anecdote is that pre-occupation with one's own sin is never adequate as a way to overcome guilt and guilt-feelings. "What matters is only that, starting with the fact of guilt, life be lived as a reconciling, a 'making good.' "[65] Atonement in this case is a matter of what Buber called "healing through meeting."[66]

Buber, the Zionist. The great decision which confronted Buber as he entered into the ranks of the Zionists was between Jewish nationalism which strove to create a Jewish state in Palestine (they succeeded in 1948, and triumphed again in 1967) and his own program of "Hebrew humanism." He noted that, *"sociologically* speaking, modern nationalism goes back to the French Revolution. The effects of the French Revolution were such that the old state systems which had weighed so heavily on the people of Europe were shaken and the subject nations were able to emerge under the yoke."[67] In addition to this we need to be aware that

61 Martin Buber, *Tales of the Hasidim. The Later Masters,* trans. Olga Marx (New York: Schocken Books, 1961), p. 277.

62 *Ibid.,* p. 60.

63 *Ibid.,* p. 267.

64 *Ibid.,* p. 294.

65 Martin Buber, "Healing Through Meeting," *Pointing the Way,* trans. and ed. M. Friedman (New York: Harper, 1957), p. 96.

66 *Ibid.,* p. 93.

67 Martin Buber, "Nationalism," *Israel and the World* (New York: Schocken Books, 1963), p. 215.

the *psychological* origin of modern nationalism consisted in this that in "the individual, the original feeling of allegiance to a people, alive in the depth of his soul long before modern national awareness, changed from a creative power to the challenging will-to-power of the individual as a member of the community. The group-egoism of the individual emerged in its modern form."[68]

Buber rejected the identification of Zionism with the group-egoism of modern nationalism. "Judaism," he said, "is not mere being a nation. It is being a nation, but because of its own peculiar connection with the quality of being a community of faith, it is more than that."[69] Zion is both a people and a community of religious faith. Buber maintains that "a people need not necessarily be the fusion of kindred stems; it can be the fusion of un-related stems just as well. But the concept 'people' always implies unity of fate. It presupposes that in a great creative hour throngs of human beings were shaped into a new entity by a great molding fate they experienced in common."[70] Briefly put, " a people is a phenomenon of life, a nation one of awareness, nationalism one of overemphasized awareness."[71]

Are the Jews a people or are they a nation? If they are a people, they can continue to live in dispersion all over the face of the earth. But if they are a nation, they must possess and control exclusively land, as do other nations. Buber feels that through work and suffering a people makes the transition to nationhood.

> It is decisive activity and suffering, especially in an age of migrations and land conquests, which produces a *people*. A *nation* is produced when its acquired status undergoes a decisive inner change which is accepted as such in the people's self-consciousness.[72]

Out of the self-consciousness of a people grows a national ideology like "the American way of life," or "Zionism."

> National ideology, the *spirit* of nationalism, is fruitful just so long as it does not make the nation an end in itself; just so long as it remembers its part in the building of a greater structure. The moment national ideology makes the nation an end in itself, it annuls its own right to live, it grows sterile.[73]

Buber feared that Zionism might succumb to the temptation to use the procedure of making the Jewish state an end in itself. This procedure, which is a legitimate form of nationalism perhaps for every other nation on earth, is not a legitimate procedure for Israel. He stressed that

[68] *Ibid.*, p. 216.
[69] *Ibid.*, p. 222.
[70] *Ibid.*, p. 217.
[71] *Ibid.*, 219.
[72] *Ibid.*, p. 218.
[73] *Ibid.*, p. 221.

when Jewish nationalism holds aloof from such procedure, which is alien
to it, it is legitimate, in an especially clear and lofty sense. It is the nationalism of a people without land of its own, a people which lost its country.
Now, in an hour rife with decision, it wants to offset the deficiency it
realized with merciless clarity only when its faith became rootless; it wants
to regain its natural holy life.[74]

But it cannot hope to regain its "natural holy life" by severing the
concept of the people from that of the community of faith, as does modern
nationalism. Buber emphasizes that

> Israel cannot be healed, and its welfare cannot be achieved by severing the
> concepts of people and community of faith, but only by setting up a new
> order including both as organic and renewed parts.
> A Jewish national community in Palestine, a desideratum toward which
> Jewish nationalism must logically strive, is a station in this healing process.
> We must now however forget that in the thousands of years of its exile
> Jewry yearned for the Land of Israel, not as a nation like others, but as
> Judaism (*res sui generis*), and with motives and intentions which cannot be
> derived wholly from the category "nation." That original yearning is back
> of all the disguises which modern national Judaism has borrowed from the
> modern nationalism of the West.[75]

The constant danger accompanying the modern state of Israel is that it
will fall into the error of making an idol of the Jewish people and thus
confusing legitimate with arbitrary nationalism. This confusion would
distort Israel's sense of election and rob it of its universal religious significance. The idea that the people of Israel is God's chosen people "does
not indicate a feeling of superiority but a sense of destiny. It does not
spring from a comparison with others, but from the concentrated devotion
to the task which molded the people into a nation when they attempted to
accomplish it in their earlier history."[76]

This task is obedience to the commandment of God. Buber holds that
the will of God for Israel is to demonstrate to the world that understanding,
goodwill, and peace is a feasible alternative to conflict between nations,
races, and groups of peoples. The immediate context of the fulfillment of
the commandment is the reconciliation of Jews and Arabs in Palestine.
"I belong to a group of people," Buber once said to Mahatma Gandhi,

> who from the time Britain conquered Palestine have not ceased to strive for
> the concluding of a genuine peace between Jew and Arab.
> By a genuine peace we inferred and still infer that both peoples together
> should develop the land without the one imposing its will on the other. In

[74] *Ibid.,* p. 223.
[75] *Ibid.*
[76] *Ibid.*

view of the international usages of our generation this appeared to us to be very difficult but not impossible. We were and still are well aware that in this unusual—yes, unprecedented case, it is a question of seeking new ways of understanding and cordial agreement between the nations. Here again we stood and still stand under the sway of a commandment.[77]

Buber insisted that the commandment of peace and reconciliation is binding upon Jews not only in Palestine but throughout the world:

He who makes peace, our sages taught, is God's fellow worker. But addressing conciliatory words to others and occupying oneself with humane projects is not the way to make peace. We make peace, we help bring about world peace, if we make peace wherever we are destined and summoned to do so: in the active life of our own community and in that aspect of it which can actively help determine its relationship to another community. The prophecy of peace addressed to Israel is not valid only for the days of the coming of the Messiah. It holds for the day when the people will again be summoned to take part in shaping the destiny of its earliest home; it holds for today.[78]

The prophecy of peace, Buber believes, will be realized when and if the Zionist movement adopts "national humanism," or "Hebrew humanism," as its program for a life of friendly cooperation with the Arabs. "I am setting up Hebrew humanism," Buber declared,

in opposition to that Jewish nationalism which regards Israel as a nation like unto other nations and recognizes no task for Israel save that of preserving and asserting itself. But no nation in the world has this as its only task, for just as an individual who wishes merely to preserve and assert himself leads an unjustified and meaningless existence, so a nation with no other aim deserves to pass away.

By opposing Hebrew humanism to a nationalism which is nothing but empty self-assertion, I wish to indicate that, at this juncture, the Zionist movement must decide either for national egoism or national humanism. If it decides in favor of national egoism, it too will suffer the fate which will soon befall all shallow nationalism, i.e., nationalism which does not set the nation a true supernational task. If it decides in favor of Hebrew humanism, it will be strong and effective long after shallow nationalism has lost all meaning and justification, for it will have something to say and to bring to mankind.

Israel is not a nation like other nations, no matter how much its representatives have wished it during certain eras. Israel is a people like no other, for it is the only people in the world which, from its earliest beginnings, has been both a nation and a religious community.[79]

---

[77] Martin Buber, "The Land and Its Possessors," *Israel and the World*, p. 231.
[78] Martin Buber, "And If Not Now, When?" *Israel and the World*, p. 239.
[79] Martin Buber, "Hebrew Humanism," *op. cit.*, p. 248.

The spiritual roots of the Western world, which are to a large extent of Hebrew origin, cannot sustain themselves as vital and relevant values for contemporary Western culture if Judaism becomes identified with an idolatrous and selfish nationalism. "The great values we have produced," Buber stressed, "issued from the marriage of a people and a faith. We cannot substitute a technical association of nation and religion for this original marriage, without incurring barrenness. The values of Israel cannot be reborn outside the sphere of this union and uniqueness."[80]

Highest among the values of Israel ranks the magnificent vision of the redemption of mankind. This is for Buber the core of the Messianic idea of the prophets of Israel. He maintains that "a Messianic idea without the yearning for the redemption of mankind and without the desire to take part in its realization, is no longer identical with the Messianic visions of the prophets of Israel, nor can that prophetic mission be identified with a Messianic ideal emptied of belief in the coming of the kingdom of God."[81] The historical process, Buber believes, will vindicate the prophets, for "the depths of history, which are continually at work to rejuvenate creation, are in league with the prophets."[82] He is quite partial to the universalism of the prophetic tradition of Judaism. His concept of Zionism is that of a movement which opens up before the eyes of all nations the vision of universal peace and genuine cooperation between all peoples on earth. "Today, under such manifoldly aggravated circumstances, the command of the spirit is still to prepare the way for the cooperation of the peoples."[83] To help fulfill this command is, according to Buber, the historical mission of modern Zionism.

[80] *Ibid.*, p. 252.

[81] Martin Buber, "Israel's Mission and Zion," *op. cit.*, p. 263.

[82] Martin Buber, 'Prophecy, Apocalyptic, and the Historical Hour," *Pointing the Way*, p. 207.

[83] Martin Buber, "Israel and the Command of the Spirit," *Israel and the World*, p. 257.

Chapter IX

Eastern Orthodoxy: Berdyaev

One of the most dynamic and creative voices of Eastern Orthodoxy in the twentieth century is that of the Russian Orthodox philosopher and theologian Nicolas Berdyaev. Born in 1874, the son of the privileged class of the Russian nobility, he soon became known as an advocate of liberal reforms in Czarist Russia. For this he was placed under sentence of permanent exile to Siberia by the government of the Czar. When the Communists or Bolsheviks seized power in Russia, Berdyaev was freed from his exile to Siberia. But in 1922, five years after the Communist revolution, he was exiled again. From then on Berdyaev spent all but two of the remaining years of his life in France. He died in exile in 1948. Theology, philosophy, history, and literature were his chief areas of interest. His contributions in these fields have made him one of the most outstanding interpreters of Eastern Orthodox Christianity to the Western world.

St. Athanasius of Alexandria said that God became man in order that man might become God. This line of thought has been developed in the Eastern Orthodox Church in the direction of the divinization of human nature. The goal of the Christian life is so to transfigure human life that it will be the divine life of heaven. The divine liturgy is a foretaste of this transfiguration here on earth, but its final and complete consummation is the goal of Christianity.

Berdyaev shares the basic Orthodox vision of the transfiguration of humanity into divinity. "Russia," he suggests,

> was a country of enigmatical destiny harbouring the passionate thought of a religious transfiguration of life. Our will to culture was always accompanied by the will to "life." It had two aspects which were often confused: a striving after a social transfiguration of life in civilization and after a religious transfiguration, a miracle in the destinies of human society or a people. We are facing the crisis of culture without having fully experienced the latter. Russians have always tended to be dissatisfied with culture as an intermediary stage of existence. Pushkin and the Alexandrian age constitute the peak of Russian culture. The Russian literature and thought of the later nineteenth century were no longer representative of culture, but rather of an urge to "life" and religious transfiguration. That was the case of Gogol, Tolstoy and Dostoievsky as well as of Soloviev, Leontiev and Federov; and that, too, was the character of the more recent religious-philosophical currents. Our cultural traditions had always been too weak. As a result we are creating an ugly civilization, for the barbarian element in us is always strong and our will to religious transfiguration stricken with a sort of diseased vision. But the Russian consciousness is more acutely and deeply aware of the cultural crisis and tragedy of historical destiny than that of the more fortunate peoples of the West. The Russian soul has, perhaps, also a greater capacity for asserting its will to achieve a miracle or religious transfiguration. Like all the peoples of the world today we lack culture and are destined to tread the path of civilization. But we shall never be so hide-bound by either cultural symbolism or the pragmatism of civilization as the peoples of the West. The will of the Russian people has need of purification and tempering; and our people has a great expiation in store for it. Only then will its will to transfigure life give it the right to determine its mission in the world.[1]

From Berdyaev's religious analysis of the spirit of the Russian people it is easy to see how the Communist attempt to transform society and transfigure life had a deep and pervasive appeal to Russia. However, Russians did not undertake the transfiguration of life in the exuberant optimistic spirit of the Renaissance and its humanism. Indeed, Berdyaev maintains that the Russian Revolution of 1917, in which the Bolsheviks triumphed, is an eschatological interpretation of the humanistic tradition

---

[1] Nicolas Berdyaev, *The Meaning of History* (New York: Charles Scribner's Sons, 1936), pp. 223–224.

which goes back to the period of the Renaissance and the end of the Middle Ages. He stresses that

> Russia, of course, occupies a unique position in relation to the Renaissance and its decline. For Russia, although she had never experienced the Renaissance, has been more acutely aware of the humanist crisis than any Western European country. This fact explains the peculiarity of her historical destiny. The Russians have never either experienced the exuberant joy of Renaissance creation or been inspired by an authentic enthusiasm for humanism. Russia's great literature, so far her most important contribution to the world, is not Renaissance in spirit. There was only one moment in her history when the glimmer of a Renaissance appeared possible. That was in the age of Alexander I on which Pushkin set the stamp of his creative genius. Pushkin did, indeed, represent a flash of the Renaissance spirit. But this epoch of authentic culture proved but a brief interlude which did not ultimately determine the destiny of the Russian spirit.
>
> Later nineteenth-century Russian literature did not develop on the lines laid down by Pushkin, but served rather to demonstrate the impossibility of continuing his tradition. For Russian creation is on the whole the product of sorrow and suffering; and Russia's great literature is founded upon the thirst for expiating the sins of the world and bringing about its salvation. The joy of free exuberant creation was never the hallmark of the Russian spirit. The lives of its geniuses proved this. Gogol's life and work were both profoundly sorrowful and tormented. So were the lives of Dostoievsky and Tolstoy. Their work as a whole is neither humanist nor Renaissance in spirit. Russian thought, philosophy, morality and politics all express a deep sense of anguish directly opposed to the joyous spirit of both the Renaissance and humanism.
>
> Russia at the present time is experiencing the crisis of humanism in all the spheres of her communal and cultural life. Paradoxical as it may seem, Russia was destined to react against and give expression to this crisis in its most acute form. Dostoievsky in particular lays bare the contradictions inherent in the humanist ideal whose bankruptcy he demonstrates. Tormented by the problem of human destiny, which was the unique theme of his creative work, Dostoievsky revealed the profound tragedy underlying humanism. His whole dialectic is concerned to make its exposure as complete as possible. His own tragic humanism is very different from that expounded by the great European humanists.
>
> It would, indeed, appear as if to Russian thought had been reserved the special mission of speculatively resolving the urgent European problems raised by the decline of the Renaissance and the crisis of humanism. Its constant concern with the goal of history makes this task peculiarly appropriate to it. Nor is it an accident that Russian speculation in the higher spheres of religious philosophy has always tended to be apocalyptic. This was the case of Chaadayev as well as Dostoievsky, Leontiev and Soloviev. In its metaphysical aspect therefore the Russian Revolution illustrates the

bankruptcy of humanism which it interprets apocalyptically. It thus brings us nearer to the ultimate metaphysical problems of the goal and progress of history.[2]

The meaning, goal, and progress of history was one of the central concerns of Berdyaev's theology. He approached this subject from a number of different angles: theology of culture, especially as disclosed by literature; philosophy; theology. History, according to Berdyaev, gives us the clue to the nature of man. "Man is in the highest degree an historical being. He is situated in history and history is situated in him."[3] In other words, history is both a subjective process in man and an objective process outside and around man in which he "lives, moves, and has his being."

History gives us the most concrete picture of man. Therefore the philosophy of history gives us more concrete knowledge about man than either psychology or sociology.

> The philosophy of history examines man in relation to the world-forces which act upon him, that is, in his greatest fulness and concreteness. By comparison all other ways of approaching man are abstract.
> Human destiny can be grasped only through this concrete knowledge of the philosophy of history. Other sciences do not set out to study the human destiny, which is a complex of the actions of all the world-forces. This complex of world-forces gives rise to that reality of a higher and special order which we term historical reality.[4]

Berdyaev denied that history was an objective empirical realm of data and facts which could be examined with the methods of the natural sciences, that is, without regard to the spiritual dimension of life. He insisted that

> in order to grasp the mystery of the "historical," I must have a sense of it and history as something that is deeply *mine*, that is deeply *my* history, that is deeply *my* destiny. I must situate myself within historical destiny and it within my own human destiny. The presence of the historical destiny then becomes revealed in the very depths of the human spirit. All historical epochs, from the very earliest to that at the topmost peak of modern history, represent my historical destiny; they are all mine.[5]

Berdyaev is here saying that history is a continuous process in and through which I am related to all that ever happened in the history of the world and to all future events. My history therefore cannot be bracketed off from the rest of history by giving the dates of my death and birth, thus

[2] *Ibid.*, pp. 183–185.
[3] *Ibid.*, p. 15.
[4] *Ibid.*
[5] *Ibid.*, p. 16.

making my history an objective historical datum empirically limited and defined within the span of three score and ten years or so. History, Berdyaev maintains, "is not an objective empirical datum; it is a myth."[6]

Myth for Berdyaev is the incarnation of the inner meaning of history. For him to say that history is a myth is not the expression of that cynical skepticism which was attributed to Napoleon I who reportedly said that "history is the lies men have chosen to believe about it." Rather, Berdyaev conceives the essence of history to be the divine revelation of the Spirit. Without this the modern historical sense could not have arisen out of the soil of our Judaic-Christian Western culture. "History and its conception," Berdyaev holds, "are possible only when the world process is conceived as a catastrophic one. The catastrophic interpretation of history postulates a central fact—that of the divine revelation by which the interior becomes the exterior and the Spirit incarnate."[7]

Berdyaev's view of history as process is rooted in the biblical interpretation of history as the story of the mighty acts of God by which he reveals himself to man in history. Man being essentially historical, the most effective way for the Spirit to manifest itself would be through and in history. To have discovered this is the great contribution of Judaism and Christianity. Berdyaev observes that the Jews have played an all-important role in history. They are preeminently an historical people and their destiny reflects the indestructibility of the divine decrees.[8] Christianity supplies the process of history with a central point of reference from which all history is measured and interpreted: the coming of Christ in the incarnation. Berdyaev notes that "the exclusively historical character and dynamism of Christianity are the result of the Coming of Christ, which constitutes the central fact of Christian history. This fact is unique and non-recurring—the essential quality of everything historical. And it focusses the whole of world history.[9]

Berdyaev distinguished between Hebrew and Greek elements in Christianity. The Judaic dimension of the church and Christianity is dynamic, the Greek dimension is static and contemplative. He argued that

it may be said that, on the whole, the Church is essentially and pre-eminently an historical force. It introduces revelation into the historical organization of mankind and guides the religious destinies of the national masses. It is thus an historical guiding force traditionally bound up with those Judaic principles which constitute the pre-eminently historical elements of Christianity. The Hellenistic elements are also a rich source of Christianity, but

6 *Ibid.*, p. 21.
7 *Ibid.*, p. 34.
8 *Ibid.*, p. 86.
9 *Ibid.*, p. 108.

are less dynamic. They are mainly related to the contemplative side of Christianity,[10]

illustrated best by the great contemplative mystics of the church.

The secret of the Judaic dynamism of history is the discovery of freedom as the soul of the divine *logos* or reason. This secret of freedom was taken up by Christianity and transformed into a doctrine of divine providence which exploded the fatalism of the ancient world. Berdyaev emphasizes that

> the exceptionally dynamic and historical character of Christianity is the result of the fact that it conclusively revealed for the first time the existence of the principle of freedom, which was ignored by both the ancient and the Hebrew worlds. Christian freedom postulates the fulfilment of history through the agency of a free subject and spirit. And such a fulfilment constitutes the essential nature of both Christianity and history, because the structure of the latter is impossible without the postulate of a freely-acting subject determining the historical destinies of mankind.[11]

Creativity and freedom are the forces which turn the wheels of history. Berdyaev says that

> Christianity affirmed that freedom is the highest achievement of the higher divine reason and that it determines the destiny of both man and the world, and thus makes history. Christian Providence is synonymous with freedom and not fatality. Unlike the ancient world, Christianity is not content to submit to fate. Such submissiveness as the highest wisdom attainable to man had been expressed in both Greek tragedy and philosophy. But the Christian spirit is based upon a principle that rebels against such submission. The freedom to choose and affirm the good, rooted in the will and not in reason, presupposes in its turn that freedom of the creative and active subject without which a true dynamism of history is impossible.[12]

However, man uses the freedom of the creative and active subject not only for good but also for evil, thus betraying his higher spiritual calling. Consequently man's freedom in history leads him into ever new forms of bondage. The human race is unable to achieve its divine calling in history. History is the failure of man to reach the spiritual goal of the world process. Berdyaev remarks that his "interpretation of history as a profound failure [does not] imply that it is devoid of significance, for I consider its failure to be sacred. It helps to demonstrate that the higher calling of both man and mankind is super-historical, and that only this realization can

[10] *Ibid.,* p. 109.
[11] *Ibid.,* p. 110.
[12] *Ibid.,* p. 111.

resolve the fundamental antithesis of history."[13] In history man lives in creativity, freedom, suffering, and failure.

Redemption is for Berdyaev not the flight from the failure of history into a supra-historical realm where the pious rest as contented slaves of the divine monarch. He holds that "redemption is the meeting with the suffering and sacrificial God, with a God, i.e., who shares the bitter destiny of the world and of man. Man is a free being and there is in him an element of primeval, uncreated, pre-cosmic freedom. But he is powerless to master his own irrational freedom and its abysmal darkness."[14]

Freedom is another one of the dominant themes of Berdyaev's theology. He sees the root of freedom in non-being. "Creativeness," he argues,

> presupposes non-being, *mē on* (and not *ouk on*), which is the source of the primeval, pre-cosmic, pre-existent freedom in man. The mystery of creativeness is the mystery of freedom. Creativeness can only spring from fathomless freedom, for such freedom alone can give rise to the new, to what had never existed before. Out of being, out of something that exists, it is impossible to create that which is completely new; there can only be emanation, generation, redistribution. But creativeness means breaking through from non-being, from freedom, to the world of being.[15]

By the "world of being" Berdyaev means the cosmos, the God-given, creative, free order of the universe. The given world, the world immediately accessible to empirical observation, is governed by necessity, it is the phantom-world of the multiverse which binds man with the chains of necessity and blinds him with sin and thus keeps him in the prison cave of the given world. Berdyaev emphatically maintained that

> the human spirit is in prison. Prison is what I call this world, the given world of necessity. "This world" is not the cosmos; it is a non-cosmic condition of divisions and enmity, the atomization and falling apart of the living monads of the cosmic hierarchy. And the true way is that of spiritual liberation from "the world," the liberation of man's spirit from its bondage to necessity. The true way is not a movement to right or left in the plane of "the world," but rather movement upward and downward on lines of the ultra-worldly, movement in spirit and not in "the world." Freedom from the reactions of "the world" and from opportunistic adaptations to it is the great achievement of the spirit. This is a way of great spiritual contemplation, spiritual collectedness and concentration. The cosmos is true being, but the "given world" is a phantom and so is the necessity of the given world. This phantom "world" is born of our sin.[16]

[13] *Ibid.,* p. 183.
[14] Nicolas Berdyaev, *The Destiny of Man* (New York: Scribner's, 1937), p. 133.
[15] *Ibid.,* p. 163.
[16] Nicolas Berdyaev, *The Meaning of the Creative Act,* trans. Donald E. Lowrie (New York: Collier, 1962), p. 11.

How can we overcome the given world in order to penetrate to the world of being itself? In his early book on *The Meaning of the Creative Act* Berdyaev points to the way of philosophy, knowledge, and truth as the way of freedom from the bondage of necessity which governs the given world. "The philosophy of the future," he predicts,

> will recognize the creative overcoming and transfiguring nature of knowledge, for in knowledge it will see the dawn and the flowering of being itself. Philosophy will recognize its spiritually revolutionary nature, will recognize that it is in conscious rebellion against the captivity of necessity and against the slavery which conceals the secret and the meaning of being. In the creative, knowing act of philosophy there is an upsurge towards another being, another world, daring to approach the ultimate mystery.[17]

The approach to "the ultimate mystery" of the Spirit discloses the interrelationship of freedom and truth. "Truth is comprehension and liberation of being; it presupposes the creative act of the knower within being; truth is meaning and may not deny meaning. To deny meaning in the world means to deny truth, to recognize nothing but darkness. Truth makes us free. To deny freedom is to deny truth."[18] Berdyaev's defense of freedom is a reaction against the deterministic philosophies of Marx, Freud, and others who dominated thought at the beginning of the twentieth century. He is passionately convinced that "there cannot be truth in the idea that the world is merely a meaningless necessity, for the exclusive power of necessity is the power of darkness in which there is neither truth nor any way to liberation."[19]

In order to free himself from the necessity of economic and social determinism the Christian is called to free himself from bondage to this world and be ready to sacrifice security and economic advantage. Berdyaev states that

> the Christian consciousness and world outlook require an ascetic attitude toward the good things of this world, the renunciation of bourgeois values. The Christian attitude toward society is one of readiness to sacrifice: it turns away from the kingdom of this world, while every state, every law, all economics are matters of the good order of this world, and presuppose the acceptance of bourgeois values in life.[20]

Even the communists will not be able to free themselves from bourgeois values, Berdyaev predicted; only the Christian readiness to sacrifice as we see it in the lives of men like St. Francis can free man from the weight of the cares of "this world." Therefore Berdyaev declared that

17 *Ibid.*, p. 42.
18 *Ibid.*, p. 43 (italics omitted).
19 *Ibid.*
20 *Ibid.*, p. 262.

a truly radical universal revolution in society will only be realized when the Christian world matures to the point of collective readiness to sacrifice, the point of renunciation of the ancient social theories of this world which still guarantee and protect the goods of the bourgeois world. Not only Christian personality but Christian society as well has to pass through the sacrificial truth of St. Francis. This sacrifice is liberation from the disproportionate heaviness of this world, from the power of natural necessity; for, up to now, all social orders, from the most conservative to the most revolutionary, have been obedient to the weight of natural necessity, have never been an outbreaking into another world.

Regarding the kingdom not of this earth, the creative society is subterranean, of the catacombs. It is not a kingdom of this world; it overcomes the world, sacrifices its goods for the sake of another, freer life.[21]

There is no genuine freedom, according to Berdyaev, without the radical preparedness to sacrifice "security and guaranteed well-being."[22]

Thus far it has been seen how Berdyaev's ideas of history and freedom illumine the basic Eastern Orthodox principle that salvation means the transfiguring of life and the making divine of humanity. It now remains to be shown in what ways this principle also animates his conceptions of creativity, spirit, and man.

Creativity, according to Berdyaev, "is only possible, because the world is created, because there is a Creator. Man, made by God in His own image and likeness, is also a creator and is called to creative work."[23] "Creativeness," he notes,

is a complex fact. It presupposes, first, man's primary, meonic, uncreated freedom; secondly, the gifts bestowed upon man the creator by God the Creator, and, thirdly, the world as the field of his activity. Thus three elements are involved in human creativeness: the element of freedom, owing to which alone creation of new and hitherto non-existent realities is possible, gifts and vocations connected with them, and the already created world from which man can borrow his materials.[24]

But creativity must not limit its vision to the present; it must look forward to, and work toward the end of "this world" and the coming of the kingdom of God.

Christ's second coming presupposes intense creative activity on our part, preparing both mankind and the world for the end. The end itself depends upon man's creative activity and is determined by the positive results of the cosmic process. We must not passively wait for the Kingdom of Christ,

21 *Ibid.*, p. 263.
22 *Ibid.*, p. 264.
23 Berdyaev, *The Destiny of Man* (New York: Scribner's, 1937), p. 163.
24 *Ibid.*

any more than for that of antichrist, but must actively and creatively struggle against the latter and prepare for the Kingdom of God which is taken by force.[25]

The possibility of a creative struggle for the kingdom of Christ is given with freedom. Freedom allows the genuinely new to emerge in history. It discloses the universe as a dynamic process striving toward completion.

> To be aware of the fact that man does not exist within a finished and stabilized system of being is fundamental to the philosophy of creativeness, and it is only on that understanding that the creative act of man is possible and intelligible. Another fundamental position consists in the realization that the creative act of man is not simply a regrouping and redistribution of the matter of the world. Nor is it merely an emanation, an outflowing of the primary matter of the world. Nor again is it just a shaping of the material in the sense of imposing ideal forms upon it. In the creative act of man, a new element is introduced, something which was not there before, which is not contained in the given world, and is not part of its make-up, but which breaks through from another scheme of the world, not out of the eternally given ideal forms, but out of freedom; and not out of dark freedom, but out of an illuminated freedom.[26]

Freedom allows room for the creative advance into novelty.

Creativity in the full sense of the word is the shaping of something out of nothing. For Berdyaev, freedom, nothing, and spirit are related terms in this context. He states that

> creativeness in art, like every other form of creative activity, consists in triumph over given, determined, concrete life, it is a victory over the world. Objectification knows a humdrum day-to-day concreteness of its own, but creative power finds its way out from this imposed concreteness, into concreteness of another kind. Creative activity does not consist merely in the bestowal of a more perfect form upon this world; it is also liberation from the burden and bondage of this world. Creativeness cannot be merely creation out of nothing, it presupposes the material which the world supplies. But the element "out of nothing" does enter into creative activity. For it is creativeness out of the freedom of the other world. This means that what is most important, most mysterious and most creatively new, comes not from "the world," but from spirit.[27]

Creativity which comes from the Spirit signifies the end of security and obedience to the laws of economic and social stabilization. Berdyaev points out the revolutionary implications for society of the creative drive toward new forms of social order and justice. He recognizes that "the move from

[25] Ibid., p. 335.
[26] Nicolas Berdyaev, The Beginning and the End (London: G. Bles, 1592), p. 171.
[27] Ibid., p. 173.

obedience over to creativeness in the social order is possible here as everywhere, only by sacrificing security and guaranteed well-being."[28] Whether it is the Russian Revolution of 1917, or the current civil rights revolution in America, we are faced in either case with the need of, and demand for creativity in the social order. According to Berdyaev this demand cannot be met without civil disobedience and the willingness to sacrifice the security of the established order.

The ultimate driving power in the creative advance of social change and justice comes, as Berdyaev says, "not from 'the world,' but from Spirit." Spirit is the creative and redemptive presence of the divine in the world. In accordance with the basic Orthodox vision of the divinization of human nature Berdyaev affirms that "Spirit is a constant transcending of human life."[29] Furthermore, "Spirit is *being-in-itself* or being not determined from without."[30] Berdyaev is here protesting again against the determinism of much of modern economic, social, and psychological theory. The dimension of spirit signifies the inward power of creativity in contrast to the external coercion of determinism. "Everything spiritual emanates from within," he declares, "from the inner depths. But this inwardness comes to be exteriorized."[31]

The danger against which spirit must be on a constant watch is that its incarnation and exteriorization will trap spirit in the forms of culture and thus rob it of its freedom. Berdyaev holds that "spirit is incarnated both really and existentially in the human personality, in its creatively intuitive attitude to life, in a fraternal communion with other men. In objectifying itself in culture and in social life spirit easily foregoes its freedom."[32] It ceases to be creative in its expressions and merely repeats the forms of the established order. Thus it betrays its very nature as spirit, for, according to Berdyaev, "spirit is creative activity: every creative act is a spiritual act. But the creative act of the subjective spirit is an exteriorization of self in the world. In every creative act there is an element of the primordial freedom inherent in the subjective spirit, an element free from external determination."[33]

Berdyaev is careful to emphasize that "there is a difference between Spirit and the Holy Spirit, but they are one and the same reality in different degrees."[34] The activity of the Spirit is disclosed in every act of creativity and freedom. But

---

[28] Berdyaev, *The Meaning of the Creative Act*, pp. 263–264.
[29] Nicolas Berdyaev, *Spirit and Reality* (New York: Scribner's, 1939), p. 48.
[30] *Ibid.*
[31] *Ibid.*, p. 49.
[32] *Ibid.*, p. 59.
[33] *Ibid.*, p. 58.
[34] Nicolas Berdyaev, *Truth and Revelation* (London: G. Bles, 1953), p. 141.

the Holy Spirit, in the age of the Spirit, the Father and the Son must be revealed in another way since that will mean the revelation of the Holy Trinity, which has not really happened yet. The light will be thrown backwards. According to the divine plan and according to the divine idea man is a spiritual being. The spirituality in him must be disclosed, the spirituality which may hitherto have been in an unawakened and merely potential state. The realization of personality is the realization of the spiritual nature of man and this realization means a divine-human process within him. But the awakening of the spiritual nature takes place in secret ways.[35]

The secret of the ways of the spirit is that it both has revealed itself in every age since the dawn of creation and at the same time the manifestation of the ways of the spirit belongs to the future age of the Spirit. Therefore, "the era of the Spirit or the third revelation must not be taken in an entirely chronological sense. There have always been people of the Spirit, there have always been those who prepare the way for the era of the Spirit, there have always been men of prophetic spirit."[36]

The prophetic spirit testifies to the reality of the coming divine mystery of the transfiguration of human life, and all life, by the Spirit. It is a living witness to the need of men to put an end to the old world and its ways and to begin living in the new world of the spirit, of freedom, and of creativity. In typically Eastern Orthodox fashion Berdyaev states that

the primary mystery is the mystery of the birth of God in man (who includes the world in himself) and the birth of man in God. In our imperfect language this means that there is in God a need for a responsive creative act on the part of man. Man is not merely a sinner; the consciousness of sin is but an experience which moves him as he treads his path; man is also a creator. The human tragedy from which there is no escape, the dialectic of freedom, necessity and grace finds its solution within the orbit of the divine Mystery, within the Deity, which lies deeper than the drama between Creator and creature, deeper than representations of heaven and hell.

Here the human tongue keeps silence. The eschatological outlook is not limited to the prospect of an indefinable end of the world, it embraces in its view every moment of life. At each moment of one's living, what is needed is to put an end to the old world and to begin the new. In that is the breath of the Spirit. The aeon of the end is the revealing of the Spirit.[37]

There are theologians today who argue that we have entered the post-Christian era. Buber grants that "in a certain sense it may be said that Christianity, historical Christianity, is coming to an end, and that a rebirth is to be looked for only from a religion of the Holy Spirit which will bring

---

[35] *Ibid.*, p. 142.
[36] *Ibid.*, p. 145.
[37] Berdyaev, *The Beginning and the End*, p. 254.

Christianity itself to birth again, since it is the fulfillment of Christianity."[38] We are today, he observes, "passing through a stage of God-forsakenness."[39] This God-forsakenness takes many different forms; there are today even professional theologians who maintain that "God is dead," and who confidently proclaim "the gospel of Christian atheism." But, according to Berdyaev, "the most terrible forms of godlessness are certainly not those which are displayed in the militant and passionate struggle against the idea of God and against God himself, but those which are shown in the godlessness of practical life, in indifference and coldness."[40] They are the most devastating and destructive forms of godlessness because they deny the reality of the process of divine revelation without which there is no knowledge of God and no Christianity. "Revelation," Berdyaev holds, "is the fact of the Spirit in me, in the subject; it is spiritual experience, spiritual life."[41] To smother this life with coldness and indifference is to smother the Spirit and the life of the Christian religion. If this is done, then the hope of transfiguring human life is extinguished.

The concern for man and the transformation of humanity is one of the great themes of Berdyaev's thought. Since in the mystery of the incarnation God became man in order that man might become God, Berdyaev sees in God the most adequate expression of humanity. Against the Aristotelian God, the unmoved Mover, and against the traditional substance-concept of God according to which he is an unchanging substance which needs nothing but himself in order to exist, Berdyaev argues that "the revelation of a suffering and yearning God is higher than the revelation of a God whose sufficiency and satisfaction are in himself. Thus the loftiest humanity of God is revealed; humanity becomes his unique attribute. God is mystery and freedom. God is love and humanity."[42] His thoughts here are close to those of Archbishop Söderblom who stressed the suffering of God on behalf of, and together with, mankind. This emphasis on "the humanity of God" leads Berdyaev to say that "God is human whereas man is unhuman."[43]

With this strong emphasis on the relatedness of God and man goes the stress on the relatedness of truth. Truth is not an abstract and self-existent reality which the individual seeks and perchance finds. Truth, according to Berdyaev, "is communal, that is, it postulates a sense of community and brotherhood among men."[44] Moreover, "truth is human, and can be born

[38] Nicolas Berdyaev, *The Divine and the Human* (London: G. Bles, 1949), p. 1.
[39] *Ibid.*
[40] Berdyaev, *Truth and Revelation*, p. 92.
[41] Berdyaev, *The Divine and the Human*, p. 14.
[42] Berdyaev, *Truth and Revelation*, p. 53.
[43] *Ibid.*, p. 57.
[44] *Ibid.*, p. 25.

only of human effort, of the endeavor of every human being."[45] "But truth is also divine, it belongs to God-manhood."[46] that is, truth is a matter of incarnation, a matter of being true.

Not to be true, that is, not living in and according to the truth, is to be on the way to death and hell. But the righteous are also on their way to death. Berdyaev maintains that

> death is the most profound and significant fact of life, raising the least of mortals above the mean commonplaces of life. The fact of death alone gives true depth to the question as to the meaning of life. Life in this world has meaning just because there is death; if there were no death in our world, life would be meaningless. The meaning is bound up with the end. If there would be no end, i.e. if life in our world continued for ever, there would be no meaning in it. Meaning lies beyond the confines of this limited world, and the discovery of meaning presupposes an end here. It is remarkable that although men rightly feel the horror of death and rightly regard it as the supreme evil, they are bound to connect with it the final discovery of meaning. Death—the supreme horror and evil—proves to be the only way out of the "bad time" into eternity; immortality and eternity prove to be attainable only through death. Man's last hope is connected with death, which manifests so clearly the power of evil in the world. This is the greatest paradox of death. According to the Christian religion death is the result of sin and is the last enemy, the supreme evil which must be conquered. And at the same time in our sinful world death is a blessing and a value. It inspires us with terror not merely because it is an evil, but because the depth and the greatness of it shatter our everyday world and exceed the powers accumulated by us in this life to meet this world's requirements. Spiritual enlightenment and an extraordinary intensity of spiritual life are needed to give us a right attitude towards death.[47]

The reason why death is evil is that it tries to depress being to the level of non-being. And although death does have a positive significance,

> at the same time it is the most terrible and the only evil. Every kind of evil in the last resort means death. Murder, hatred, malice, depravity, envy, vengeance are death and the seeds of death. Death is at the bottom of every evil passion. Pride, greed, ambition are deadly in their results. There is no other evil in the world except death and killing. Death is the evil result of sin. A sinless life would be immortal and eternal. Death is the denial of eternity and therein lies its ontological evil, its hostility to existence, its striving to reduce creation to non-being.[48]

[45] *Ibid.*, p. 28.
[46] *Ibid.*
[47] Berdyaev, *The Destiny of Man*, pp. 317–318.
[48] *Ibid.*, pp. 320–321.

Death is a mystery, perhaps the ultimate mystery of life. It is paradoxical, both good and evil. Berdyaev points out that "death proves to be the greatest paradox in the world, which cannot be understood rationally. Death is folly that has become commonplace."[49] But

> if death is accepted as a part of the mystery of life, it is not final and has not the last word. Rebellion against death in our world is rebellion against God. But at the same time we must wage a heroic struggle against death, conquer it as the last evil and pluck out its sting. The work of Christ in the world is in the first instance victory over death and preparation for resurrection and eternity.[50]

Christ's victory is not only over death but also over hell. "Hell," for Berdyaev,

> is not eternity at all but endless duration in time. The torments of hell are temporal, for they are in the "bad infinity" of time; they do not mean abiding in an eternity different from the eternity of the Kingdom of God. In hell are those who remain in time and do not pass into eternity, those who remain in the subjective closed-in sphere and do not enter the objective realm of the Kingdom of God. In itself hell is illusory, phantasmagorical and unreal, but it may be the great psychological subjective reality for the individual. Hell is a phantasm, a nightmare which cannot be eternal but may be experienced by man as endless. Phantasms created by human passions plunge the self into hell. Passions weave the illusory web of dreams and nightmares from which man cannot wake in eternity, but which for that very reason cannot be eternal. There is nothing objectively real in those nightmares. It is not God's objective justice that dooms man to the experience of them, but man's irrational freedom which draws him to preexistential non-being. After the experience of the living in God's world, that non-being proves to be of the nature of hell.[51]

Berdyaev's picture of hell gives us the impression that he is speaking about something which actually exists in the experience of contemporary man. "Hell," he insists,

> is immanent and subjective through and through, there is nothing transcendental and ontological about it. It is the state of being utterly closed in, of having no hope of breaking through to anything transcendent and of escaping from oneself. Hell is the experience of hopelessness, and such an experience is entirely subjective. The rise of hope is the way out.[52]

In Berdyaev's view the rise of hope testifies to the awakening superconsciousness of man. He maintains that "the existence of hell as a sub-

49 *Ibid.*, p. 321.
50 *Ibid.*
51 *Ibid.*, p. 342.
52 *Ibid.*, p. 354.

jective realm depends upon the correlation between subconsciousness, consciousness, and superconsciousness, i.e., the spiritual life."[53] Hell and the alienation of the human from the divine is overcome in the realm of superconscious, spiritual life. "The Holy Spirit," Berdyaev points out, "is the principle of union between God and the creature, and it is in Him that the mystery of creation, a mystery which is anthropological and cosmological, must be revealed."[54] The revelation of the spiritual principle will make clear that "the separation and opposition of the divine and the human will be overcome in the Spirit, although the distinction between them will be preserved.[55]

For Berdyaev the overcoming of the separation of the divine and the human takes place in the community of the Spirit. In this spiritual communion the creative mystery of divine humanity will be disclosed. "The creation of a new communion or communality presupposes," according to Berdyaev,

> an anthropological revelation, a revelation of divine humanity, a Christology of humanity. The creative mystery of the social order, the mystery of communion both human and cosmic, could not be unveiled before the creative mystery of man and of humanity had been revealed. And we have seen that in Christianity the anthropological revelation has not yet taken place. The final anthropological secret will be revealed, not in obedience but in creativeness. In creativeness rather than in obedience will be revealed the mystery of society, the mystery of a new communion in love, communion in the Spirit, communion not only human but cosmic as well.[56]

The magnificent vision of a human and cosmic communion in Spirit and love is the capstone of Berdyaev's prophetic interpretation of the spirit of Eastern Orthodoxy in general, and of Russian Orthodoxy in particular.

[53] *Ibid.,* p. 343.
[54] Berdyaev, *The Divine and the Human,* p. 184.
[55] *Ibid.,* p. 183.
[56] Berdyaev, *The Meaning of the Creative Act,* pp. 264–265.

CHAPTER X

EXISTENTIALIST THEOLOGY: TILLICH AND BULTMANN

What is existentialism? Generally speaking existentialism is a theological, literary, and philosophical movement emphasizing human existence beset by anxiety, guilt, boredom, loneliness, inauthenticity, and longing for freedom, authentic existence, and the reunion of estranged and alienated mankind with itself and with its God.

The father of modern existentialism is the Danish Lutheran theologian Søren Kierkegaard (1813–1855). Reacting against Hegel's philosophy, he emphasized the personal commitment of the individual in opposition to the spectator attitude of modern science and speculative philosophy. Where Hegel outlined a magnificent vision of the unfolding of the universal process of the Idea (*Geist*), Kierkegaard spoke of radical inwardness, despair, anxiety, loneliness, and guilt as well as the almost absolute difference between the divine Spirit and the human existence. He argued that anxiety, loneliness, and guilt are more basic and powerful factors of human existence than the speculative contemplation of a vast, impersonal process in which the absolute Idea realizes itself.

Next to Kierkegaard, the most significant nineteenth-century existentialist was the Russian Orthodox writer Fyodor Dostoievsky (1821–1881). His famous novels *Crime and Punishment* and *The Brothers Karamazov,* present genuine Christianity as the transfiguring of human life which in this world is characterized by violence, cruelty, distortion, absurdity, meaninglessness, loneliness, madness, and idolatry. He was a vigorous opponent of the materialistic athesism and nihilism of modern European civilization.

In the twentieth century existentialism became the dominant philosophy on the European continent. It developed along both theistic and atheistic or nontheistic lines. The theologians Karl Barth, Paul Tillich, and Rudolf Bultmann as well as the philosophers Karl Jaspers and Gabriel Marcel are examples of the former. The philosophers Martin Heidegger and Jean-Paul Sartre are examples of nontheistic existentialists.

Both Paul Tillich and Rudolf Bultmann, the two theologians who will be considered in this presentation of contemporary existentialist theological thought, were profoundly influenced by the philosophy of Martin Heidegger's monumental fragment entitled *Being and Time (Sein und Zeit),* judged by many historians of modern philosophy to be the most profound and influential philosophical writing of the twentieth century. Heidegger makes human existence, or *Dasein* as he calls it, the focus of his inquiry. He then proceeds to analyze human existence in typically existentialist fashion in terms of "care," "being-toward-death," "resoluteness," and "authenticity." His basic philosophical concern is to go behind the speculative world of idealistic metaphysics to what is most basic in reality: Being. "The question of the meaning of Being must be *formulated,"* he declares. "If it is a fundamental question, or indeed *the* fundamental question, it must be made transparent, and in an appropriate way."[1] The clarification of the meaning of being is the main theme of Heideggerian philosophy.

The theme of being has been picked up and developed theologically by *Paul Tillich.* In a sense, Tillich's great work, the *Systematic Theology,* is a theological commentary on Heidegger and the history of Christian thought. God, according to Tillich, is Being, or the Ground of Being, or the Power of Being. Man is a mixture of being and non-being, and this gives rise to anxiety over his finitude, and hence leads to alienation from the Ground of man's being. "The being of God is being-itself."[2] For man and the world this means that God "is the power of being in everything and

---

[1] Martin Heidegger, *Being and Time,* trans. J. Macquarrie and E. Robinson (New York: Harper & Row, 1962), p. 24.
[2] Paul Tillich, *Systematic Theology* (Chicago: University of Chicago Press, 1951), I, p. 235.

above everything, the infinite power of being."³ Jesus the Christ is "the New Being," and the criterion for the use of the sources of systematic theology is "the New Being in Jesus as the Christ as our ultimate concern."⁴ Wherever we turn in theology, the ultimate question is that of being and non-being.

In order to understand the systematic thought of Tillich it is helpful to know a few of the important facts about his life. Tillich was born at Starzeddel in the province of Brandenburg, Germany, on August 20, 1886, the son of a Lutheran pastor. In 1911, at the age of 25 years, he received his Ph.D. degree from the University of Breslau in Silesia. The following year he received the licentiate in theology from the University of Halle in Saxony.

Paul Johannes Tillich served as German army chaplain during the entire First World War, from 1914 to 1918. After World War I he taught at the universities of Berlin, Marburg, Dresden, and Leipzig. From 1929 to 1933 he taught at the University of Frankfurt. His opposition to the Nazi regime forced him to leave that post in 1933. He went to Union Theological Seminary in New York where he was professor of philosophical theology from 1933 to 1955.

During World War II he served on the Committee for a Democratic Germany and was chairman of the Committee on Self-Help for Refugees. From 1955 to 1962 Tillich was university professor at Harvard University, and from 1962 to 1965 he served as Nuveen Professor at the Divinity School of the University of Chicago. He died at Chicago on October 22, 1965.

Tillich wrote his Ph.D. thesis on the German philosopher Schelling. Schelling, Böhme, and Heidegger were the most important philosophical influences on Tillich's thought. The characteristic involvement in the social and political and cultural affairs of his society came out already while Tillich was still in Germany. During the so-called Weimar Republic, which ruled Germany from the end of World War I to the rise of Hitler in 1933, Tillich was an active and leading member of the Religious Socialists' movement of German intellectuals.

Tillich belongs, from the point of view of the history of Christian thought, in the camp of the synthesizers of faith and philosophy. He continues the great tradition which leads from Origen and St. Augustine to St. Thomas Aquinas and Friedrich Schleiermacher, the father of modern theology.

The three most famous contributions of Tillich to contemporary reli-

³ *Ibid.*, p. 236.
⁴ *Ibid.*, p. 50.

gious thought are: (1) the "Protestant principle," (2) the method of "correlation," and (3) the theology of "Being."

The Protestant principle, according to Tillich, maintains that nothing is sacred but God alone. It tends to relativize all other claims to divine dignity and to expose them as more or less subtle manifestations of idolatrous human pride. Tillich insists with Luther and other leaders of the Reformation that

> the central principle of Protestantism is the doctrine of justification by grace alone, which means that no individual and no human group can claim a divine dignity for its moral achievements, for its sacramental power, for its sanctity; or for its doctrine. If, consciously or unconsciously, they make such a claim, Protestantism requires that they be challenged by the prophetic protest, which gives God alone absoluteness and sanctity and denies every claim of human pride. This protest against itself on the basis of an experience of God's majesty constitutes the Protestant principle.[5]

For Tillich the Protestant principle is binding on all Protestants. It is their historic contribution to the spiritual and temporal well-being of the whole church on earth.

> This principle holds for Lutheranism as well as for Calvinism and even for modern Protestant denominationalism. It is the principle which made the accidental name "Protestant" an essential and symbolic name. It implies that there cannot be a sacred system, ecclesiastical or political; that there cannot be a sacred hierarchy with absolute authority; and that there cannot be a truth in human minds which is divine truth in itself. Consequently the prophetic spirit must always criticize, attack, and condemn sacred authorities, doctrines, and morals. And every genuine Protestant is called upon to bear personal responsibility for this. Each Protestant, each layman, each minister (the minister in Protestantism is a qualified layman and nothing else), has to decide for himself whether a doctrine is true or not, whether a prophet is a true or a false prophet, whether a power is demonic or divine. Even the Bible cannot liberate him from this responsibility, for the Bible is subject to interpretation: there is no doctrine, no prophet, no priest, no power, which has not claimed biblical sanction for itself. For the Protestant, individual decision is inescapable.[6]

Tillich holds that "the Protestant principle is in contradiction to the newly emerging principles of social organization."[7] There is in the contemporary world, he notes, a strong trend toward centralization of power and standardization of opinion. Mass media of news and advertising are

---

[5] Paul Tillich, "The End of the Protestant Era?" *The Protestant Era,* trans. James Luther Adams (Chicago: University of Chicago Press, 1948), p. 226.
[6] *Ibid.*
[7] *Ibid.,* p. 222.

favorable toward the claims to absolute power and almost divine efficacy
which modern communism, socialism, and nationalism claim for themselves. Individual decision and responsibility are reduced to a minimum
by modern advertising. The prophetic protest of Protestantism against
sacred wars to maintain certain ideals, against governments and hierarchies
claiming absolute authority, against absolute moral principles and doctrines
runs counter to the modern trend toward uniformity and conformity.
Tillich predicted that "the traditional form of the Protestant attitude cannot outlast the period of mass disintegration and mass collectivism—that
the end of 'the Protestant era' is a possibility."[8]

From the Protestant principle, which describes the basic theological
stance of Tillich, we now move to the "method of correlation." The basic
idea underlying this method is that a man cannot and will not receive
answers to questions he has never really asked. In Tillich's words, "the
method of correlation explains the contents of the Christian faith through
existential questions and theological answers in mutual interdependence."[9]
No matter what religious question we wish to consider, we must always
begin with the questions implied in man's existential situation. It is this
existential starting point which places Tillich squarely into the existentialist
camp. All the ways of theology lead to an analysis of human existence.

Given this existential starting of the way in which theology is carried
on, it might seem as though God were dependent on human receptivity.
And this is precisely what Tillich maintains; God and man are interdependent and interrelated. This means that "although God in his abysmal
nature is in no way dependent on man, God in his self-manifestation to
man is dependent on the way man receives his manifestation."[10]

The method of correlation is amazingly simple and has universal scope:
there is no conceivable religious or theological issue to which it cannot be
applied. In every religion on earth, "symbolically speaking, God answers
man's questions, and under the impact of God's answers man asks them."[11]
There is a dynamic interchange between man's existential questions, God's
theological answers, and the synthesis of the two which in turn gives rise
to a new triadic process of existential question, theological answer, and a
further synthesis. We may suspect that Tillich's theological method is a
variation of the Hegelian dialectical method of thesis, antithesis, and synthesis.

"In using the method of correlation," Tillich explains, "systematic theology proceeds in the following way: it makes an analysis of the human

8 *Ibid.*
9 Tillich, *Systematic Theology,* I, p. 60.
10 *Ibid.,* p. 61.
11 *Ibid.,* p. 62.

situation out of which the existential questions arise, and it demonstrates that the symbols used in the Christian message are the answers to these questions."[12] The human situation is characterized by self-estrangement and by alienation from God. Therefore, "in so far as man's existence has the character of self-contradiction or estrangement, a double consideration is demanded, one side dealing with man as he essentially is (and ought to be) and the other dealing with what he is in his self-estranged existence (and should not be)."[13]

The method of correlation dictates that the five parts of Tillich's theological system exhibit the question-and-answer pattern. The five parts are: (1) Reason and Revelation, (2) Being and God, (3) Existence and the Christ, (4) Life and the Spirit, and (5) History and the Kingdom of God. Within these five parts Tillich encloses the entire range of Christian thought. He does so by means of a method which "requires that every part of the system should include one section in which the question is developed by an analysis of human existence and existence generally, and one section in which the theological answer is given on the basis of the sources, the medium, and the norm of systematic theology."[14]

The sources of systematic theology, according to Tillich are (1) the Bible, (2) the history of Christian thought, (3) the history of religion, and (4) the history of culture, including contemporary culture. "The Bible, however, is the basic source of systematic theology because it is the original document about the events on which the Christian church is founded."[15]

The medium of systematic theology is experience. "Experience is the medium through which the sources 'speak' to us, through which we can receive them."[16] Theology needs an existential relation to the truth of the Christian faith.

Following the Christocentric tradition of Lutheran theology, Tillich states in his *Systematic Theology:*

> The material norm of systematic theology, used in the present system and considered the most adequate to the present apologetic situation, is the "New Being in Jesus as the Christ." If this is combined with the critical principle of all theology, one can say that the material norm of systematc theology today is the New Being in Jesus as the Christ as our ultimate concern. This norm is the criterion for the use of all the sources of systematic theology.[17]

The most significant events of the life of Jesus are the cross and the resurrection, according to Tillich. They are "the central symbols of the uni-

---

[12] *Ibid.*
[13] *Ibid.,* p. 66.
[14] *Ibid.*
[15] *Ibid.,* p. 35.
[16] *Ibid.,* p. 40.
[17] *Ibid.,* p. 50.

versal significance of Jesus as the Christ."[18] Tillich stresses that "the story of the Cross of Jesus as the Christ does not report an isolated event in his life but that event toward which the story of his life is directed and in which the others receive their meaning. Their meaning is that he who is the Christ subjects himself to the ultimate negation of existence and that they are not able to separate him from his unity with God."[19]

Tillich makes the analogous observations with respect to the resurrection.

> Like the story of the Cross, the story of the Resurrection of the Christ does not report an isolated event after his death. It reports the event which is anticipated in a large number of other events and which is, at the same time, their confirmation. The Resurrection, as well as the historical, legendary, and mythical symbols corroborating it, show the New Being in Jesus as the Christ as victorious over the existential estrangement to which he has subjected himself. This is their universal significance.[20]

The purpose of the cross and resurrection of Jesus the Christ is to bring salvation to all men. Tillich distinguishes three aspects of salvation: (1) "salvation as participation in the New Being," traditionally known as "regeneration," (2) "salvation as acceptance of the New Being," formerly known as "justification," and (3) "salvation as transformation by the New Being," before Tillich generally referred to as "sanctification."[21]

Tillich argues that "the saving power of the New Being in Jesus as the Christ is dependent on man's participation in it. The power of the New Being must lay hold of him who is still in bondage to the old being."[22] When this happens, regeneration is taking place. "Regeneration is the state of having been drawn into the new reality manifest in Jesus as the Christ. The subjective consequences are fragmentary and ambiguous and not the basis for claiming participation in the Christ. But the faith which accepts Jesus as the bearer of the New Being is this basis."[23]

To Tillich justification means acceptance of the fact that we are accepted by God despite our unacceptability. If you would be saved, you must accept by faith that you are accepted by grace. Tillich emphasizes that it is misleading to speak of justification by faith, "for it gives the impression that faith is an act of man by which he merits Justification. This is a total and disastrous distortion of the doctrine of Justification. The

[18] Paul Tillich, *Systematic Theology, II* (Chicago: University of Chicago Press, 1957), 153.
[19] *Ibid.*, p. 158.
[20] *Ibid.*, p. 159.
[21] *Ibid.*, pp. 176, 177, 179.
[22] *Ibid.*, p. 176.
[23] *Ibid.*, p. 177.

cause is God alone (by grace), but the faith that one is accepted is the channel through which grace is mediated to man (through faith)."[24]

Sanctification is the process which is initiated by justification and regeneration, "the reunion of what is estranged."[25] For Tillich, "sanctification is the process in which the power of the New Being transforms personality and community, inside and outside the church. Both the individual Christian and the church, both the religious and the secular realm, are objects of the sanctifying work of the divine Spirit, who is the actuality of the New Being."[26] Thus the actuality of the New Being in Jesus as the Christ transforms human life through its "Spiritual Presence,"[27] which is Tillich's term for the traditional "Holy Ghost." The Spiritual Presence creates the "Spiritual Community,"—Tillich's concept of the church—through faith and love. "Whereas faith is the state of being grasped by the Spiritual Presence, love is the state of being taken by the Spiritual Presence into the transcendent unity of unambiguous life."[28] This "unambiguous life" is eternal life, the goal of salvation and of Christianity.

We conclude that the union of Reformation theology and existential philosophy is the basic presupposition, the working hypothesis, and the final outcome of Tillich's work. Philosophy elaborates the questions arising out of human existence. Theology gives the answer to these questions. But since for Tillich culture determines the form of religion, philosophy also shapes the form of the theological answer.

From Paul Tillich, the systematic theologian and philosopher of being, we now move to *Rudolf Bultmann,* the New Testament scholar and pioneer of modern form criticism. That which unites the philosopher and the biblical thinker is their common ground in existentialist philosophy. The formative existentialist work for Bultmann was Heidegger's *Being and Time.* The existentialist analysis of human existence found in that work became for Bultmann the closest approximation to the New Testament view of human existence which he could find in contemporary culture.

Rudolf Bultmann was born on August 20, 1884 at Wiefelstede in the province of Oldenburg, Germany. He studied at the universities of Marburg, Tübingen, and Berlin. He was professor of New Testament studies at the universities of Breslau (1916–1920), Giessen (1920–1921), and Marburg (1921–1951). Since 1951 he has lived in retirement, but has continued to participate in the great debate initiated by his program for demythologizing the New Testament. This debate has brought Bultmann's

[24] *Ibid.,* p. 179.
[25] *Ibid.*
[26] *Ibid.,* pp. 179–180.
[27] Paul Tillich, *Systematic Theology,* III (Chicago: University of Chicago Press, 1963), p. 111.
[28] *Ibid.,* p. 134.

theology so much to the foreground of German theological interests that he has replaced Karl Barth as the center of theological attention in German-speaking countries.

Together with Martin Dibelius and K. L. Schmidt Bultmann was one of the pioneers of modern form criticism. Form criticism is the study of the origins and development of the oral tradition behind the four Gospels of the New Testament. In his famous *History of the Synoptic Tradition,* which appeared in 1921, and of which an English translation was made available in 1963, Bultmann sought to show that the Gospels are not biographical accounts of Jesus' life and teachings, but rather religious products of the believing Christian community of the first century.

Bultmann believes that the attempt to reconstruct the life of Jesus after the fashion of a biography misses the point that Jesus really had at heart.

> However good the reasons for being interested in the personalities of significant historical figures, Plato or Jesus, Dante or Luther, Napoleon or Goethe, it still remains true that this interest does not touch that which such men had at heart; for *their* interest was not in their personality but in their *work.* And their work was to them not the expression of their personality, nor something through which their personality achieved its "form," but the cause to which they surrendered their lives. Moreover, their work does not mean the sum of the historical effects of their acts; for to this their view could not be directed. Rather, the "work" from *their* standpoint is the end they really sought, and it is in connection with their life purpose that they are the proper objects of historical investigation. This is certainly true if the examination of history is no neutral orientation about objectively determined past events, but is motivated by the question how we ourselves, standing in the current of history, can succeed in comprehending our own existence, can gain clear insight into the contingencies and necessities of our own life purpose.[29]

Bultmann is saying that an objective and neutral observation of historical events after the manner of the objective and neutral observation of natural events studied by science is impossible. The reason for this lies in the basic distinction which Bultmann believes we must make between nature and history. He argues that

> man, if he rightly understands himself, differentiates himself from nature. When he observes nature, he perceives there something objective which is not himself. When he turns his attention to history, however, he must admit himself to be a part of history; he is considering a living complex of events in which he is essentially involved. He cannot observe this complex objectively as he can observe natural phenomena; for in every word which he says about history he is saying at the same time something about himself.

[29] Rudolf Bultmann, *Jesus and the Word,* trans. L. P. Smith and E. H. Lantero (New York: Scribner's, 1958), pp. 9–10.

Hence there cannot be impersonal observation of history in the same sense as there can be impersonal observation of nature.[30]

How, then, can we deal with history? Bultmann answers: by means of dialogue, interrogation of history, and listening to the demand which history makes upon us. For him

> the actual encounter with history takes place only in the dialogue. We do not stand outside historical forces as neutral observers; we are ourselves moved by them; and only when we are ready to listen to the *demand* which history makes on us do we understand at all what history is about. This dialogue is no clever exercise of subjectivity on the observer's part, but a real *interrogating* of history, in the course of which the historian puts this subjectivity of his in question, and is ready to listen to history as an authority. Further, such an interrogation of history does not end in complete relativism, as if history were a spectacle wholly dependent on the individual standpoint of the observer. Precisely the contrary is true: whatever is relative to the observer—namely all the presuppositions which he brings with him out of his own epoch and training and his individual position within them—must be given up, that history may actually speak. History, however, does not speak when a man stops his ears, that is, when he assumes neutrality, but speaks only when he comes seeking answers to the questions which agitate him. Only by this attitude can we discover whether an objective element is really present in history and whether history has something to say to us.[31]

The concern with history, and not with nature, has led Bultmann to be critical of the traditional methods of science which were dominated by an objectivistic understanding of nature and ignored the historical dimension of human existence and human understanding. He felt that existential philosophy had realized, together with recent theology, that the scientific modes of thought are objectivistic and therefore inadequate. The working together of theology and philosophy is therefore not a matter of individual, personal preference but a necessity of the contemporary historical situation in which science has failed to perceive the historical nature of its own enterprise. Bultmann insists that "whether theology is advanced or not by its recourse to modern philosophy depends not on arbitrary choice or individual preference, but on the historical situation: for both theology and philosophy have begun to realize how questionable is the thinking that has prevailed in science down to the present time.[32] Philosophy and theology are fellow workers in the common quest for a more adequate and comprehensive statement of the problems and prospects of human existence.

30 *Ibid.*, p. 3.
31 *Ibid.*, pp. 4–5.
32 Rudolf Bultmann, "The Case for Demythologizing: A Reply," *Kerygma and Myth*, II, ed. H.-W. Bartsch, trans. R. H. Fuller (London: S.P.C.K., 1962), p. 182.

The basic existential concern with human existence determines also Bultmann's perspective as a biblical scholar. His work in form criticism, which exposed the Gospels as products of many sources and redactors rather than the work of one writer, say, St. Mark or St. Matthew, lent biblical support to his pervasive concern with the humanity of the Holy Scriptures. In the course of his scholarly investigations by means of the modern method of form criticism, Bultmann came to the conclusion that

> the whole tradition about Jesus which appears in the three synoptic gospels is composed of a series of layers which can on the whole be clearly distinguished, although the separation at same points is difficult and doubtful. (The Gospel of John cannot be taken into account at all as a source for the teachings of Jesus. . . .) The separating of these layers in the synoptic gospels depends on the knowledge that these gospels were composed in Greek within the Hellenistic Christian community, while Jesus and the oldest Christian group lived in Palestine and spoke Aramaic. Hence everything in the synoptics which for reasons of language or content can have originated only in Hellenistic Christianity must be excluded as a source for the teaching of Jesus. The critical analysis shows, however, that the essential content of these three gospels was taken over from the Aramaic tradition of the oldest Palestinian community. Within this Palestinian material again different layers can be distinguished, in which whatever betrays the specific interests of the church or reveals characteristics of later development must be rejected as secondary. By means of this critical analysis an oldest layer is determined, though it can be marked off with only relative exactness. Naturally we have no absolute assurance that the exact words of this oldest layer were really spoken by Jesus. There is a possibility that the contents of this oldest layer are also the result of a complicated historical process which we can no longer trace.[33]

The events of Jesus' life are uncertain; the only sure thing we have is the biblical record. Bultmann states that

> by tradition Jesus is named as bearer of the message [or the kerygma]; according to the overwhelming probability he really was. Should it prove otherwise, that does not change in any way what is said in the record. I see then no objection to naming Jesus throughout as the speaker. Whoever prefers to put the name of "Jesus" always in quotation marks and let it stand as an abbreviation for the historical phenomenon with which we are concerned, is free to do so.[34]

At first the scholarly researches of form critics like Bultmann greatly upset more literal Protestant and Catholic interpretations of the Scriptures. Today, however, they are more or less completely accepted by the overwhelming majority of biblical scholars in the Roman Catholic, Eastern

---

[33] Bultmann, *Jesus and the Word*, pp. 12–13.
[34] *Ibid.*, p. 14.

Orthodox, and Protestant branches of Christendom. However, the theological shock-wave created by Bultmann's 1941 essay on "New Testament and Mythology,"[35] is still felt with great apprehension in many sections of the church universal. In this programmatic essay he demands the demythologization of the church's preaching. He argues that Christian doctrines like the Incarnation, Resurrection, Ascension, and the Second Coming of Christ are modelled after the pattern of mythologies created by Jewish apocalyptics and Hellenistic gnostics. What the New Testament really wants to do is to confront the inauthentic existence of man with the decision for or against the way of Christ which is the way to authentic human existence.

The way of Christ, according to Bultmann, is an event, namely, the act of God in Christ which the New Testament proclaims. The meaning of authentic existence is described in language most easily accessible to modern man by the existentialist philosophy of Martin Heidegger. Bultmann maintains that

> above all, Heidegger's existentialist analysis of the ontological structure of being would seem to be no more than a secularized, philosophical version of the New Testament view of human life. For him the chief characteristic of man's Being in history is anxiety. Man exists in a permanent tension between the past and the future. At every moment he is confronted with an alternative. Either he must immerse himself in the concrete world of nature, and thus inevitably lose his individuality, or he must abandon all security and commit himself unreservedly to the future, and thus alone achieve his authentic Being. Is not that exactly the New Testament understanding of human life? Some critics have objected that I am borrowing Heidegger's categories and forcing them upon the New Testament. I am afraid this only shows that they are blinding their eyes to the real problem. I mean, one should rather be startled that philosophy is saying the same thing as the New Testament and saying it quite independently.[36]

The authentic life of man, according to Bultmann, is a life of self-commitment, which is the gift of God. Inauthentic human life is a life of self-glorification and self-assertion. To Bultmann this is the very essence of sin.

> For as a result of his self-assertion man is a totally fallen being. He is capable of knowing that his authentic life consists in self-commitment, but is incapable of realizing it because however hard he tries he still remains what he is, self-assertive man. So in practice authentic life becomes possible only when man is delivered from himself. It is the claim of the New Testament that this is exactly what has happened. This is precisely the meaning of that

---

[35] Rudolf Bultmann, "New Testament and Mythology," trans. R. H. Fuller, *Kerygma and Myth* (New York: Harper & Row, 1961), pp. 1–44.
[36] *Ibid.*, pp. 24–25.

which was wrought in Christ. At the very point where man can do nothing, God steps in and acts—indeed he has acted already—on man's behalf.[37]

The New Testament gospel proclaims the redemptive action of God which alone can free man from the bondage to self-assertion and liberate him for the authentic life of self-commitment. The natural man can know what authentic existence is, but he cannot reach it by his own power. The philosophers are not in agreement with the gospel when they maintain that "all man needs is to be told about his authentic nature."[38] Only by faith and obedience "he has become a free man."[39] The challenge of the gospel is the challenge of faith in "the event in Jesus Christ . . . the revelation of the love of God. It makes a man free from himself and free to be himself, free to live a life of self-commitment in faith and love."[40]

Bultmann's goal is to present modern man clearly with the challenge of faith, not the impossible demand to accept an obsolete mythology belonging to the ancient world.

> He must be confronted with the issue of decision, be provoked to decision by the fact that the stumbling-block to faith, the *skadalon,* is peculiarly disturbing to man in general, not only to modern man (modern man being only one species of man). Therefore my attempt to demythologize beings . . . by clearing away the false stumbling-blocks created for modern man by the fact that his world-view is determined by science.[41]

While modern man has accepted more or less fully the process view of modern cosmology, the world-view of the ancient world provides the cosmology of the New Testament. According to Bultmann,

> the cosmology of the New Testament is essentially mythical in character. The world is viewed as a three-storied structure, with the earth in the centre, the heaven above, and the underworld beneath. Heaven is the abode of God and of celestial beings—the angels. The underworld is hell, the place of torment. Even the earth is more than the scene of natural, everyday events, of the trivial round and the common task. It is the scene of the supernatural activity of God and his angels on the one hand, and of Satan and his daemons on the other. These supernatural forces intervene in the course of nature and in all that men think and will and do. Miracles are by no means rare. Men is not in control of his own life. Evil spirits may take possession of him. Satan may inspire him with evil thoughts. Alternatively, God may inspire his thought and guide his purposes. He may grant him heavenly visions. He may allow him to hear his word of succour or demand. He may

[37] *Ibid.,* p. 31.
[38] *Ibid.,* p. 29.
[39] *Ibid.,* p. 32.
[40] *Ibid.*
[41] Bultmann, "The Case for Demythologizing," *op. cit.,* p. 183.

allow him the supernatural power of his Spirit. History does not follow a smooth unbroken course; it is set in motion and controlled by these supernatural powers. This aeon is held in bondage by Satan, sin, and death (for "powers" is precisely what they are), and hastens towards its end. That end will come very soon, and will take the form of a cosmic catastrophe. It will be inaugurated by the "woes" of the last time. Then the Judge will come from heaven, the dead will rise, the last judgment will take place, and men will enter into eternal salvation or damnation.[42]

Thus the New Testament presents the event of salvation in the langauge of a mythology which claims

that the last time has now come. "In the fulness of time" God sent forth his Son, a pre-existent divine Being, who appears on earth as a man. He dies the death of a sinner on the cross and makes atonement for the sins of men. His resurrection marks the beginning of the cosmic catastrophe. Death, the consequence of Adam's sin, is abolished, and the daemonic forces are deprived of their power. The risen Christ is exalted to the right hand of God in heaven and made "Lord" and "King." He will come again on the clouds of heaven to complete the work of redemption, and the resurrection and judgment of men will follow. Sin, suffering and death will then be finally abolished. All this is to happen very soon; indeed, St. Paul thinks that he himself will live to see it.[43]

According to the mythological New Testament view,

all who belong to Christ's Church and are joined to the Lord by Baptism and the Eucharist are certain of resurrection to salvation, unless they forfeit it by unworthy behaviour. Christian believers already enjoy the first instalment of salvation, for the Spirit is at work within them, bearing witness to their adoption as sons of God, and guaranteeing their final resurrection.[44]

Bultmann emphasizes that

all this is the language of mythology, and the origin of the various themes can be easily traced in the contemporary mythology of Jewish Apocalyptic and in the redemption myths of Gnosticism. To this extent *the kerygma is incredible to modern man, for he is convinced that the mythical view of the world is obsolete.* We are therefore bound to ask whether, when we preach the Gospel to-day, we expect our converts to accept not only the Gospel message, but also the mythical view of the world in which it is set. If not, does the New Testament embody a truth which is quite independent of its mythical setting? If it does, theology must undertake the task of stripping the Kerygma from its mythical framework, of "demythologizing" it.[45]

---

[42] Bultmann, "New Testament and Mythology," *op. cit.,* pp. 1–2.
[43] *Ibid.,* p. 2.
[44] *Ibid.*
[45] *Ibid.,* p. 3.

Only when the New Testament message of forgiveness and salvation is demythologized can the theologian and preacher come to the real point of Christianity which is to confront mankind with the challenge of decision. "It is this," Bultmann maintains, "—to disclose what the Christian faith is, to disclose the issue of decision—that seems to me the only, the crucial thing that the theologian must accomplish"[46] today in our modern, scientific and technological culture.

In order to penetrate through the thicket of preliminary irrelevancies to to the heart of the gospel we must recognize that it would be both senseless and impossible to expect modern man to accept the ancient mythical *Weltanschauung,* or world-view, as true.

It would be senseless, because there is nothing specifically Christian in the mythical view of the world as such. It is simply the cosmology of a pre-scientific age. Again, it would be impossible, because no man can adopt a view of the world by his own volition—it is already determined for him by his place in history. Of course such a view is not absolutely unalterable, and the individual may even contribute to its change. But he can do so only when he is faced by a new set of facts so compelling as to make his previous view of the world untenable. He has then no alternative but to modify his view of the world or produce a new one. The discoveries of Copernicus and the atomic theory are instances of this, and so was romanticism, with its discovery that the human subject is richer and more complex than enlightenment or idealism had allowed, and nationalism, with its new realization of the importance of history and the tradition of peoples.[47]

Bultmann stresses that

man's knowledge and mastery of the world have advanced to such an extent through science and technology that it is no longer possible for anyone seriously to hold the New Testament view of the world—in fact, there is no one who does. What meaning, for instance, can we attach to such phrases in the creed as "descended into hell" or "ascended into heaven"? We no longer believe in the three-storied universe which the creeds take for granted. The only honest way of reciting the creeds is to strip the mythological framework from the truth they enshrine—that is, assuming that they contain any truth at all, which is just the question that theology has to ask. No one who is old enough to think for himself supposes that God lives in a local heaven. There is no longer any heaven in the traditional sense of the word. The same applies to hell in the sense of a mythical underworld beneath our feet. And if this is so, the story of Christ's descent into hell and of his Ascension into heaven is done with. We can no longer look for the return of the Son of Man on the clouds of heaven or hope that the faithful will meet him in the air (I Thess 4:15 ff.).[48]

46 Bultmann, "The Case for Demythologizing," *op. cit.,* p. 183.
47 Bultmann, "New Testament and Mythology," *op. cit.,* p. 3.
48 *Ibid.,* p. 4.

Moreover,

now that the forces and the laws of nature have been discovered, we can no longer believe in *spirits, whether good or evil.* We know that the stars are physical bodies whose motions are controlled by the laws of the universe, and not daemonic beings which enslave mankind to their service. Any influence they may have over human life must be explicable in terms of the ordinary laws of nature; it cannot in any way be attributed to their malevolence. Sickness and the cure of disease are likewise attributable to natural causation; they are not the result of daemonic activity or of evil spells. The *miracles of the New Testament* have ceased to be miraculous, and to defend their historicity by recourse to nervous disorders or hypnotic effects only serves to underline the fact. And if we are still left with certain physiological and psychological phenomena which we can only assign to mysterious and enigmatic causes, we are still assigning them to causes, and thus far are trying to make them scientifically intelligible. Even occultism pretends to be a science.[49]

Given the new, modern, scientific *Weltanschauung* we need to adjust our religious thinking in order to be relevant to the space age. We must develop what I once heard the late beloved Pope John XXIII call "atomic theology." "It is impossible to use electric light and the wireless and to avail ourselves of modern medical and surgical discoveries, and at the same time to believe in the New Testament world of spirits and miracles. We may think we can manage it in our own lives, but to expect others to do so is to make the Christian faith unintelligible and unacceptable to the modern world."[50] With these words Bultmann presents one of the great problems of the Christian faith in the modern world. The stimulus of his thought has reached far beyond the confines of German Lutheranism to Anglicanism, where it prompted Bishop Robinson to write *Honest to God,* an essay in secular theology, to American Methodism, where it led process theologian Schubert Ogden to develop a theology of *Christ without Myth,* and to many other denominations on practically every continent of the globe.

[49] *Ibid.,* pp. 4–5.
[50] *Ibid.,* p. 5.

CHAPTER XI

SECULAR THEOLOGY: COX

The influence of modern science and technology has vastly accelerated the process of secularization in the West which began with the humanism of the Renaissance and the deism or atheism of the Enlightenment. The contemporary secular theologian Harvey Cox defines secularization as "the liberation of man from religious and metaphysical tutelage, the turning of his attention away from other worlds and toward this one."[1] Cox proposes to adjust theology to the new secular mood of our age in order to make Christianity relevant to our age of revolutionary process and change.

While Dr. Cox, who is currently a professor of theology at the Divinity School of Harvard University, was a teenager, at the end of World War II, he worked on UNRRA cattle and relief ships to Poland and Germany. Later he returned to this country and studied at the University of Pennsylvania, from which he received his Bachelor of Arts degree; Yale Divinity

[1] Harvey Cox, *The Secular City* (New York: Macmillan, 1965), p. 17.

School, where he earned the Bachelor of Divinity degree; and the Harvard University Divinity School, which awarded him the degree of Doctor of Philosophy. Two incidents are rather characteristic of the unconventional and revolutionary stance of Cox's *Weltanschauung*. During the academic year of 1962–1963, the year after the famous Berlin Wall went up, Cox went to Berlin as a so-called "fraternal worker" and communicated with universities and churches in East Germany. Returning from the then hottest spot in the Cold War, he took part in a civil rights demonstration in the South. He was arrested there and held in jail for five days.

Why did Cox go out in the name of God to do battle at the fronts of the Cold War in far-away Berlin and the race war in the American South? It is because he conceives of God as a revolutionary process in the world. The revolutionary action of God aims at "the liberation of man to freedom and responsibility."[2] Theology must therefore address itself to the task of transforming the church from the bulwark of religious and cultural conservatism and white racism into "God's avant-garde," the trail-blazer of a new and better future in peace, justice, and ecumenism. "Theology, in these terms, is concerned *first* of all with finding out where the action is, the 'discernment of the opening.' Only then can it begin the work of shaping the church which can get to the action. This is why the discussion of social change must precede a theology of the church."[3]

Rapid social change in the direction of increasing secularization and urbanization is, according to Cox, the central and determinative characteristic of contemporary society. Theology must gain a clear understanding of this process of change if it is to be relevant to the religious needs of modern men.

The first step in this direction is to clear away the wrong notion that secularism is opposed to biblical Christianity. Cox maintains that the Bible itself contains the seeds of secularization. He contends that

> the *disenchantment of nature* begins with the Creation; the *desacralization of politics* with the Exodus; and the *deconsecration of values* with the Sinai Covenant, especially with its prohibition of idols. The discussion is designed to make amply clear that, far from being something Christians should be against, secularization represents an authentic consequence of biblical faith. Rather than oppose it, the task of Christians should be to support and nourish it.[4]

In order to support the process of secularization in an intelligent and constructive manner, it is important to observe the distinction which Cox makes between secularization and secularism.

[2] *Ibid.*, p. 125.
[3] *Ibid.*, p. 126.
[4] *Ibid.*, pp. 17–18.

Secularization implies a historical process, almost certainly irreversible, in which society and culture are delivered from tutelage to religious control and closed metaphysical world-views. We have argued that it is basically a liberating development. Secularism, on the other hand, is the name for an ideology, a new closed world-view which functions very much like a new religion. While secularization finds its roots in the biblical faith itself and is to some extent an authentic outcome of the impact of biblical faith on Western history, this is not the case with secularism. Like any other ism, it menaces the openness and freedom secularization has produced; it must therefore be watched carefully to prevent its becoming the ideology of a new establishment. It must be especially checked where it pretends not to be a world-view but nonetheless seeks to impose its ideology through the organs of the state.[5]

Secularization is not an ideology but a process of demythologization. For instance,

> where in the Babylonian accounts, the sun, moon, and stars are semidivine beings, partaking the divinity of the gods themselves, their religious status is totally rejected by the Hebrews. In Genesis, the sun and moon become creations of Yahweh, hung in the sky to light the world for man; they are neither gods nor semidivine beings. The stars have no control over man's life. They too are made by Yahweh. None of the heavenly bodies can claim any right to religious awe or worship.[6]

In a sense, therefore,

> the Genesis account of Creation is really a form of "atheistic propaganda." It is designed to teach the Hebrews that the magical vision, by which nature is seen as a semidivine force, has no basis in fact. Yahweh, the Creator, whose being is centered outside the natural process, who calls it into existence and names its parts, allows man to perceive nature itself in a matter-of-fact way. . . . The mature secular man neither reverences nor ravages nature. His task is to tend it and make use of it, to assume the responsibility assigned to The Man, Adam.[7]

Just as the process of biblical secularization frees man from bondage to nature, so it liberates him from the oppressive weight of real and imaginary kinship ties.

> The lines of kinship in the Bible are temporal, not spatial. Instead of reaching out to encompass kangaroos and totem shrubs, they reach back to the sagas of the fathers and forward to the fortunes of the children's children. The structure of Hebrew kinship is linear; it is historical, not cosmological. The Bible, with one or two quaint exceptions (Eve's serpent and Balaam's ass), is devoid of the animal fables which abound in the legends and myths

5 *Ibid.*, pp. 20–21.
6 *Ibid.*, p. 22.
7 *Ibid.*, p. 23.

of magical peoples. Just after his creation man is given the crucial responsibility of naming the animals. He is their master and commander. It is his task to subdue the earth. Nature is neither his brother nor his god. As such it offers him no salvation. When he looks up to the hills, Hebrew man turns from them and asks where he can gain strength. The answer is: Not from the hills, but from Yahweh, who *made* heaven and earth. For the Bible, neither man nor God is defined by his relationship to nature. This not only frees both of them for history, it also makes nature itself available for man's use.[8]

Cox argues that

this disenchantment of the natural world provides an absolute precondition for the development of natural science. Since we have already shown that technopolis, today's technical city, would not have been possible without modern science, disenchantment is also an essential precondition for modern urbanization. Science is basically a point of view. However highly developed a culture's powers of observation, however refined its equipment for measuring, no real scientific breakthrough is possible until man can face the natural world unafraid. Wherever nature is perceived as an extension of himself or his group, or as the embodiment of the divine, science as we know it is precluded. This is evident in Assyrian culture, where an uncanny accuracy in astronomical observation developed, but in which the heavenly bodies were still experienced as the determinants of human destiny; hence no real scientific astronomy emerged.[9]

Furthermore,

it remains true in so-called under-developed cultures today that the mere introduction of modern technological devices and procedures will never suffice to produce a scientific culture. Somehow nature must be disenchanted, which means the destruction of many traditional religions. This destruction took place in the past century mainly under the auspices of Christian missions. More recently, it occurred as a result of the spread of Communist ideology. In this instance, Christianity and communism, despite their differences, played nearly identical roles in the removal of traditional religious restraints on scientific and technological change. Both are historically oriented ways of perceiving natural reality. Both exorcise the magical demons and open nature for science. More recently still, less precise socialistic ideologies of a vague planned welfare state have had the same influence. The disenchantment of nature is one of the essential components of secularization.[10]

From the disenchantment of nature we move to the second component of secularization: the desacralization of politics. Cox makes the observation that

[8] *Ibid.*
[9] *Ibid.*, p. 24.
[10] *Ibid.*

no one rules by divine right in secular society. In presecular society, everyone does. Just as nature is perceived by tribal man both as a part of his family and as the locus of religious energy, so the political power structure is accepted as an extension of familial authority and as the unequivocal will of the gods. The identification of the political with the religious order, whether in a primitive tribe where the chief is also the sorcerer, or in the Roman Empire where the emperor is both political ruler and pontifex maximus, betrays the same sacral legitimation of political power.[11]

The result of surrounding the social and political order with the halo of divine respectability is that

significant political and social change is almost impossible in societies in which the ruling regime is directly legitimated by religious symbols, in which the ruler is believed to be divine or a direct expression of the divine intention. Political change depends on a previous desacralization of politics. The process is closely related to the disenchantment of nature. Since nature always repeats itself, while history never does, the emergence of history rather than nature as the locus of God's action opens a whole new world of possibilities for political and social change.[12]

Cox emphasizes that

in tracing the desacralization of politics to its biblical roots, the Exodus must be the focal point of study. For the Hebrews Yahweh had spoken decisively not in a natural phenomenon, such as a thunderclap or an earthquake, but through a historical event, the deliverance from Egypt. It is particularly significant that this was an event of social change, a massive act of what we might today call "civil disobedience." It was an act of insurrection against a duly constituted monarch, a pharaoh whose relationship to the sungod Re constituted his claim to political sovereignty. There had no doubt been similar escapes before, but the Exodus of the Hebrews became more than a minor event which happened to an unimportant people. It became the central event around which the Hebrews organized their whole perception of reality. As such, it symbolized the deliverance of man out of a sacral-political order and into history and social change, out of religiously legitimated monarchs and into a world where political leadership would be based on power gained by the capacity to accomplish specific social objectives.[13]

Thus the sacredness of political order was abolished in favor of a secular view of political power based on pragmatic adequacy and effective performance. The process of the secularization of politics initiated at the Exodus continues until today. In the United States, for instance, remnants of sacral politics are still in evidence. For example, "the President is

[11] *Ibid.*, p. 25
[12] *Ibid.*
[13] *Ibid.*, pp. 25–26.

installed with an oath spoken while his hand rests on a Bible. Priests, rabbis, and ministers intone prayers in a kind of ritual vestiture. But here too the matter is all effect with no substance. Significantly, the Chief Justice of the Supreme Court who holds the Bible presides over a body which . . . has ruled that its reading cannot be required in public schools."[14] Thus politico-religious ceremonial, emptied of its sacred substance, continues in even so secularized a nation as the United States. All this goes to show that "secularization is a process, not a state of affairs."[15]

The third major component in the process of secularization initiated by the Judaic-Christian scriptural tradition has to do with the deconsecration of values. The key to the deconsecration of values is their relativization which

> stems in part from the biblical opposition to idolatry. Beginning with the prohibition against 'graven images' which is part of the Sinai Covenant, the Old Testament is characterized by an uncompromising refusal to allow any replication of the deity. The enormous revelance of this prohibition is frequently misunderstood by modern readers. Since, for the ancients, god and value systems were the same thing, this interdiction against idols has real import for the question at hand. It means that the Jews were forbidden to worship (that is, to take with any real moral seriousness) anything which could be fashioned by man himself. It was not that the Jews feared that by making an idol religious worship might be cheapened or misled. Rather, it was believed that Yahweh, the Holy One of Israel, was by his very nature impossible of replication by human effort. The commandment against idolatry is a clue to Yahweh's essence. Any deity which could be expressed in the form of an idol was *ipso facto* not Yahweh. The gods were thereby demoted. The Bible does not deny the reality of the gods and their values; it merely relativizes them. It accepts them as human projections, as "the work of man's hand," and in this sense is very close to the modern social sciences. It was because they believed in Yahweh that, for the Jews, all human values and their representations were relativized.
>
> The same observation holds for the continuing tradition of iconaclasm in Christian history. Iconoclasm is a form of deconsecration. It represents the extension of the commandment against idols.[16]

Given these Judeo-Christian roots of the process of secularization it is clear that

> those whose present orientation to reality is shaped by the biblical faith can hardly in good faith enter the lists as adversaries of secularization. Our task should be to nourish the secularization process, to prevent it from hardening into a rigid world-view, and to clarify as often as necessary its roots in

14 *Ibid.*, p. 29.
15 *Ibid.*
16 *Ibid.*, p. 32.

the Bible. Furthermore, we should be constantly on the lookout for movements which attempt to thwart and reverse the liberating irritant of secularization.[17]

Cox maintains that

this means that we should oppose the romantic restoration of the spirits of
the forest. It may seem pleasant at first to reinstate the leprechauns, but—
as Hitler made all too clear—once the Valkyries return, they will seek a
bloodthirsty revenge on those who banished them. We should also be wary
of any attempt to resacralize politics. Political leaders and movements should
never be granted any sacred significance, and all efforts to use the public
authority to support traditional religious beliefs or the quasi-religious beliefs
of ideological secularists must be resisted."[18]

There are good reasons to believe that

it is in the realm of values and ethics that the nurture of secularization becomes most ambiguous and problematical. Yet even here the broad lines of
action are clear. Of course, no group can be prevented from claiming that its
values are ultimate. But it can be prevented from employing state power or
cultural coercion to validate its case. No one can deny a Mississippi cafe pro-
prietor his right to believe that Negroes suffer the curse of Ham. But he
can be prevented from utilizing the property the state protects and regulates
for him to humiliate Negroes because of his far-fetched religious opinion.
A highly disparate conglomerate of value systems can co-exist in a society
so long as they all repudiate the privilege of winning the others over by rack
and thumbscrew. But even this repudiation demands a huge step for those
still ensnarled in mythical and metaphysical sureties. Releasing them to maturity is the work of the God of Creation, Exodus, and Sinai. Calling them
to maturity is the task of the community of faith.[19]

But it must be remembered that the maturity in question is always that of
the process of secularization, never that of the pseudo-maturity of ideological secularism.

From Cox's perspective the church appears as God's avant-garde in the
secular city. "The church, like any avant-garde, has a story it is trying to
get across. It is telling people what is coming, what to expect next. Employing political terminology, the church broadcasts the fact that a revolution is under way and that the pivotal battle has already taken place."[20]

Cox believes that

this broadcasting function of the church is crucial. It makes the church different from any other avant-garde. It has no plan for rebuilding the world.

[17] *Ibid.*, p. 36.
[18] *Ibid.*
[19] *Ibid.*
[20] *Ibid.*, p. 127.

It has only the signal to flash that the One who frees slaves and summons men to maturity is still in business. It flashes this signal not in the form of general propositions but in the language of specific announcements about where the work of liberation is now proceeding and concrete invitations to join in the struggle.[21]

In more traditionally Christian terminology Cox's point can be expressed by saying that

the message of the church is that God has defeated the "principalities and powers" by Jesus and has made it possible for man to become the "heir," the master of the created world. This sounds foreign to us now, but nothing could be closer to the center of human existence in twentieth-century urban society. These "principalities and powers" actually signify all the forces in a culture which cripple and corrupt human freedom. In various ages men have experienced these forces in different ways. Sometimes they have denied their existence, but this has not happened often. In the tribal era which colors much of the New Testament, they were perceived as demons, spirits, and astral forces. They were believed to be linked up with individuals and especially with rulers. Each person had his own "star" (we still read horoscopes today) and astronomical symbols were often associated with kings. In the transition period of town culture these forces were either denied or were reduced to regular movements and predictable patterns. Newton's spheres and Adam Smith's invisible hand are good examples. Still, the nineteenth century as a whole was skeptical about such forces, and only in our own time have they been rediscovered under such concepts as the id, the collective unconscious, the dialectic of history, or even statistical probability. One could sum up all these fields of force insofar as they impair or imperil man's free exercise of responsibility in the single word *fate*. When Proudhon claimed, . . . that the impact of biblical faith is to "defatalize" the world, he was right. What is meant by the kerygmatic assertion that Jesus has defeated the "principalities and powers" is not that they have been annihilated. Ids and economic pressures still roam through history. What is meant is that these forces do not have the power to determine man. Rather, man has the power and the responsibility to rule over them and use them in responsibility before God.[22]

Secularization is the process of maturation which liberates technopolitan man from the oppression of the "principalities and powers" of the secular city. Cox argues that

these principalities and powers, according to the New Testament, were originally intended to be a part of the world, to be dominated and utilized by man. But man's freedom is so complete that he "worshipped and served the creature rather than the Creator" (Romans 1:24). Man thus fell captive to

[21] *Ibid.*, pp. 127–128.
[22] *Ibid.*, p. 128.

forces over which he was intended to "have dominion." Things he was meant to control controlled him. He had to be extricated. God's action, which goes on all the time but was made known in Jesus of Nazareth, is to call man to freedom *from* the powers and principalities, and to summon him at the same time to responsibility *over* and *for* them.[23]

God's action in Christ must not be understood as a static fact, but as a continued process.

Man is always tempted to surrender his freedom to the powers. God is ever at work making freedom and personhood possible. There is no neutral ground. Man either masters and manages his environment or he is mastered and managed by it. The call to freedom is at the same time a call to responsibility. In terms of modern urban life, this means that we should never seriously ask "Is New York City governable?" or "Can nuclear war be prevented?" or "Can racial justice be achieved?" The fact is that man is placed in an environment of problems which he is called to master. God has not stacked the cards against man the way fate does in Greek tragedy or a Thomas Hardy novel. To believe the kerygma is to believe that man not only *should* but *can* "have dominion over the earth." For the Bible, there are no powers anywhere which are not essentially tameable and ultimately humanizable. To deny this, in word or deed, is to "worship the creature rather than the Creator," to open the door and readmit the banished furies, to genuflect before some faceless Kismet.[24]

Concretely this means that

the kerygma itself is articulated only when a man knows that he really is free from dependence on the fates and recognizes that his life is now being placed in his own hands. The kerygma comes to a people when they stop blaming economic forces or psychological pressures for social injustice and family strife and begin to do battle against the causes of woe. The taming of the powers means that man is invited to make the whole universe over into a human place. He is challenged to push forward the disenchantment and desacralization which have expelled the demons from nature and politics.[25]

And "because the avant-garde announces the coming of a new era which has already begun but is not yet complete, its message is in the indicative mood, not the imperative. It does not urge or exhort people. It simply makes known what has happened, that 'the acceptable year of the Lord' has arrived."[26] Thus

[23] Cox, *The Secular City* (New York: Macmillan, 1965), pp. 128–129.
[24] *Ibid.*, p. 129.
[25] *Ibid.*, p. 130.
[26] *Ibid.*

the church's announcement produces what theologians call the "crisis of the Kingdom." It results in a catalytic gap in which people have to make a decision. It is the coming of the new regime into the midst of the old which requires this response.

To express it in wholly political terminology, the revolutionary regime has seized power but the symbols of authority are still in the hands of the old displaced rulers. Like the inhabitant of a country torn by revolution, each man is confronted by a choice, a crisis. Shall he obey the new authority announced by the avant-garde, though it does not yet possess the symbols (legal legitimation, ceremonial inauguration, etc.); or shall he obey the "duly constituted authorities" who still claim the right to govern?

The illustration is a particularly apt one because the citizen cannot answer the question theoretically. He must cooperate either with the new regime or with the old. His choice is expressed in what he *does*. Nor can he merely evade the issue. Even neglecting to oppose one regime, for example, could at some time be interpreted as collaboration.[27]

The influence of modern existentialism is quite evident in Cox's emphasis on the issue of decision. He is intent to point out that

a biblical theology begins by viewing all of history since the coming of Jesus as the beginning of a new regime. But the new regime takes shape in the midst of the old. Consequently, a crisis of choice is presented which eventually confronts every man who hears about the new reality. In this respect it is essential to notice that Christian theology, unlike the Old Testament vision, claims that the seizure of power *has* already taken place. The revolutionary deliverer *has* come and *has* won the decisive battle. For this reason, all of human history takes place between the achievement of *de facto* power and the appearance of visible *de jure* authority. History does not take place between the black noon of Good Friday and the bright dawn of Easter. It takes place, rather, between Easter Day and the Last Day. History is a permanent crisis in which the defeated old regime still claims power while the victorious new regime has still not appeared publicly on the balcony. The New Testament looks forward not to the victory of Jesus, since that has already been won, but to the day when "every knee shall bow and every tongue confess" that Jesus is Victor.[28]

For Cox, therefore,

Exodus and Easter remain the two foci of biblical faith, the basis on which a theology of the church must be developed. The exodus is the event which sets forth "what God is doing in history." He is seen to be liberating people from bondage, releasing them from political, cultural, and economic captivity, providing them with the occasion to forge in the wilderness a new symbol system, a new set of values, and a new national identity. Easter

27 *Ibid.*, p. 131.
28 *Ibid.*, pp. 131–132.

means that the same activity goes on today, and that where such liberating activity occurs, the same Yahweh of Hosts is at work. Both Exodus and Easter are caught up in the inclusive symbol of the Kingdom, the realization of the liberating rule of God. In our terms, God's action today, through secularization and urbanization, puts man in an unavoidable crisis. He must take responsibility in and for the city of man, or become once again a slave to dehumanizing powers.[29]

If man is to "take responsibility in and for the city of man" he must have an adequate understanding of the form, structure, and dynamics of the secular city. For Cox two of the most characteristic components of the social shape of the city of man (as opposed to its physical shape) are anonymity and mobility.

The city of man is the secular city shaped by technology. Cox calls it the "technopolis" in which

technopolitan man sits at a vast and immensely complicated switchboard. He is *homo symbolicus,* the man the communicator, and the metropolis is a massive network of communications. A whole world of possibilities for communication lies within his reach. The contemporary urban region represents an ingenious device for vastly enlarging the range of human communication and widening the scope of individual choice. Urbanization thus contributes to the freedom of man. This is perfectly evident when we think for example of cinema theatres and restaurants. Residents of a city of 10,000 may be limited to one or two theatres, while people who live in a city of a million can choose among perhaps fifty films on a given night. The same principle holds for restaurants, schools, and even in some measure for job opportunities or prospective marriage partners. Urban man is free to choose from a wider range of alternatives. Thus his manhood as *homo symbolicus* is enhanced.[30]

The greater freedom of urban man brings with it a greater need for self-discipline. Thus Cox stresses that "the mere availability of such a wide spectrum of possibilities requires an adjustment of urban man's behavior. He must exercise choice more frequently, and choice always means exclusion. He doesn't just 'go to the movies' on a free evening, as his more rural counterpart might; he must choose one from among the fifty films now showing. This means a conscious decision *not* to see the other forty-nine."[31]

Technopolitan man in the secular city must learn to discipline himself to make conscious choices if he is to enjoy his freedom to its fullest extent. He must be highly selective.

[29] *Ibid.,* p. 132.
[30] *Ibid.,* p. 40.
[31] *Ibid.,* p. 41.

In the area of personal relationships this selectivity becomes more demanding. Urban man has a wider variety of "contacts" than his rural counterpart; he can choose only a limited number for friends. He must have more or less impersonal relationships with most of the people with whom he comes in contact precisely in order to choose certain friendships to nourish and cultivate. This selectivity can best be symbolized perhaps by the unplugged telephone or the unlisted number. A person does not request an unlisted number to cut down on the depth of his relationships. Quite the opposite; he does so to guard and deepen the worthwhile relationships he has against being dissolved in the deluge of messages that would come if one were open on principle and on an equal basis to anyone who tried to get through, including the increasing army of telephone salesmen who violate one's privacy so arrogantly. Those we want to know have our number; others do not: We are free to use the switchboard without being victimized by its infinite possibilities.[32]

Thus for many people life in the modern technopolis "is a glorious liberation, a deliverance from the saddling traditions and burdensome expectations of town life and an entry into the exciting new possibilities of choice which pervade the secular metropolis."[33] What we need, therefore, is not laments over the urbanization of modern culture, but rather the development of "a viable theology of anonymity."[34]

We also must come to terms with the vital role which mobility plays in the modern city. Cox notes that

there are many critics of residential and occupational mobility. They use different rhetoric but quite frequently paint verbal landscapes of home and vocation which are laden with religious sentiments. For many people these images have a real appeal. To be born and reared in the same clapboard house where one may even grow old and die does have a certain cozy attractiveness. To work at the same job in the same place through all one's adult years might also provide elements of comfort. But those who bewail the passing of the era in which this stable, idyllic condition was supposed to have obtained forget one important fact: only a tiny minority of people ever really enjoyed such pastoral permanence. The majority of people in premobile societies lived and worked in ways we would not want to return to. Most of us today would vigorously object to living in the house or doing the job our great-grandfathers did. The fact is that most people's great-grandparents were dirt-poor and lived in hovels. Most of us are much better off today because our forebears *were* mobile. Mobility is always the weapon of the underdog. The desire to combat mobility, to encourage residential and occupational *im*mobility, is a romantic distortion which springs from a reactionary mentality.[35]

[32] *Ibid.*
[33] *Ibid.*, p. 49.
[34] *Ibid.*, p. 48.
[35] *Ibid.*, p. 52.

In fact, "mobility is closely linked to social change; so guardians of the status quo have always opposed mobility. They are perfectly consistent in doing so. They sense that changes in one area of life—job or residence—will lead to other kinds of change; and they are against change."[36] For example,

> in our own country the emergence of the Negro Freedom Movement provides a particularly good example of the link between mobility and social change. Many observers believe that the movement of large numbers of Negroes out of rural areas in the South and into urban industrial centers, plus the experience of thousands of young Negroes in the military service, supplied the indispensable social exposure which has resulted in the civil rights revolution. Negroes discovered that things did not have to be the way they were. Those who acted against oppression were young, and they were geographically and occupationally mobile. Their battles, unlike those of the Civil War which took place at heretofore unknown villages—Bull Run and Gettysburg—now took place in urban centers such as Birmingham, and spread to the provinces. Mobility has unlocked the cage.[37]

What is the theological significance of mobility? "Let us admit at once," Cox remarks,

> that high mobility does play havoc with traditional religion. It separates people from the holy places. It mixes them with neighbors whose gods have different names and who worship in different ways. But since we have already noted the important connection between urbanization and secularization, we need not pause to lament this process. What we do wish to say is that, from a biblical perspective, mobility can also be viewed positively. Without ignoring the dangers it can bring or the problems it creates, it must be insisted that mobility offers positive possibilities for individuals.[38]

In our attempt to understand the theological meaning of mobility

> it is well to remember that the whole Hebrew view of God arose in the social context of a nomadic, essentially homeless people. Only for relatively brief periods in their history did the Jews have a "home of their own," and these periods were usually viewed as the least creative periods in their career as a people. The experience of the escape from Egypt, the wandering in the wilderness, and the battles in Canaan supplied the axial events on which the Israelite faith was based. The greatest prophets, Jeremiah and Second Isaiah, did their work either as the security of the homeland was being crushed or in political exile. Israel's level of prophetic insight after they returned to their former homes under Ezra and Nehemiah dropped to an all-time low. Indeed, the universalism which broke through during the exile

---

[36] *Ibid.*
[37] *Ibid.*, p. 53.
[38] *Ibid.*, p. 54.

was almost lost sight of during the regressive period of the return. In short, when they were wandering and homeless the Jews seem to have been closest to fulfilling their calling.[39]

The same is true of the Judaic concept of God. Cox states that

the key characteristics of Yahweh, the Old Testament God, are linked to his mobility. He is the Lord of history and time. He is not spatially placed. It was because Yahweh, like the Jews, was a nomad, that the period of settlement in Canaan sparked the titanic battle between Yahweh and the baal. The struggle arose because the Baalim were the recognized deities of Canaan, and when the nomadic children of Israel finally settled there, they had to face the question of what to do with these local gods. The word *baal* itself means "possessor" or "inhabitant." The Baalim of Canaan were the proprietors of certain activities or more frequently of particular towns and places. They were *immobile* gods. A particular baal expected deference from people only so long as they were within its territorial jurisdiction. The Baalim were the gods of a sedentary people who were suspicious of any sort of change.[40]

Not so Yahweh, the God of Israel.

True, He had appeared at particular places such as Sinai or in the burning bush, but He was certainly not restricted to these places. He not only moved with His people, but "went before them." Although the view of Yahweh as a nomadic, non-spatial God was constantly threatened by syncretism with the Canaanite Baal, it finally withstood the test. With the Second Isaiah, it became clearly established that not even the rock of Zion in Jerusalem had any claim to Yahweh, that He ruled over all peoples and moved wherever he wanted to. This was a crucial victory for the Yahwist faith, since the historical character of Israel's vision of life depends on Yahweh's stalwart refusal to be a hearth god of some home-sweet-home.[41]

Cox maintains that

one of the clearest evidences of Yahweh's mobility is the Ark of the Covenant, about which biblical archeologists have speculated. It is described in several places in the Old Testament. Some believe the Ark was a chest in which sacred stones were carried by the Hebrews into battle. Others believe it was a throne on which the invisible Yahweh rode with His people. Regardless of what it actually looked like, it is clear that the Ark was mobile. Unlike the Inca temples, the Egyptian sphinxes, or the Babylonian ziggurats, it could be picked up and carried wherever the people went. Unlike the baal, it was not stationary. Most important, however, when the Ark was finally captured by the Philistines, the Jews began to realize that

[39] *Ibid.*, pp. 54–55.
[40] *Ibid.*, p. 55.
[41] *Ibid.*, pp. 55–56.

Yahweh was not localized even in it. The seizure of the Ark prepared them for the eventual destruction of the Temple and the loss of their homeland. This whole historical movement by which Yahweh was divested of spatiality has enormous theological significance. It meant that Yahweh could not be localized at any given geographic spot. He traveled with his people and elsewhere.[42]

The Israelites refused to localize God but located his presence in certain historical events. Here, as Cox insists,

the nomadic life of the early Israelites provided the necessary social setting for the emergence of a view of God that was startlingly at variance with those of Israel's neighbors. Yahweh was a God of history, not of nature. He disclosed Himself in political and military events, including defeats. He spoke through events of social change. For this reason, during the settlement of Canaan and the confrontation with the fertility gods of that culture, it was the farmers and the ruling elites who flirted with abandoning Yahweh and turning to the Baalim. The farmers did so because they were the most sedentary group, the rulers because they were the most conservative. The rural "high places" and the sad saga of Queen Jezebel provide the clearest examples. Yahweh won the contest with the agricultural deities not by becoming one but by absorbing many of the harvest and procreation festivals into what still remained an essentially nonspatial, historical faith. The rise of a monarchy with its requisite ideology put an even more fearful strain on the Yahwist faith. But still Yahwism survived. Diluted during the monarchy, it was renewed in military defeat, captivity, and exile. Thus the faith was strengthened and revived precisely by a new period of homelessness and mobility.[43]

Christianity carried on the Judaic concept of divine mobility. Cox stresses that

Jesus picked up the tradition of opposing sacred places and holy homelands. Thus he rejected the promptings of the Zealots, chiefly Judas Iscariot, to save the sacred homeland from the pagan Romans; he refused to allow his disciples, in the story of the Transfiguration, to build permanent monuments to him; he repeatedly promised to destroy the Temple of Jerusalem, the existence of which was always on the verge of respatializing God. His identifying the new temple with the risen body must be seen as his way of carrying the despatialization motif to its ultimate conclusion. The early church's belief in the Ascension can be read as its refusal to allow its Lord to be localized or spatially restricted. The Ascension in its simplest terms means that Jesus is mobile. He is not a baal, but the Lord of all history.[44]

From all this it can be concluded that

[42] *Ibid.*, p. 56.
[43] *Ibid.*, pp. 56–57.
[44] *Ibid.*, p. 57.

mobility is not the menace religious romantics paint it. It has its pitfalls. Endless movement from place to place can betray the same kind of unwillingness to take responsibility for decisions which can be seen in switching wives. But by and large the mobile man is less tempted than the immobile man to demote Yahweh into a baal. He will usually not idolatrize any town or nation. He will not be as likely to see the present economic and political structure as the unambiguous expression of how things always have been and always should be. He will be more open to change, movement, newness. There is no reason why Christians should deplore the accelerating mobility of the modern metropolis. The Bible does not call man to renounce mobility, but to "go to a place that I will show unto you." Perhaps the mobile man can even hear with less static a Message about a Man who was born during a journey, spent his first years in exile, was expelled from his own home town, and declared that he had no place to lay his head. High mobility is no assurance of salvation, but neither is it an obstacle to faith.[45]

The conclusion of our examination of Cox's theology of the secular city is a confirmation of Paul Tillich's observation: Religion is the substance of culture, and culture is the form of religion. The increasing secularization of our culture must lead to a pervasive secularization of theological form. This explains the immense popularity of Cox. His *Secular City* has become the "bible" of thousands of young Christians and theologians in our day. For Cox has been able to speak finally a theological word relevant to the modern world, and thus he has redeemed the promise of Bonhoeffer's religionless Christianity, with particular emphasis on the social and ethical relevance of theology. Urban man finds Cox's theology of the city more helpful in his situation than the entire corpus of the ancient Church Fathers and the sixteenth-century Reformers. Thus his theology of secularity offers the opportunity to go around the stalemate of Catholic Church Fathers versus Protestant Reformers and to forge ahead boldly into the unlimited ecumenical future of the coming great church.

[45] *Ibid.*, p. 58.

CHAPTER XII

THEOLOGY OF THE NEW MORALITY: FLETCHER

In the previous chapter Harvey Cox spoke, for himself. The same approach will be used in the following examination of situation ethics as proposed in the new morality of Joseph Fletcher. But in order to understand why Fletcher sees a need for a new morality, it is necessary to make a few concluding observations regarding the secular city, which is the soil out of which the new morality grew. In a very real sense situation ethics is the moral answer given to the problem of the secular city as posed and analyzed by theologians like Harvey Cox.

If we are to get a real grasp of the substance and sum of Fletcher's new situation ethics we need to keep before us the dimensions of anonymity, mobility, practicality, and profanity of the secular city of modern technopolitan man. According to Cox's theology of the secular city, technopolitan man not only thrives on anonymity and mobility, but his style of life is shaped by "pragmatism" and "profanity."

By *pragmatism* we mean secular man's concern with the question "Will it work?" Secular man does not occupy himself much with mysteries. He is little interested in anything that seems resistant to the application of human energy and intelligence. He judges ideas, as the dictionary suggests in its definition of pragmatism, by the "results they will achieve in practice." The world is viewed not as a unified metaphysical system but as a series of problems and projects.[1]

The term "profanity" in Cox's secular theology refers to

secular man's wholly terrestrial horizon, the disappearance of any supre-mundane reality defining his life. Pro-*fane* means literally "outside the temple"—thus "having to do with his world." By calling him profane, we do not suggest that secular man is sacrilegious, but that he is unreligious. He views the world not in terms of some other world but in terms of itself. He feels that any meaning to be found in this world originates in this world itself. Profane man is simply *this*-worldly.[2]

Cox grants that

the contrast, even the contradiction, between the style of the secular city and our traditional faith appears at first glance to be serious. Indeed, if we do accept man as pragmatic and profane, we seem to sabotage the corner-stone of the whole theological edifice. If secular man is no longer interested in the ultimate mystery of life but in the "pragmatic" solution of particular problems, how can anyone talk to him meaningfully about God? If he discards suprehistorical meanings and looks in his "profanity" to human history itself as the source of purpose and value, how can he comprehend any religious claim at all? Should not theologians first divest modern man of his pragmatism and his profanity, teach him once again to ask and to wonder, and *then* come to him with the Truth from Beyond?[3]

"No," Cox replies.

Any effort to desecularize and deurbanize modern man, to rid him of his pragmatism and his profanity, is seriously mistaken. It wrongly presupposes that a man must first become "religious" before he can hear the Gospel. It was Dietrich Bonhoeffer who firmly rejected this erroneous assumption and pointed out that it bore a striking parallel to the long-discarded idea that one had to be circumcised a Jew before becoming a Christian. Bonhoeffer insisted that we must find a nonreligious interpretation of the Gospel for secular man. He was right.[4]

The pragmatism and profanity of modern man enable him to see in a new light elements of traditional Christianity which have been buried for

[1] Harvey Cox, *The Secular City* (New York: Macmillan, 1965), p. 60.
[2] *Ibid.*, pp. 60–61.
[3] *Ibid.*, p. 61.
[4] *Ibid.*, pp. 61–62.

centuries. They are the elements which today have political connotations. Cox emphasizes that "in the epoch of the secular city, politics replaces metaphysics as the language of theology."[5]

This means that

we speak of God politically whenever we give occasion to our neighbor to become the responsible, adult agent, the fully post-town and post-tribal man God expects him to be today. We speak to him of God whenever we cause him to realize consciously the web of interhuman reciprocity in which he is brought into being and sustained in it as a man. We speak to him of God whenever our words cause him to shed some of the blindness and prejudice of immaturity and to accept a larger and freer role in fashioning the instrumentalities of human justice and cultural vision. We do not speak to him of God by trying to make him religious but, on the contrary, by encouraging him to come fully of age, putting away childish things.[6]

Cox emphasizes that

to say that speaking of God must be political means that it must engage people at particular points, not just "in general." It must be a word about their own lives—their children, their job, their hopes or disappointments. It must be a word to the bewildering crises within which our personal troubles arise—a word which builds peace in a nuclear world, which contributes to justice in an age staked by hunger, which hastens the day of freedom in a society stifled by segregation. If the word is not a word which arises from a concrete involvement of the speaker in these realities, then it is not a Word of God at all but empty twaddle.[7]

Cox stresses that

we speak of God to secular man by speaking about man, by talking about man as he is seen in the biblical perspective. Secular talk about God occurs when we are away from the ghetto and out of costume, when we are participants in that political action by which He restores men to each other in mutual concern and responsibility. We speak of God in a secular fashion when we recognize man as His partner, as the one charged with the task of bestowing meaning and order in human history.[8]

Cox concludes the discussion of the problem of how to speak of God in a secular fashion appropriate to the mode of thought which rules in the modern technopolis by noting that such speaking is

a political issue. It entails our discerning where God is working and then joining His work. Standing in a picket line is a way of speaking. By doing

---

[5] *Ibid.*, p. 255.
[6] *Ibid.*, p. 255.
[7] *Ibid.*, p. 256.
[8] *Ibid.*

it a Christian speaks of God. He helps alter the word "God" by changing the society in which it has been trivialized, by moving away from the context where "God-talk" usually occurs, and by shedding the stereotyped roles in which God's name is usually intoned.[9]

The pragmatic emphasis on the particular and concrete situation of modern man in the secular city, as opposed to metaphysical generalities, is carried into the realm of ethical decision and action by Joseph Fletcher.

Fletcher has been Professor of Christian Ethics at Episcopal Theological School, Cambridge, Massachusetts, since 1944. Among his books are: *Church and Industry* and *Morals and Medicine*. His new morality is for the situationist, and "the situationist, whether a Christian or not, follows a strategy that is pragmatic."[10] With the pragmatist philosophy of William James, the situationist "turns away from abstraction and insufficiency, from verbal solutions, from bad *a priori* reasons, from fixed principles, closed systems, and pretended absolutes and origins. He turns toward concreteness and adequacy, toward facts, toward actions, and toward power."[11]

Fletcher's approach to morality is not only pragmatic, it is also relativistic.

As the strategy is pragmatic, the tactics are relativistic. Perhaps the most pervasive culture trait of the scientific era and of contemporary man is the relativism with which everything is seen and understood. Our thought forms are relativistic to a degree that our forebears never imagined. We have become fully and irreversibly "contingent," not only about our particular ideas, but about the very idea of ideas themselves (cognitive value) and about goodness itself (moral value). The situationist avoids words like "never" and "perfect" and "always" and "complete" as he avoids the plague, as he avoids "absolutely."[12]

For the new morality

to be relative, of course, means to be relative *to* something. To be "absolutely relative" (an uneasy combination of terms) is to be inchoate, random, unpredictable, unjudgeable, meaningless, amoral—rather in the antinomian mode. There must be an absolute or norm of some kind if there is to be any true relativity. This is the central fact in the normative relativism of a situation ethic. It is not anarchic (i.e., without an *archē*, an ordering principle). In *Christian* situationism the ultimate criterion is . . . "agapeic love." It relativizes the absolute, it does not absolutize the relative![13]

Fletcher observes that

9 *Ibid.*, pp. 256–257.
10 Joseph Fletcher, *Situation Ethics* (Philadelphia: Westminster Press, 1966), p. 43.
11 William James, *Pragmatism*, quoted in Fletcher, *op. cit.*, p. 43.
12 Fletcher, *op. cit.*, pp. 43–44.
13 *Ibid.*, pp. 44–45.

ethical relativism has invaded Christian ethics progressively ever since the simultaneous appearance in 1932 of Emil Brunner's *The Divine Imperative* and Reinhold Niebuhr's *Moral Man and Immoral Society*. Both theologians built their conceptions of the Christian ethic on the principle that the divine command is always the same in its *Why* but always different in its *What*, or changeless as to the *What* but contingent as to the *How*. We are always, that is to say, commanded to act lovingly, but how to do it depends on our own responsible estimate of the situation. Only love is a constant; everything else is a variable. The shift to relativism carries contemporary Christians away from code ethics, away from stern iron-bound do's and don'ts, away from prescribed conduct and legalistic morality.[14]

The Pharisaic code of ethics, the legalistic morality of the Torah, in Fletcher's view "is now suffering a second eclipse, a far more radical one than it endured under Jesus' and Paul's attacks. Our milieu and era are far unfriendlier to law ethics than were the apostolic and patristic times, to say nothing of the medieval period."[15]

Therefore,

contemporary Christians should not underestimate this relativism, in either its secular or its Christian form. Christian ethics was drawn into it long ago when Jesus attacked the Pharisees' principle of statutory morality, and by Paul's rebellious appeal to grace and freedom. Even earlier, the Biblical doctrine of man as only a finite creature of imperfect powers and perceptions was voiced in the docta ignorantia of Isa 55:8: "For my thought are not your thoughts, neither are your ways my ways, says the Lord." This concept of human creatureliness at the very heart of Christian ethics cries, "Relativity!" in the face of all smug pretensions to truth and righteousness. Christians cannot go on trying to "lay down the law" theologically, about either creed or code.[16]

Besides pragmatism and relativism, Fletcher's situation ethics is built on "theological positivism." In this "positive theology"

faith propositions are "posited" or affirmed voluntaristically rather than rationalistically. It is a-rational but not ir-rational, outside reason but not against it. Its starting point is like Anselm's *Credo ut intellegam* in the *Proslogion* (first chapter); thinking supported by faith rather than faith supported by thinking. Although it does not exclude reason, reason goes to work because of the commitment and in its service. Thus Christian ethics "posits" faith in God and *reasons* out what obedience to this commandment to love requires in any situation. God's existence and belief that Christ is God in man cannot be proved, any more than a Marxist can prove that

---

[14] *Ibid.*, p. 45.
[15] *Ibid.*, pp. 45–46.
[16] *Ibid.*, p. 46.

history is headed for Communism and that labor is the sole source of commodity value."[17]

For the Christian situationist

the faith comes first. The Johannine proposition (I John 4:7–12) is not that God is *love* but that *God* is love! The Christian does not understand God in terms of love; he understands love in terms of God as seen in Christ. "We love, because he first loved us." This obviously is a faith foundation for love. Paul's phrase (Gal 5:6), "faith working through love," is the essence and pith of Christian ethics. *Nevertheless,* a perfectly sincere man, in every way as intelligent and wise as any Christian might be, can refuse to put any stock whatever in Christ, in which case he might in all seriousness also doubt the hope and love that Paul linked to faith in his triad of theological virtues (I Cor, ch. 13). But still, these are the faith commitments which identify the Christian.[18]

A fourth characteristic of the new morality for the secular city is its personalism.

Ethics deals with human relations. Situation ethics puts people at the center of concern, not things. Obligation is to person, not to things; to subjects, not objects. The legalist is the what asker (What does the law say?); the situationist is a *who* asker (Who is to be helped?). That is, situationists are *personalistic*. In the Christian version, for example, a basic maxim is that the disciple is commanded to love people, not principles or laws or objects or any other *thing*.[19]

Consequently, for Fletcher,

there are no "values" in the sense of inherent goods—value is what *happens to* something when it happens to be useful to love working for the sake of persons. Brunner declared that the notion of value apart from persons is a "phantasmagoria." There are no intrinsic values, he says, being a blunt situationist. Anything, material or immaterial, is "good" only because it is good for or to somebody. (Pius XII warned against "personalistic morality," but its influence continues to grow among Catholic theologians [*Acta Apostolicae Sedis*, XLV (1953), 278]).[20]

Fletcher observes that

in *Christian* situation ethics, there is also a theological side to personalism, since God is "personal" and has created men in his own image—imago Dei. Personality is *therefore* the first-order concern in ethical choices. Kant's second maxim holds: Treat persons as ends, never as means. Even if in

[17] *Ibid.,* p. 47.
[18] *Ibid.,* pp. 49–50.
[19] *Ibid.,* p. 50.
[20] *Ibid.*

some situations a material thing is chosen rather than a person, it will be (if it is Christianly done) for the sake of the person, not for the sake of the thing itself. If a man prefers to keep his money invested instead of giving it to his son who needs it, it could only be because he believes his son will need it far more urgently later on. To repeat, values are only extrinsically, never intrinsically, "valuable." Love is of people, by people, and for people. Things are to be used; people are to be loved. It is "immoral" when people are used and things are loved. Loving actions are the *only* conduct permissible.[21]

Therefore,

the Christian situationist says to the non-Christian situationist who is also neighbor—or person—concerned: *"Your* love is like mine, like everybodies; it is the Holy Spirit. Love is not the work of the Holy Spirit, it *is* the Holy Spirit—working in us. God *is* love, he doesn't merely *have* it or *give* it; he gives himself—to all men, to all sorts and conditions: to believers and unbelievers, high and low, dark and pale, learned and ignorant, Marxists and Christians and Hottentots."[22]

For Fletcher, "this is what is meant by 'uncovenanted' grace. This is the 'saving' truth about themselves which the faithless, alas, do not grasp! It is not the unbelieving who invite 'damnation' but the unloving. Temple insisted that 'the atheist who is moved by love is moved by the spirit of God; an atheist who lives by love is saved by his faith in the God whose existence (under that name) he denies.' "[23] The important thing for the situationalist is not what a man believes but how he acts in specific, concrete situations. "If we put these working principles," says Fletcher,

(pragmatism, relativism, positivism, and personalism), their shape is obviously one of action, existence, eventfulness. The situation ethic, unlike some other kinds, is an ethic of *decision*—of *making* decisions rather than "looking them up" in a manual of prefab rules. . . . Situation ethics is more Biblical and verb-thinking than Greek and noun-thinking. It does not ask *what* is good but *how* to do good for *whom;* not what *is* love but how to *do* the most loving thing possible in the situation. It focusses upon *pragma* (doing), not upon *dogma* (some tenet). Its concern is with behaving according to the believing. It is an activity, not a feeling, an "activistic" ethic. Kant's phrase for ethics, "practical reason," is precisely correct. We can agree with G. E. Moore at least about this: that "casuistry is the goal of ethical investigation"—i.e., that an ethic is inauthentic until it gets down to cases.[24]

21 *Ibid.,* p. 51.
22 *Ibid.*
23 *Ibid.,* p. 52.
24 *Ibid.*

In order to move quickly to authentic ethics according to Fletcher, let us look at a concrete case told by him:

> I was reading Clinton Gardner's *Biblical Faith and Social Ethics* on a shuttle plane to New York. Next to me sat a young woman of about twenty-eight or so, attractive and well turned out in expensive clothes of good taste. She showed some interest in my book, and I asked if she'd like to look at it. "No," she said, "I'd rather talk." What about? "Me." That was a surprise, and I knew it meant good-by to the reading I needed to get done. "I have a problem I can't get unconfused about. You might help me to decide," she explained. This was probably on the strength of what I was reading.
>
> I learned that she had been educated in church-related schools, a first-rate college, and was a now a buyer in women's shoes for a Washington store. We agreed, however, to remain mutually anonymous. Her problem? "O.K. This is it. One of our intelligence agencies wants me to be a kind of counterespionage agent, to lure an enemy spy into blackmail by using my sex." To test her Christian sophistication, I asked if she believed Paul's teaching about how our sex faculties are to be used, as in First Corinthians. Quickly she said, "Yes, if you mean that bit in the sixth chapter—your body is the temple of the Holy Spirit. *But,*" she added, "the trouble is that Paul also says, 'The powers that be are ordained of God.' "
>
> The defense agency wanted her to take a secretary's job in a western European city, and under that cover "involve" a married man who was working for a rival power. Married men are as vulnerable to blackmail as homosexuals. They did not put strong pressure on her. When she protested that she couldn't put her personal integrity on the block, as sex for hire, they would only say: "We understand. It's like your brother risking his life or limb in Korea. We are sure this job can't be done any other way. It's bad if we have to turn to somebody less competent and discreet than you are."
>
> So. We discussed it as a question of patriotic prostitution and personal integrity. In this case, how was she to balance loyalty and gratitude as an American citizen over against her ideal of sexual integrity?[25]

The answer to this question Fletcher would have had to evolve out of his four basic presuppositions of pragmatism, relativism, positivism, and personalism as well as out of his absolute norm, which is love.

Having discussed the basic presuppositions of the new morality, its pragmatism, relativism, positivism, and personalism, as well as its absolutistic love norm, we are now ready to apply these insights to a specific problem, that of conscience. According to Fletcher,

> situation ethics is interested in conscience (moral consciousness) as a function, not as a faculty. It takes conscience into account only when it is working, practicing, deciding. There have been four theories about what "conscience" is, but situationism takes none of them seriously. Some have

[25] *Ibid.,* pp. 163–164.

said it is an innate, radarlike, built-in faculty—intuition. Others have thought of it as inspiration from outside the decision maker—guidance by the Holy Spirit or a guardian angel or a Jimmy Cricket. The popular theory nowadays is "introjection"—that conscience is the internalized value system of the culture and society. The Thomists have followed Aquinas' definition, that it is the reason making moral judgments or value choices. But situationism has no ontology or being theory for conscience, whatsoever.[26]

According to Fletcher,

the traditional error lies in thinking about conscience as a noun instead of as a verb. This reflects the fixity and establishment-mindedness of all law ethics as contrasted to love ethics. There *is* no conscience; "conscience" is merely a word for our attempts to make decisions creatively, constructively, fittingly. If, with Huckleberry Finn, we were to suppose that conscience is a faculty, with a bag of reliable rules and principles, then we should have to say what Huck said when he wrestled over whether it was right to befriend Jim, the runaway slave: "If I had a yaller dog that didn't know more than a person's conscience does, I would pison him. It takes up more room than all the rest of a person's insides, and yet ain't no good, nohow. Tom Sawyer he says the same." Thomas Aquinas' description is the best (leaving aside his faculty idea [which tied conscience to a faculty, synteresis]): the reason making moral judgments.[27]

In dealing with the question of conscience, the situationist is concerned

with antecedent rather than consequent conscience, i.e., with prospective decision-making rather than with retrospective judgment-passing. The ancient world ordinarily thought of conscience (*syneidēsis*) as a review officer, weighing an action ex post facto and rendering approval or disapproval. (We all do this, head on pillow, after a long, hard day!) An example is Ernest Hemingway's famous definition, "What's good is what I feel good after, and what's bad is what I feel bad after." Savage cultures have often thought of conscience with the model of a sharp stone in the breast under the sternum, which turns and hurts when we have done wrong. Conscience is here remorse or reassurance.[28]

Situation ethics follows biblical, specifically Pauline ethics.

Paul spoke of conscience in two of his letters, to Rome and Corinth, and tended to give a new twist to the Greco-Roman idea by treating it as a *director* of human decisions rather than simply a reviewer. It acquired a future reference, directive and not merely reactive. So it is with situation ethics. By contrast, the morality of the confessional is ex post facto and retrospective, backward-looking.[29]

[26] Fletcher, *Situation Ethics* (Philadelphia: Westminster Press, 1966), pp. 52–53.
[27] *Ibid.*, p. 53.
[28] *Ibid.*, p. 54.
[29] *Ibid.*

Fletcher contrasts the old, traditional, abstract morality of historical Christian ethics with the new empirical attitude of situation ethics.

Historically, man's ethical struggle (including Christian ethics) has worked out theories in the abstract about the nature of the good and about right conduct. It has tried, then, to apply these theories as rules prescribing actions. Christian thought and practice, for example, has tackled Christian ethics first, elaborating the *ideal* as based on systems of Biblical, historical, and dogmatic theology. The second stage has been moral theology, an attempt to formulate and articulate (i.e., systematize) working principles or rules, from the ideal. The third stage has been to use these rules and principles as prescriptions and directives in actual cases (casuistry).

This strategy produced a bed of Procrustes onto which the decisions of life had to be forced and cut to fit the bed's iron shape and size. The *aggiornamento* spirit has led Father C. E. Curran to speak of a "need for a life-centered and not a confession-oriented moral theology," explaining that "theologians have begun to react against the manualistic treatment of conscience." "God," he says, "has called each person by his own name. In one sense, every individual is unique; every concrete situation is unique. . . . Frequently there are no easy solutions. After prayerful consideration of all values involved, the Christian chooses what he believes to be the demands of love in the present situation."[30]

Traditional Christian ethics proceeds by deduction from abstract ideals to specific cases.

The pragmatic-empirical temper of situation ethics, on the other hand, calls for a radical reversal of the classic approach. It focuses on cases and tries experientially, not propositionally, to adduce, not deduce, some "general" ideas to be held only tentatively and lightly. It deals with cases in all their contextual particularity, deferring in fear and trembling only to the rule of love. Situation ethics keeps principles sternly in their place, in the role of advisers without veto power![31]

For the new morality

only one "general" proposition is prescribed, namely, the commandment to love God through the neighbor. . . . And this commandment is, be it noted, a normative ideal; it is *not* an operational directive. All else, all other generalities (e.g., "One should tell the truth" and "One should respect life") are at most only *maxims*, never rules. For the situationist there are no rules —none at all.[32]

While there are no rules in situation ethics, there are half-a-dozen moral propositions or ethical maxims upon which Fletcher's new morality rests.

[30] *Ibid.*, pp. 54–55.
[31] *Ibid.*, p. 55.
[32] *Ibid.*

"The First Proposition: 'Only one "thing" is intrinsically good; namely, love: nothing else at all.' "[33]

"The Second Proposition: 'The ruling norm of Christian decision is love: nothing else.' "[34]

"The Third Proposition: 'Love and justice are the same, for justice is love distributed, nothing else.' "[35]

"The Fourth Proposition: 'Love wills the neighbor's good whether we like him or not,' "[36]

"The Fifth Proposition: 'Only the end justifies the means; nothing else.' "[37]

"The Sixth Proposition: 'Love's decisions are made situationally, not prescriptively.' "[38]

Let us now briefly look at each one of these ethical propositions individually. Fletcher's first proposition says that love is the only intrinsic good. He remarks that "the rock-bottom issue in all ethics is 'value.' Where is it, what is its locus? Is the worthiness or 'worthness' of a thing inherent *in* it? Or is it contingent, *relative* to other things than itself? Is the good or evil of a thing, and the right or wrong of an action, intrinsic or extrinsic?"[39] Fletcher answers that "no law or principle or value is good as such—not life or truth or chastity or property or marriage or anything but love. *Only one thing is intrinsically good, namely, love: nothing else at all.*"[40]

According to Fletcher's second moral proposition love is the only norm of ethical decision making, not law. For the new moralist

> the plain fact is that love is an imperious law unto itself. It will not share its power. It will not share its authority with any other laws, either natural or supernatural. Love is even capable of desecrating the Holy of Holies, the very tabernacle of the altar, if human hunger cries for help. Imagine an Anglo-Catholic or Roman Catholic being told that in serious need of food it is all right to open the pyx and eat the Blessed Sacrament! What a shock to law-bound piety! The pericope Matt. 12:1–8 (and parallels Mark 2:23–28; Luke 6:1–5) left no doubt about Jesus' willingness to follow the radical decisions of love. He puts his stamp of approval on the translegality of David's paradigm or exemplary act: "Have you never read what David did, when he was . . . hungry, he and those who were with him: how he entered the house of God . . . and ate the bread of the Presence, which it is not lawful

[33] *Ibid.*, p. 57 (italics omitted).
[34] *Ibid.*, p. 69 (italics omitted).
[35] *Ibid.*, p. 87 (italics omitted).
[36] *Ibid.*, p. 103 (italics omitted).
[37] *Ibid.*, p. 120 (italics omitted).
[38] *Ibid.*, p. 134 (italics omitted).
[39] *Ibid.*, p. 57.
[40] *Ibid.*, p. 68.

for any but the priests to eat and also gave it to those who were with him?" At least the *Christ* of the Christian ethic leaves no doubt whatsoever that *the ruling norm of Christian decision is love: nothing else.*[41]

The third proposition of situation ethics identifies justice with distributive love. Fletcher makes this identification because he is convinced that

it will not do merely to keep love and justice separate and then to give one or the other priority. Nathaniel Micklem relates a story of Canon Quick's about an Indian deeply in debt who inherited a fortune and gave it away to the poor, leaving his creditors unpaid. The "moral" drawn was that something is wrong with charity (love) when it is at variance with justice, since charity does more than justice, not less. This is, of course, a very badly drawn lesson. It is true, yes, that love and justice should not be at variance. The reason, however, is not that one should excel the other but, rather, that they are one and the same thing and *cannot* vary! The Indian failed in *agape,* and was therefore unjust.[42]

The case of the Indian illustrates the importance of "love using its head."[43] Justice, for the situationist,

is Christian love using its head, calculating its duties, obligations, opportunities, resources. Sometimes it is hard to decide, but the dilemmas, trilemmas, and multilemmas of conscience are as baffling for legalists as for situationists. Justice is love coping with situations where distribution is called for. On this basis it becomes plain that as the love ethic searches seriously for a social policy it must form a coalition with utilitarianism. It takes over from Bentham and Mill the strategic principle of "the greatest good of the greatest number."[44]

Fletcher's fourth moral proposition makes the point that the decisive thing for Christian ethics is not whether we like but whether we love our neighbor. He stresses that "to love Christianly is a matter of attitude, not of feeling. Love is discerning and critical; it is not sentimental. . . . That is, it is neighbor-concerned, outgoing, not self-concerned or selective."[45]

This is why Rudolf Bultmann is so positive in his statement: "In reality, the love which is based on emotions of sympathy, or affection, is self-love; for it is a love of preference, of choice, and the standard of the preference and choice is the self."

A young unmarried couple might decide, if they make their decisions Christianly, to have intercourse (i.e., by getting pregnant to force a selfish parent to relent his overbearing resistance to their marriage). But as Chris-

[41] *Ibid.,* pp. 85–86.
[42] *Ibid.,* p. 89.
[43] *Ibid.,* p. 95.
[44] *Ibid.*
[45] *Ibid.,* p. 103.

tians they would never merely say, "It's all right if we *like* each other!" Loving concern can make it all right, but mere liking cannot.[46]

Fletcher remarks that

to love is not necessarily to please. *Agape* is not gratification. It has often been remarked that the golden rule should read, "Do unto others as they would have you do unto them"—that its classic form "as you would have them do unto you" is self-centered, cutting its cloth according to what *you* want rather than what the neighbor wants. But to accept this revision would be too close to "disinterested" love; it would be *neutral* love, which is too close to indifference. For *agape* is concerned for the neighbor, ultimately, for God's sake; certainly not for the self's but not even for the neighbor's own sake only. Christian love, for example, cannot give heroin to an addict just because he wants it. Or, at least, if the heroin is given, it will be given as part of a cure. And the same with all pleasures—sex, alms, food, anything. All parents know this.[47]

They know it because they realize that "love's business is not to play favorites or find friends or to 'fall' for some one-and-only. It plays the field, universalizes its concern, has a social interest, is no respecter of persons. . . . Disinterested love can only mean impartial love, inclusive love, indiscriminate love, love for Tom, Dick, and Harry."[48]

In his fifth ethical proposition Fletcher attacks the traditional Christian idea that the end does not justify the means.

We grow cynical or despairing, depending on our temper, when we see the way Christian ethics down through the centuries has clung stubbornly to the doctrine that "the end does not justify the means." It is an absurd abstraction, equivalent to saying that a thing is not worth what it costs, that *nothing* is, that use or usefulness is irrelevant to price.[49]

Fletcher observes that

in the perspective of situation ethics it is amazing that almost unanimously this sententious proposition has managed to hand on with bland and un-challenged acceptance. Just as Socrates saw that the unexamined life is not worth living, we can say that unexamined ethical maxims are not worth living by. Therefore we have to raise the question, implicit in all that has gone before, "If the end does not justify the means, what does?" The answer is, obviously, "Nothing!"

    Unless some purpose or end is in view to justify or sanctify it, any action we take is literally meaningless—i.e., means-less, accidental, merely random, pointless. Every action without exception is haphazard if it is without an

[46] *Ibid.,* p. 104.
[47] *Ibid.,* p. 117.
[48] *Ibid.,* p. 119.
[49] *Ibid.,* p. 120.

end to serve: it only acquires its status as a means, i.e., it only becomes meaningful by virtue of an end beyond itself.[50]

As a concrete example of what is meant by the proposition that the end alone justifies the means, Fletcher relates the following instance:

If, for example, the emotional and spiritual welfare of the parents and children in a *particular* family could best be served by a divorce, then, wrong and cheap-jack as divorce often is, love justifies a divorce. Love's method is to judge by particularity, not to lay down laws and universals. It does not preach pretty propositions; it asks concrete questions, situation questions. Getting a divorce is sometimes like David's eating the reserved Sacrament; it is what Christ would recommend. The fact that Jesus is reported in the Gospels as having blessed David's act on the basis of the situation, while he also absolutized the prohibition of divorce, poses a problem for Biblical scholarship (especially troublesome to the literalizers and legalists) but it does not confuse Christian ethics, at least of the situationist stamp. We are quite clear about it: to will the end is to will the means.[51]

The sixth and last moral proposition of Fletcher's situationism argues for a situational decision of love and against the prescriptive application of the love norm. Fletcher deplores that

too many people at heart long for an ethical *system* of prefabricated, pre-tailored morality. They want to lean on strong, unyielding rules. It was all very well, they complain, for Paul to say that living by the law is like slavery (Gal 4:21–26), "but after all, *we* aren't St. Pauls." Even if he did say that those who stick to the law are no better than slaves, we still need law—and if not the Torah, then something like it, something more "Christian."[52]

The situation ethicist contrasts the security of law-bound morality with the anguish, ambiguity, freedom, and creative insecurity of the new morality without law. Fletcher notes that

people like to wallow or cower in the security of the law. They cannot trust themselves too much to the freedom of grace; they prefer the comfortableness of law. Better the policy of the Grand Inquisitor; better bread and circuses. If, as the philosophers say, man became "the tragic animal" by transcending instinctually determined choices and acquiring conscience, then it's at least better to keep that tragic burden of conscience to a safe minimum! In a way they are right; moving over from law to love (Paul called it "grace") is a painful and threatening step to take.[53]

50 *Ibid.*, pp. 120–121.
51 *Ibid.*, p. 133.
52 *Ibid.*, p. 134.
53 *Ibid.*, pp. 134–135.

On the other hand,

the situationist, cutting himself loose from the dead hand of unyielding law, with its false promises of relief from the anguish of decision, can only determine that as a man of goodwill he will live as a free man, with all the ambiguities that go along with freedom. His moral life takes on the shape of adventure, ceases to pretend to be a blueprint. In all humility, knowing that he cannot escape the human margin of error, he will—in Luther's apposite phrase—sin bravely.[54]

As an application of Luther's saying Fletcher gives the following illustration.

When a lady in Arizona learned, a few years ago, that she *might* bear a defective baby because she had taken thalidomide, how was she to decide? She asked the court to back her doctor and his hospital in terminating the pregnancy, and it refused, to the judge's chagrin, since the law prohibits nonmedically indicated abortions without exception. Her husband took her to Sweden, where love has more control of law, and there she was aborted. God be thanked, since the embryo was hideously deformed. But nobody could know for sure. It was a brave and responsible and right decision, even if the embryo had been all right. It was a *kairos,* a fullness of time, a moment of decision.[55]

The primary aim of situation ethics is to be adequate to the particular circumstances of the ethical situation. This aim overrules the concern for upholding standards of public or private morality.

[54] *Ibid.,* p. 135.
[55] *Ibid.,* pp. 135–136.

Chapter XIII

The Negro Contribution to American Theology:
King

The theological contribution of Afro-Americans has been long neglected. In our time we are beginning to recognize the significant contribution that they have made and continue to make. From the devotional power of the great Negro spirituals to the dynamic theology of rapid social change of a Martin Luther King, Afro-American religious poets and thinkers have covered the spectrum of the great themes of American theology: freedom, love, justice, and the church's social responsibility. In the theological vision and philosophical personalism of King, the American Negro has achieved his most valuable and relevant expression of Christian religion.

King saw in Gandhi a Christ-figure of overwhelming contemporary relevance. To apply Jesus' teaching to the social problems of the day was his underlying concern. As a pastor of the church he wished to make the church relevant for the redemption of mankind. But unlike Jesus, who kept his messianic secret within the inner circle of twelve chosen disciples, King consciously addressed himself to the masses. Jesus withdrew from large crowds; King sought mass meetings and mass leadership through the agencies of the Southern Christian Leadership Conference. But King shared Christ's concern for an ethic based on love, justice, and freedom. He also followed the Nazarene's nonviolent concept of redemptive messiahship.

It has been said with a great deal of justification that "Martin Luther King was the most important theologian of our time not because of the plenitude of his literary production, but because of his creative proposals for dealing with the structure of evil."[1] Over against the modern social evils of racism, violence, oppression, discrimination, and the refusal to adapt fairly to social change "King created not only a new theology, but also new types of piety, new styles of Christian living."[2] He demonstrated the overwhelming relevance of secular Christianity loyal to Christ and the church and adamantly opposed cooperation with evil. He saw himself in the great line that stems from Moses, who stood before the mighty Pharoah pleading for the freedom of his people. He thundered against social evil in the spirit of the ancient prophet Amos.

Martin Luther King was born on January 15, 1929 at Atlanta, Georgia. "Through an error, apparently, the baby born that day was listed officially as Michael Luther King, Jr., and remained so, officially, until 1957 when he received his first passport. But to the father and, later, to the world, the baby was Martin Luther King, Jr."[3]

King's father was pastor of Ebenezer Baptist Church of Atlanta, Georgia. His ancestry included American Indians, Irish, and Africans. He had an older sister, Christine, and a younger brother, Alfred Daniel. His childhood surroundings were those of the Negro middle class. Although he lived through the Great Depression, when two-thirds of the Negroes of Atlanta were on public relief, his life was protected from economic suffering and insecurity. "There was always meat on the King table, and bread and butter. 'We've never lived in a rented house,' the elder King has said, 'and never ridden too long in a car on which payment was due.' "[4]

People who knew the young King were impressed by the fact that, like the great Reformer from whom he took his name, he was a master of words.

Watching his father and other ministers dominate audiences with artfully chosen words, the young boy tingled with excitement; and the urge to speak,

---

[1] Herbert Warren Richardson, "Martin Luther King—Unsung Theologian," *Commonweal* (May 3, 1968), p. 201a.

[2] *Ibid.*

[3] Lerone Bennett, Jr., *What Manner of Man* (New York: Pocket Books, 1968), p. 4.

[4] *Ibid.*, p. 14.

to express himself, to turn and twist and lift audiences, seized him and never afterwards left him. To form words into sentences, to fling them out on the waves of air in a crescendo of sound, to watch people weep, shout, *respond:* this fascinated young Martin. His mother has said that she cannot recall a time when he was not fascinated by the sound and power of words. "You just wait and see," he told his mother at the age of six, "I'm going to get me some *big* words." The idea of using words as weapons of defense and offense was thus early implanted and seems to have grown in King as naturally as a flower. In time, this idea would become a central component of his life style.[5]

Like the parents of the magnificent Lutheran Reformer, King's family, too, had won success through thrift, hard work, and staying out of trouble. And like the father of the Protestant Reformation, King, Jr. dissented from the craving for success and economic security which his parents had. He had a profound sympathy for the suffering and downtrodden masses of Afro-Americans, and rejected the aloofness of the prosperous Negro middle class. Young Martin also was repelled by the irrelevant emotionalism of Negro Baptist religion. Therefore he vowed not to become a minister, like his father, but rather a doctor of medicine.

King, Jr. was a brilliant student in school. He skipped 9th and 12th grades and finished his high school work at the age of 15. In 1944 he entered Morehouse College, where his father had gone to school. "Morehouse was an all-men's school, famous for molding leading members of the Negro leadership group. At Morehouse, the pursuit of excellence in the classroom was supplemented by daily chapel periods and a vigorous and exceptionally free campus life. Two things were drilled into Morehouse men from their first day on the campus to their last: 1) that they were Morehouse men, and 2) that they were expected to succeed in life."[6]

King majored in sociology. He was a scholastically outstanding student, but made little impact on the life of the school. "He sang in the glee club but joined only a few organizations, none of which elected him to high office. He was also active as an orator, winning a prize in the annual college oratorical contest."[7]

In 1948 the 19-year-old King graduated from Morehouse College, and in the fall of the same year he entered Crozer Theological Seminary of Chester, Pennsylvania. He was an A student for the three year course there.

The years at the seminary were magnificently rich in spiritual growth for King. "Of all the authors he read in this period (Reinhold Niebuhr, Marx, Sartre, Jaspers, Heidegger), two impressed him most. The first

[5] *Ibid.,* p. 13.
[6] *Ibid.,* p. 20.
[7] *Ibid.,* p. 21.

was Hegel, whose analysis of the dialectical process and of progress and growth through pain became central elements in his emerging personal philosophy. King was impressed, too, by Hegel's theory that "world-histori-cal individuals' were the agents by which 'the will of the World Spirit' is carried out."[8]

The second was the Baptist theologian, Walter Rauschenbusch.

In 1950, during his senior year at Crozer, King came across a copy of Rauschenbusch's *Christianity and the Social Crisis,* a book which, he said, "left an indelible imprint on my thinking." Although King did not agree with the whole of Rauschenbusch's philosophy, he was "fascinated" by the great preacher's application of the social principles of Jesus to the problems of the modern world. Thereafter, the main thrust of the "social gospel"— the idea that the church should take a direct, active role in the struggle for social justice—became a pivotal element in King's personal philosophy.[9]

In 1950, during his final year as a seminarian, King heard several speakers on Gandhi's nonviolent techniques, such as, fasts, general strikes, boycotts, mass marches, and massive civil disobedience. He bought six books on or about the Indian prophet of nonviolence and his philosophy of suffering and self-sacrifice. These he studied diligently, and it began to dawn on him that Gandhi's methods could be used effectively in the struggle of Afro-Americans for social justice and recognition.

On June 18, 1953, King married Coretta Scott, a "pretty, long-haired soprano."[10] The ceremony took place "in a fashionable garden wedding in Heiberger, Alabama. Martin Luther King, Sr., officiated."[11] The ethos of Protestant middle class religion and social values continued to surround King during his formative years. His wife returned to the Boston Conservatory after their honeymoon, and they rented a four-room apartment near there. "By this time King had completed most of the requirements for the Ph.D. degree. He therefore kept the house and cooked dinner for his student-wife on Thursday evenings."[12]

King's attraction to Boston had reasons other than the musical ambitions of his wife.

As a result of his reading and thinking, he had adopted the philosophical posture of personalism. Boston University at the time was a germinal center of this philosophy, which holds that personality is the key to the meaning of the universe and that not only man but also God is, as King puts it, "supremely personal." . . . "This personal idealism remains today my basic philosophical position. Personalism's insistence that only personality—finite

8 *Ibid.,* p. 27.
9 *Ibid.,* p. 28.
10 *Ibid.,* p. 31.
11 *Ibid.,* p. 37.
12 *Ibid.*

and infinite—is ultimately real strengthened me in two convictions: it gave me metaphysical and philosophical grounding for the idea of a personal God, and it gave me a metaphysical basis for the dignity and worth of all human personality."[13]

Having completed the preliminary requirements for the Ph. D., King, in 1953, began work on his thesis, entitled "A Comparison of the Conceptions of God in the Thinking of Paul Tillich and Henry Nelson Wieman." He completed the project in two years on 343 type-written pages. "As a personal idealist, King disagreed with both Tillich and Wieman, one of whom (Tillich) contended that God was transcendent (i.e., outside things) while the other stressed God's immanence (i.e., His penetration of all things)."[14]

In 1954, King became pastor of Dexter Avenue Baptist Church of Montgomery, Alabama. His wife favored the offers he had received from Northern pastorates, but King's messianic consciousness drew him to the South. There "from the beginning King stressed social action, organizing a social and political action committee within the church and urging every member to become a registered voter and a member of the NAACP. Although King had a passion for social justice, his approach to the racial problem at that time was strictly conventional;"[15] that is, it centered on protest and legal means to gain equality and justice for Afro-Americans in the South.

The May, 1957, Prayer Pilgrimage to Washington, D.C., marked King's rise as a national Negro leader. He was the soul of the Pilgrimage, which was the greatest civil rights gathering in American history up to 1957. His leadership of the freedom movement brought him into conflict with the Southern white establishment. Many arrests were his lot. After one of these, in 1958, he addressed a protest meeting at Dexter Avenue Baptist Church in which he enunciated his vision of Christianity active through nonviolence in furthering social change. "Meet physical force with soul force," he said, in accordance with Gandhi's famous principle of nonviolent resistance.

Blood . . . may flow in the streets of Montgomery before we receive our freedom, but it must be our blood that flows and not that of the white man. We must not harm a single hair on the head of our white brothers. . . . Some day—it may be a year, ten years or even longer—but some day all the people of Montgomery are going to live together as brothers. There may be some delays, but one day we shall all live on an integrated basis.[16]

13 *Ibid.*
14 *Ibid.*, p. 38.
15 *Ibid.*, p. 42.
16 *Ibid.*, p. 77.

The year 1959 saw King in India as the personal guest of Prime Minister Nehru, in whom King saw the embodiment of all that Gandhi had stood for. At his arrival King said, "To other countries I may go as a tourist, but to India, I come as a pilgrim."[17] King was especially impressed by Nehru's efforts to stop discrimination against India's untouchables. He wished that the President of the United States might show a similarly vigorous espousal of the cause of minority groups which are the victims of discrimination, segregation, and social injustice. "My privilege of traveling to India," King remarked,

> had a great impact on me personally, for it was invigorating to see firsthand the amazing results of a nonviolent struggle to achieve independence. The aftermath of hatred and bitterness that usually follows a violent campaign was found nowhere in India, and a mutual friendship, based on complete equality, existed between the Indian and British people within the Commonwealth. . . . I am sure that many of our white brothers in Montgomery and throughout the South are still bitter toward the Negro leaders, even though these leaders have sought to follow a way of love and nonviolence. But the nonviolent approach does something to the hearts and souls of those committed to it. It gives them new self-respect. It calls up resources of strength and courage that they did not know they had. Finally, it so stirs the conscience of the opponent that reconciliation becomes a reality.[18]

The year following his return from his pilgrimage to India King resigned as pastor of Dexter Avenue Baptist Church. Now he wanted to be free to devote himself fully to the pragmatic test of the truth of his theology of rapid social change through nonviolence and Christian love. The immediate opportunity for this testing was the sit-in movement led by the Southern Chrsitian Leadership Conference. "Recognized by almost everyone as the 'spiritual father' of the sit-in students, King stepped forward immediately as a spokesman and symbol of the movement."[19]

During the years from 1960 on

> King and SCLC were involved in a number of programs (voter registration, leadership training, etc.) but their foremost emphasis, as King said, was "to spread the philosophy of nonviolence and to demonstrate through action its operational techniques." To an extent unprecedented in the civil rights field, King was the organization he headed. Despite that fact, he refused to accept a salary from the organization. He was paid $1.00 a year by SCLC and $6,000.00 annually by Ebenezer Baptist Church. The bulk of his income came from speaking engagements, royalties, and magazine articles.[20]

[17] *Ibid.*, p. 80.
[18] Martin Luther King, *Strength to Love* (New York: Pocket Books, 1964), p. 170.
[19] Bennett, *op. cit.*, p. 170.
[20] *Ibid.*, p. 134.

As the years went by, King's major concerns and theological motifs emerged in a clearly distinguishable pattern. "In speeches and interviews, King dwelt almost always on four major themes: 1) nonviolence, 2) social change, 3) individual and collective responsibility, and 4) the price of freedom. Increasingly, in recent years, he also stressed nonracial themes, particularly the inequitable distribution of wealth and the threat of nuclear war."[21] But to all of his theological statements and philosophical visions he applied the pragmatic test of truth, which says that the meaning of an idea lies in its practical consequences. Contemporary America, indeed, the world of the twentieth century, needs a theology of social change through nonviolence based on the love of Christ because only this theology works without destroying him who uses it to promote justice and freedom.

In 1964, Martin Luther King was awarded the Nobel Peace Prize, which 34 years earlier, in 1930, that great ecumenical prince of the Church, Archbishop Nathan Söderblom of Uppsala, Sweden, had received. In his acceptance speech, King stated:

> After contemplation, I conclude that this award which I receive on behalf of that movement [for racial equality and civil rights] is a profound recognition that nonviolence is the answer to the crucial political and moral questions of our time—the need for man to overcome oppression and violence without resorting to violence and oppression. Civilization and violence are antithetical concepts. Negroes of the United States, following the people of India, have demonstrated that nonviolence is not sterile passivity, but a powerful moral force which makes for social transformation. Sooner or later, all the people of the world will have to discover a way to live together in peace, and thereby transform this pending cosmic elegy into a creative psalm of brotherhood. If this is to be achieved, man must evolve for all human conflict a method which rejects revenge, aggression, and retaliation. The foundation of such a method is love.[22]

The award of the Nobel Peace Prize was the climax of King's career as a theologian and philosopher of rapid social transformation. His call for "freedom now!" in place of the familiar "wait!" made him many enemies. But he knew that "wait" meant "never." Therefore he braved the possibility of death through violence. In April 1968, the assassin's bullet felled the most significant American Negro theologian and preacher. Like Gandhi twenty years before, he died at the hands of violence and lawlessness.

The untimely death of the foremost Negro philosopher of Christian nonviolence must not blind us to the lasting enrichment which his life and thought has meant for contemporary theology and religious thought. We

---

[21] *Ibid.*, p. 136.
[22] Martin Luther King, Jr., "The Nobel Peace Prize Speech," *What Manner of Man*, p. 141.

may sum up his chief ideas under the five headings of nonviolence, love, freedom, prophetic responsibility (individual and social), and a theology of social change and destiny.

It was Gandhi who convinced King that Jesus' love ethic could be cast into workable form by means of the technique of nonviolence. "Gandhi's politics are indistinguishable from his religion. 'My patriotism,' he said, 'is subservient to my religion.' In politics he cleaved to moral considerations, and as a saint he thought his place was not in a cave or cloister but in the hurly-burly of the popular struggle for rights and the right. Gandhi's religion made him political, and his politics were religious."[23] King, also, was convinced that theology that wants to be relevant to the secular world must be political theology. He thus took his place in the ranks of the theologians of "the secular city" for whom the touchstone of adequate philosophy and theology was the word of Christ, "By their fruits you shall know them."

For King, as for Gandhi, the greatest power in the universe is love, because the key to the universe is personality (infinite and finite), and without truth and love personality cannot exist. Gandhi made the term *satyagraha* famous. "*Satya* means truth, the equivalent of love, and both are attributes of the soul; *agraha* is firmness or force. 'Satyagraha' is therefore translated Soul Force."[24]

The great Indian apostle of nonviolence explained that *satyagraha* " 'is the vindication of truth not by infliction of suffering on the opponent but on one's self.' The opponent must be 'weaned from error by patience and sympathy.' Weaned, not crushed. Satyagraha assumes a constant beneficient interaction between contestants with a view to their ultimate reconciliation. Violence, insults, and superheated propaganda obstruct this end."[25]

The greatest enemy of nonviolence based on love and truth is fear. A *satyagrahi*, i.e., a person who practices *satyagraha* or soul force. Gandhi once explained, " 'bids good-bye to fear. He is therefore never afraid to trust the opponent. Even if the opponent plays him false twenty times, the Satyagrahi is ready to trust him the twenty-first time, for an implicit trust in human nature is the very essence of his creed.' "[26]

Gandhi was a Hindu who knew Christ. King was a Christian pastor who proclaimed the redemptive significance of Jesus the Christ. Once Gandhi was asked: "Does Hinduism permit killing an evildoer?" "One

[23] Louis Fischer, *Gandhi* (New York: New American Library, 1954), p. 35.
[24] *Ibid.*
[25] *Ibid.*
[26] *Ibid.*, p. 36.

evildoer cannot punish another," Gandhi replied.[27] One cannot help but recall the words of Jesus of Nazareth to those who wished to stone an evildoer: "Let him who is without sin among you cast the first stone." Soul force overcame physical force, and they all left, one after the other, from the greatest to the least, until only the Christ and the adulterous woman remained.

It is not difficult to understand why King was impressed by the contemporary relevance of nonviolent techniques as developed by Gandhi. As a Christian theologian, King's central emphasis rested on redemption, reconciliation, and the creation of the beloved community through mutual forgiveness. According to King the method of nonviolence not only implied the avoidance of external physical violence but also meant the avoidance of the violation of the internal spirit. It is not enough simply to refuse to shoot a man, but in the spirit of Jesus one must refuse to hate him. The gentle spirit of the forgiving Christ permeated the life and thought of King as theologian, as philosopher, and as Christian leader.

King was emphatic in his distinction between means and ends. He argued that the nonviolent resister on numerous occasions must demonstrate his protest through boycotts and noncooperation, but he maintained that these are not ends in themselves. Their purpose is to arouse a sense of moral shame in the enemy. The final goal is redemption and reconciliation. In the wake of nonviolence the beloved community grows, while in the wake of violence we reap tragic bitterness. Such a theology of social change as King proposed insisted that the end justifies the means. The end is reconciliation, forgiveness, and authentic human communion. This end justifies the means of sit-ins, demonstrations, boycotts, and the refusal to cooperate with social structures which serve unjust ends. King was aware that nonviolent direct action was not born in America, but he felt that its natural home was here. In America, refusal to cooperate with injustice is an old and honorable tradition, he maintained. Further, in America, the Christian vision of love and forgiveness is an integral part of the hearts and minds of good men. And he stressed that a theology of nonviolent, rapid social change developed on the Christian soil of America will finally bring not only the American Negro, but all men closer to the great goal of a new world of peace and justice and freedom for all men. He writes, "Nonviolence, the answer to the Negro's need, may become the answer to the most desperate need of all humanity."[28]

King called for a Christian theology of redemptive nonviolence because

---

[27] *Ibid.,* p. 181.
[28] Martin Luther King, Jr., *Why We Can't Wait* (New York: The New American Library, 1964), p. 152.

he was convinced that "the Christian doctrine of love, operating through the Gandhian method of nonviolence, is one of the most potent weapons available to an oppressed people in their struggle for freedom."[29]

Wherever there have been prophets of light in the history of mankind, there have also been the apostles of gloom, who were blinded by the reality of evil and violence to the possibilities of love, forgiveness, and redemptive reconciliation. They seized upon King's theology of nonviolent social transformation in order to advance their arguments against his ethic of nonviolence.

> The first is that it cannot work, since it seems to suppose an angelic conception of Man's dignity rarely encountered in reality. Even in the case of Gandhi, many have said, the success of his non-violence was only made possible by England's lukewarm desire to hold on to India, and by the coincidence that the English were enough a part of the moral tradition he evoked to make them susceptible to his tactics. In short, non-violence will not work and, if it does, that is just an ad hoc historical accident which cannot be repeated. The death of Martin Luther King, one could say, simply proved the irrelevance of non-violence: the fate of the non-violent is a violent death at the hands of those who live in the real and not hoped-for human world. Reality caught up with Dr. King just as it did with Gandhi.[30]

This argument against the relevance and practicality of a nonviolent theology of social change lacks persuasiveness because 1) Gandhi's assassination greatly accelerated, rather than rendered impossible, India's independence; and 2) King's assassination gave his philosophy of nonviolent social transformation the martyr symbol which may endow it with much greater significance and appeal. At the present time it is premature to say that King's theology of nonviolence did not produce results.

A second argument advanced by the critics of King's theology of social renewal

> is that the concept of non-violence can easily become just another instrument of subjugation. Faced with rising, utterly just Negro demands, stridently pushed, expensive to meet, unnerving to confront, what is more natural than for whites to embrace Dr. King's non-violence? The nice thing about it, from a nervous white viewpoint, is that it doesn't endanger property, doesn't promote costly rioting, doesn't allow blacks to get out of hand. It also means that whites can meet Negro demands at their leisure, being reasonably sure that nothing too drastic will happen in the meantime. Many blacks of course saw this kind of effect in Dr. King's non-violence. They felt it played only too nicely into white hands—and they rejected it, casting about for an

[29] Martin Luther King, Jr., *Strength to Love* (New York: Pocket Books, 1964), p. 169.
[30] *Commonweal* editorial, "Dr. King's Legacy," *Commonweal* (April 19, 1968), p. 125 b.

ethic with more bite to it, one which would allow whites less chance to put off what had to be done, less chance to go about business as usual. And violence does have a bite.[31]

Against this second argument criticizing a theology of Christian non-violence, King advanced several persuasive counterarguments. First, he reminded his opponents of the fate of the American Indian. Violence, he was sure, would give the white majority the justification to ignore all the just demands of Afro-Americans, to beat them down in "self-defense," and to lock them up in reservations where they would lose their identity, their self-respect, their freedom, and human dignity. Nonviolence, King correctly recognized, is the most effective weapon in Christian America, because it evokes a moral tradition which is irresistible in the New World.

Second, costly riots inflict more suffering on the Negro population than on the few white slumlords whose substandard houses might be destroyed in riots like those in Watts or Chicago or Washington, D.C. The white owners live in safe luxury apartments or suburban homes, far away from the plight of the Negro. Arson destroys the already inadequate housing of many Afro-Americans, it destroys Negro businesses through fire and looting; in short, it hurts the American Negro the most.

Third, King came to realize that the method of nonviolent resistance was the most powerful weapon in the world in the struggle for human dignity and freedom. Writing of his experience in Montgomery he says, "As the days unfolded, I became more and more convinced of the power of nonviolence. Nonviolence became more than a method to which I gave intellectual assent; it became a commitment to a way of life."[32] Moreover he insisted that, "In a day when vehicles hurtle through outer space and guided ballistic missiles carve highways of death through the stratosphere, no nation can claim victory in war. A so-called limited war will leave little more than a calamitous legacy of human suffering, political turmoil, and spiritual disillusionment."[33] Our choice is not simply between violence and nonviolence in our day, it is either nonviolence or nonexistence.

As a theologian and pastor of the Church, King wrote, "My mind, consciously or unconsciously, was driven back to the Sermon on the Mount and the Gandhian method of nonviolent resistance. This principle became the guilding light of our movement. Christ furnished the spirit and motivation and Gandhi furnished the method."[34] He saw himself as the leader of an army engaged in warfare.

[31] Ibid.
[32] King, Strength to Love, p. 170.
[33] Ibid., p. 35.
[34] Ibid., p. 169.

208   CONTEMPORARY PROTESTANT THOUGHT

But it was a special army, with no supplies but its sincerity, no uniform but its determination, no arsenal except its faith, no currency but its conscience. It was an army that would move but not maul. It was an army that would sing but not slay. It was an army that would flank but not falter. It was an army to storm bastions of hatred, to lay siege to the fortresses of segregation, to surround symbols of discrimination. It was an army whose allegiance was to God and whose strategy and intelligence were the simple dictates of conscience.[35]

If King shared with Martin Luther the emphasis on "the dictates of conscience," which give man no rest in the face of unrighteousness and evil, he shared with Archbishop Söderblom the concern for peace. "In measuring the full implications of the civil-rights revolution," he observed, "the greatest contribution may be in the area of world peace. The concept of nonviolence has spread on a mass scale in the United States as an instrument of change in the field of race relations. To date, only a relatively few practitioners of nonviolent direct action have been committed to its philosophy. The great mass have used it pragmatically as a tactical weapon, without being ready to live it."[36]

Looking beyond the immediate concerns of the freedom movement of Afro-Americans seeking to assert their human dignity, King philosophized about the worldwide implications of violence as a mode of settling difference and promoting rapid social change. He came to the conclusion that "more and more people . . . have begun to conceive of this powerful ethic [of nonviolence as both a theological and a practical program] as a necessary way of life in a world where the wildly accelerated development of nuclear power has brought into being weapons that can annihilate all humanity. Political agreements are no longer secure enough to safeguard life against a peril of such devastating finality. There must also be a philosophy, acceptable to the people, and stronger than resignation toward sudden death."[37]

King saw his personal, historical destiny in terms of the creation of a theology of justice and brotherhood, and the practical demonstration of its contemporary relevance and effectiveness. Echoing the words of Archbishop Söderblom in The Church and Peace (written in 1929, the year of King's birth), he stressed that we should move from "a negative peace which is the absence of tension to a positive peace which is the presence of justice."[38] Along with Söderblom, King agreed that true peace needs the positive forces of equality, justice, love, good will, unity, and brother-

[35] King, Why We Can't Wait, p. 62.
[36] Ibid., p. 152.
[37] Ibid.
[38] Ibid., p. 84.

hood. Both men also agree on the point that the Christian and the man of peace must work diligently in the cause of peace. Those who think and plan for peace must work and organize as effectively as the war hawks who scheme in favor of war and disunity.

Concluding then that true peace is not simply the absence of tension, but rather the presence of love, justice, and brotherhood, King's theology of nonviolent social change and rapid social transformation summons all men to devote their energies to the creation of the beloved community of love, justice, freedom, unity, and brotherhood. Only on this basis can the command against war be obeyed effectively and permanently. King reminds us that all through the ages a voice has been crying "Put up your sword!" The shores of history are scattered with the white bones of those who have refused to heed this command. Thus Martin Luther King's philosophy of Christian nonviolence leads through the social unrest created by demonstration and boycotts and sit-ins to a triumphant song of peace in freedom and justice for all.

CHAPTER XIV

ECUMENICAL THEOLOGY: A SUMMARY

The implications of the Teilhardian vision of evolution and process are of great significance for the future of ecumenical theology. It is well to recall in this connection Bonhoeffer's observation that if ecumenism is to be more than a passing episode in the historical development of the church universal it will have to develop an adequate ecumenical theology.

The theology of the coming great church of the ecumenical era will have to emerge out of a synthesis of Roman Catholic, Protestant, and Orthodox thought. Each of the three great historic branches of Christendom will have to make its own contribution to the new ecumenical shape of theology. It appears that the process theology of Pierre Teilhard de Chardin promises to become the most significant theological contribution of Roman Catholic ecumenism. By achieving an ecumenical synthesis with Protestant process thought based on the philosophy of Alfred North Whitehead and other process thinkers, the magnificent vision of Teilhard and Whitehead can be welded together to form the new basis of the ecumenical theology of the future.

There are those theologians today, particularly in Protestant circles, but also among Roman Catholics and Orthodox, who oppose philosophy as the handmaiden of theology and propose to fashion an exclusively biblical theology. This venture can only fail. If we are to develop an ecumenical theology for the future, we must recover and renew our philosophical theological "blik"—to use a term that Paul M. van Buren's imaginative *Secular Meaning of the Gospel* has made famous in today's theological world. Any other attempt to provide a theological foundation for the ecumenical reunion of the separated churches and denominations is too fragmentary, truncated, and incomplete to be widely useful in the secular city of what Harvey Cox has aptly called "technopolitan man."

The cooperation between Roman Catholics and Protestants in the area of biblical studies is a promising omen for future ecumenical endeavors. The emphasis on churches working together in matters of social justice and civil rights is also a genuine asset for the task of the church in our time. As magnificent as these cooperative efforts might be, they are not wholly adequate. There remains the crying need for the development of a new philosophical-theological vision for the twentieth and twenty-first centuries. Van Buren's *Secular Meaning* attempts with admirable courage to create such a vision with the tools of contemporary linguistic analysis, which is presently the ruling philosophy of many departments of philosophy in this country. Van Buren's reconstruction of the Christian "historical perspective" suffers, however, under the destructive implications of linguistic analysis applied to religious values and value judgments.

To make sense of biblical studies and to elicit the coherence of scriptural ideas requires a vast metaphysical and cosmological framework. The churches' involvements in social justice and civil rights must also be based on a *Weltanschauung* big enough to unite the biblical vision and the concern for contemporary relevance in a dynamic ecumenical synthesis. This synthesis cannot be created by rewarming old, parochial, sectarian or medieval theologies. Such warmed-over theological stews tend to be regurgitated by modern man.

When we remember what the philosophical theology of Aquinas has done for the Roman Catholic Church, it will be easier to understand that one of the greatest assets of theology for its ecumenical future will be an adequate philosophical framework. A philosophical perspective will be termed adequate in the twentieth century, when it is able to replace the old concept of substance with that of process, and the notion of the essence of man with that of the evolution of man. Pierre Teilhard de Chardin, indicated some of the theological consequences of the restatement of traditional doctrines in terms of process thought. But Teilhard was a paleontologist and thelogian rather than a systematic philosopher and theologian. The credit for a systematic statement of the philosophy of process belongs to the British-American philosopher and mathematician Alfred North Whitehead. What Aristotle, in his Metaphysics, did for the theology of Thomism, Whitehead, in his *Process and Reality,* can do for the future ecumenical theology.

Process philosophy will equip ecumenical thought with the necessary intellectual and metaphysical tools, concepts, and structure, which will enable it to give warm, rich, universal, and genuinely evangelical meaning to theological notions and Christian cultic practices, which have become, or are in danger of becoming, irrelevant, nonunderstandable, and anachronistic to twentieth-century man. The Teilhardian and Whiteheadian categories place at the disposable of ecumenical theology that indispensable philosophical metaphysics that will make possible the relevant restatement of theological ideas with a view both to the missionary role of the church in the world and to its ecumenical structure. Ecumenical theology, in its search for restatement and relevance in our century, must find something more adequate than the philosophy of substance, the philosophical presuppositions of neo-orthodoxy, and the overweening concern with existentialism. All of these reveal a kind of inadequacy in our world which is characterized by the ecumenical situation. The philosophical presuppositions and categories of Alfred North Whitehead reveal a concern for universality, adequacy, catholicity, and wholeness which is integral to the development of an ecumenical synthesis.

The spirit of ecumenism has turned the minds of men again toward the serene view of wholeness with a more balanced view of the relation between theology and philosophy than the so-called biblical theology, theology of crisis, or dialectical theology of the neo-orthodox and Barthian era would allow. Although the work of Karl Barth has attracted considerable attention among Roman Catholic theologians, they have preserved their traditional, attitude toward philosophical theology. Theologians in the Protestant branch of the church are also beginning to rediscover the value and rightful place of philosophical insight in theology. By some ecumenical theologians this shift of emphasis is deemed necessary in the interest of a deeper penetration into truth and reality, and a fresher and wider apprehension of meaning and religious value in the ecumenical era.

1. *Natural Theology.* The task of philosophical theology as the handmaiden of the future, ecumenical theology of the church universal has at least two aspects. First, ecumenical philosophical theology has to provide the basis for what traditionally has been known as Christian natural theol-

ogy. Karl Barth has denounced natural theology as an invention of the Antichrist, and declared that the Roman Catholic endorsement of natural theology was reason enough for him not to become a Roman Catholic. Nathan Söderblom pointed out that the notion of natural theology is in a sense a fictitious one, because natural theology presupposes a natural religion which in reality does not exist. Religion, in the Söderblomian perspective, is always a positive and historical phenomenon; no actually existing religion can be called natural.

However, there is a sense in which natural theology belongs in the context of the problem of revelation and reason. Both the criticism of Söderblom and that of Barth fail to take seriously the fact that this problem is of decisive importance for the future of ecumenical theology. In the context of what traditional theology referred to as the problem of revelation and reason, natural theology is a philosophical attempt to construct a theology which is basic to all religion but not identical with any one of the positive religions which have arisen in the course of history. Of central significance to this philosophical construction is a doctrine of God derived from the observation of the visible processes of nature. This means that cosmology is bound to play a key role in natural theology.

The Christian concept of God, which has emerged in the course of more than nineteen centuries of fruitful dialogue between philosophy and theology, cannot maintain its relevance and vitality without the support of some form of natural theology. In our time, however, this support has been largely taken away from it, because of the erosion of meaningful language about God. The cosmological horizons within which ancient, medieval, and sixteenth-century man understood his existence, and the concept of God which was tied to this pre-scientific cosmology, have been discredited by the nihilistic tendencies of modern cosmology. The Lutheran theologian, Rudolf Bultmann, has sought to disentangle the God of New Testament faith from the God of the three-decker universe of ancient mythology, which saw God up on top, the earth and man in the middle, and the devil and hell down below. The Anglican bishop and theologian, John A. T. Robinson, in his book *Honest to God,* has set in full relief the problem for modern man of the God "up there" or the God "out there."

The rise of the God-is-dead school and the secularizers of the gospel from within Christian theology is the result of the destructive implications of modern cosmology. These contemporary theological movements underline the urgent need for a new, ecumenical statement of Christian natural theology as an important phase in the theological struggle for the rehabilitation of the center of Christian faith, which is the doctrine of God. The philosophical categories of process thought as systematized by Whitehead are ideally suited to a fruitful and fresh approach to this task of natural theology, because the Whiteheadian cosmological scheme provides the future, ecumenical theology with an adequate alternative to the destructive tendencies of contemporary philosophical metaphysics.

The late, beloved Pope John XXIII, in his "Letter to the Venetian Clergy" of April 24, 1959, expressed the view that Christian unity can be best promoted if it is approached in three stages. The first stage is that of an ecumenical approach which is based on the large area of common ground that already exists between the three main sections of Christendom. The second stage is that of *riaccostamento,* or coming together. The third stage is that of perfect unity on the basis of an ecumenical unity in essentials and diversity and freedom in everything else. The development of a common, Christian, natural theology will be of great service to the successful attainment of the first stage of ecumenism. It will provide that additional area of common ground which is already present in Roman Catholicism, Protestantism, and Eastern Orthodoxy, and which only needs adequate, philosophical systematization and articulation in order to become an effective, ecumenical factor in the promotion of Christian unity. Process, evolution, and the scientific world-view are part of the Christian mind-set simply by virtue of the fact that they have grown up and are still living in the twentieth century, the age of atomic energy and of outer space. Whitehead's philosophy of process can provide theology with a philosophical basis on which to erect, and make explicit, a natural theology which is relevant to our age, an age which is both ecumenical and scientific. By affirming the scientific view of the universe, Whiteheadian process thought does away with the cosmological offense of the ancient mythological three-storied universe, and thus clears the deck for the launching of the abiding message of the good news. If the non-Christian world is to be offended by the gospel of Jesus Christ as God and Saviour, then let it be the real gospel, and not an outmoded and false cosmology, which constitutes the *skandalon,* the offence.

2. *Man in the Secular Age.* A second aspect of the ecumenical task of philosophical theology is the critical and constructive analysis of the human situation of man in the secular age. The Lutheran theologian, Dietrich Bonhoeffer, has argued that for the first time in the history of the human race, man has come of age. He believes that a profound change has occurred in the human situation, which makes twentieth-century man's relationship to reality different from that of ancient, medieval, and early modern man. Since reality is process, and history places every generation into a new situation, the analysis of the human situation by philosophical theology is essential to the progress of ecumenical theology as well as to the relevant proclamation of the gospel by the church. The high priestly

prayer of our Lord in the seventeenth chapter of St. John's Gospel inseparably relates the prayer for Christian unity, "that they all may be one," to the missionary task, "that the world may believe that Thou hast sent me." If the church is to advance the cause of Christianity, it must be aware of the changes in the human situation which have affected the life of the church, and how these changes have affected the world outside of the ecumenical church.

When philosophical theology explores the human situation down to its final microcosmic and macrocosmic implications, it does so with a view toward those ecumenical meanings and values which make for unity and universality. Christianity is a universal religion; its truth is catholic truth. The whole and universal truth of the Christian gospel must be spoken to the human situation. Philosophical theology must determine and specify what are the deepest and most universal problems which characterize the situation of man in the second half of the twentieth century. To these problems the evangelical and catholic Christian answer must be addressed.

The Prostestant theologian, Harvey Cox, in his sensational book, *The Secular City,* has sought to specify the human situation of "technopolitan man" in the secular city. Unfortunately, his book lacks systematic philosophical structure in a clearly articulated statement. But credit is due him for having frankly and forcefully pictured the universal situation of secular man in the technological metropolis. Whether we go to New York, London, Moscow, Tokyo, or Rio de Janeiro, everywhere we recognize the same questions and hopes giving shape and form to the human situation. They are the hopes and questions of secular man in a de-sacralized, naturalistic world. Also in this world, God has not left himself without a witness. The meaning and value of the grace of God is present even in the secular city. The task of philosophical theology in the service of ecumenical theology is, therefore, not the creation of meaning and value, but the discovery of these as they reveal themselves to the philosophically and theologically instructed and perceptive mind in the natural process of reality. Without the aid of adequate philosophical tools, Teilhard has done something of this sort in his remarkable book, *The Phenomenon of Man.* How much more could a systematical, philosophical effort do to orient the nascent ecumenical theology of our time toward the metaphysical categories of process theology!

It is hardly surprising that the human situation in a secular age should have given rise to a new morality. Sometimes referred to as situationalism, the new morality is a natural correlate of the new image of man come of age which is emerging in our time. The old, traditional morality assumed that there is a moral order written unchangeably into the universe. Objective and immutable are the natural and divine laws of Christian morality:

this assumption underlies the main thrust of traditional Roman Catholic moral theology, and is closely related to its puzzling, and from the Protestant point of view quite unrealistic, stand on the issues of divorce and birth control. One of the first real problems that ecumenical theology will encounter is the question of the status of the old, traditional moral theology in the context of that net of empirical relationships which constitutes the human situation of man in the space age.

The briefest and clearest theological statement of the new morality has been made by Bishop Robinson in his book, *Honest to God*. Although it is not his intention to outline the moral theology which is most suited to the ecumenical advancement of Christian unity and the creation of a universal, ecumenical, Christian theology, yet he does indicate forcefully that it will be impossible for ecumenical theology to hold on to the old supernaturalistic ethical framework. What has to give, however, is not Christian morality, but rather the antiquated, supernaturalistic framework. In our time this framework obscures, rather than clarifies, the old and ever new commandment of love which is the fulfillment of the moral law. It is the love of God in Jesus Christ which is at once the basic commandment and the fulfillment of the law of Christian living. When it is remembered that more than one and one-half millennia ago St. Augustine said, "Love, and then what thou wilt, do," the new, ecumenical basis of Christian ethics is much more a recovery and renewal of the central ethical affirmation of Christian moral philosophy and theology than a denial of it. The task of philosophical theology in the realm of Christian ethics is to help the future, ecumenical theology to rediscover and renew the indispensable foundation of ecumenical, moral theology.

INDEX